Academically Sound

...but Manner and Deportment
Need Improvement

Who would true valour see,
Let him come hither;
One here will constant be,
Come wind, come weather.
There's no discouragement
Shall make him once relent
His first avow'd intent,
To be a pilgrim.

John Bunyan (1628 – 1688)

Academically Sound

...but Manner and Deportment Need Improvement

———✦———

Sir James Smith's Grammar School,
Camelford, Cornwall,

1950 – 1957

James Platt

First published in Great Britain in 2014 by Creighton Books
Website: http//www.creightonbooks.nl
Email: jim.platt@planet.nl
© 2014 James Platt
ISBN – 978 90 807808 0 4

The moral right of James Platt to be identified as the author of this work
has been asserted by him in accordance with
the Copyright, Designs and patents Act 1988
British Library cataloguing in Publication Data
A catalogue record of this book is available from the British Library
Designed in the UK by Special Edition Pre-Press Services
Printed and Bound in Great Britain by Lightning Source UK Ltd.

Also by James Platt and published by Creighton Books

East of Varley Head – Stories from Port Isaac,
North Cornwall 1944 – 1950
(Published in 2003, ISBN 90 807808 1 2)

Your Reserves or Mine?
(Published in 2004, ISBN 90 807808 2 0)

South of Lobber Point – More Stories from Port Isaac,
North Cornwall 1944 – 1950
(Published in 2005, ISBN 90 807808 3 9)

The Great Tanganyika Diamond Hunt
(Published in 2007, ISBN 978 90 807808 4 2)

North Of Little Hill – Proper Talk in Port Isaac,
North Cornwall, 1944 – 1950
(Published in 2009, ISBN 978 90 807808 5 9)

West of Castle Rock – Port Isaac, For Letter or for Verse 1944 – 1950
(Published in 2011, ISBN 978 90 807808 6 6

This book is dedicated
to the eternally precious memory
of my beloved wife Maria

Maria Filomena Platt-Cornoldi
1 January 1941 – 8 July 2008
Always with us

———+———

She walks in beauty, like the night
Of cloudless climes and starry skies;
And all that's best of dark and bright
Meet in her aspect and her eyes;
Thus mellow'd to that tender light
Which heaven to gaudy day denie

'She Walks in Beauty' – Lord Byron (1788 – 1824)

North Cornwall—Principal location map

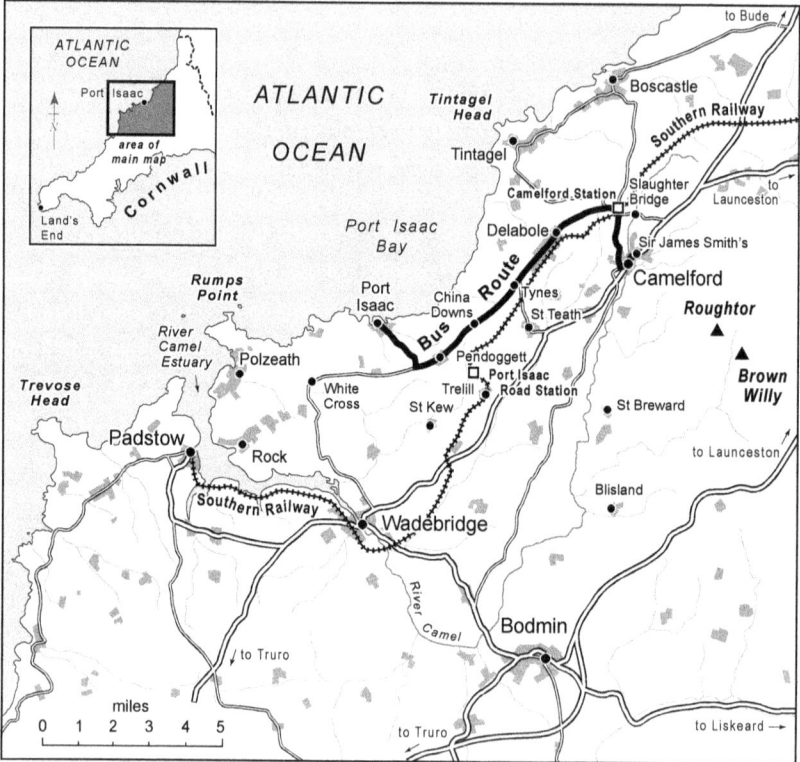

North Cornwall—Principal location map

ATLANTIC
OCEAN

Port Isaac

area of
main map

Cornwall

Land's
End

ATLANTIC

OCEAN

Port Isaac
Bay

Rumps
Point

River
Camel
Estuary

Trevose
Head

Padstow

Rock

Southern Railway

Polzeath

White
Cross

St Kew

Port
Isaac

China
Downs

Pendoggett

Trelill

Tintagel
Head

Tintagel

Camelford Station

Delabole

Tynes

St Teath

Port Isaac
Road Station

Boscastle

Southern Railway

Slaughter
Bridge

Sir James Smith's

Camelford

Roughtor

Brown
Willy

St Breward

Blisland

to Bude

to
Launceston

to Launceston

Bus Route

Wadebridge

River Camel

Bodmin

to Truro

to Truro

to Liskeard

miles

0   1   2   3   4   5

Sir James Smith's Grammar School—General layout

N

steps

7

8

9

10 steps

5

11

13

12

14   steps

29

1

15

17

19

6 **20** **21**

16

2

18

23

3

22

24

29

30

25

26

4

steps

27

28

To the buses

27

To the river

10 m

Scale (approx)

1.	First Form classroom	15.	Boys' cloakroom
2.	Second Form classroom	16.	Mr Jeal's stationery cupboard
3.	Third Form classroom	17.	School central hall
4.	Fourth Form classroom	18.	Headmaster's Study
5.	Fifth Form classroom	19.	Library
6.	Sixth Form classroom	20.	Staff Room
7.	Hedge to fields beyond	21.	Girls' lavatory block
8.	Boys' lavatory block	22.	Girls' cloakroom
9.	Physics laboratory (also Woodwork)	23.	Chemistry laboratory
10.	Milk distribution lean-to	24.	Art annex
11.	Main Assembly corridor	25.	Kitchen
12.	Principal school entry	26.	Canteen
13.	Boys' yard	27.	College Road
14.	Hall/Theatre (also Woodwork)	28.	School entry gate
		29.	Terrace embankment rim
		30.	Girls' yard

Head boy, 1956 — James Platt

Contents

Acknowledgements

This personal memoir, as with all Creighton Books' publications, was designed and prepared throughout by Corinne Orde, Principal of the media services company Special Edition Pre-Press Services. Her kindness and the quality of style, expertise and patience which she devoted to the book were exemplary. Corinne's editing skills added definitive improvements that could not have been of greater benefit to the finished work.

The location map was expertly prepared by cartographer Don Shewan, whose skill in map making and clarity of output are both gratefully acknowledged, and can be seen to speak for themselves.

The book was digitally printed and registered for Print-on-Demand orders with key trade and Internet booksellers and distributors by Lightning Source UK Limited of Milton Keynes (www.lightningsource. com). LSUK's total commitment to Creighton Books is gratefully acknowledged for its consistent professional excellence and personal consideration.

I am very much in the debt of the full seven years complement of pupils of Sir James Smith's Grammar School who accompanied me in my passage through the School from my first day in the First Form and on to A levels and the final Assembly of the Upper Sixth Form thereafter. We were all, for better or for worse, but mostly for better, a part of one another's lives for the duration, and unwitting though it may have been from time to time, we all drew undoubted strength from one another under the uniting influence of the red and green school tie. Special thanks in this regard go to my classmates for the true delight of having been one of them. I hope they will recognise the essence of the school which the book offers, even though they may not necessarily agree with some, or even more, of my opinions.

One classmate who needs to be particularly thanked is my friend Mike Ferrett. Our discussions ranging over so many of the facets and nuances and personalities of the School in recent years were a prime motivator behind this book.

Gratitude of a very high order and special kind is due to the School's Headmaster of the time, Mr Kenneth Sprayson, and all members of his teaching staff. Those teachers all carried greatness with them in their own ways, which was inevitable under a Headmaster of such stature and inspirational character. I did not always see eye with the teachers, and have myself to blame for that, but my life was enriched by the attentions of them all. In fact, with the passage of time, that enrichment deepens, as does the pleasure of having known them all, and not a day goes by without something or other that they taught and gave me being brought into the play of my life.

Finally, I am also most grateful to Jennifer Brazier (née Sprayson) for making available a short history of the School, which she researched with the admirable scholarship that would be expected from someone of her name and parentage.

Sir James Smith's Grammar School,
Camelford.

PRIZE

For *Form III*

Awarded to *J. W. Platt*

Presentation of Prizes by
J. G. HARRIES, Esq., M.A.,
Secretary for Education for the County of Cornwall.

Chairman of the Governors : Headmaster :
Sir John Molesworth-St. Aubyn, Bart. K. A. Sprayson, B.Sc.

3rd February, 1954.

A standard class prize nameplate, rendered unique by being the only one of its
kind awarded to this recipient on his long road to O Level.

1

A Bag Containing n Nuts

"In my hand", Mr Kenneth A. Sprayson declared to the First Form, "I have a bag of nuts."

We of the First Form had to take his word for the truth of that statement as he held no bag of any kind containing anything at all that could be seen, unless it was secreted behind the little textbook grasped in his right hand and opened to the first page, from which incidentally he had just read the statement. But then, he was the Headmaster, and it had to be believed without question that he knew what he was talking about.

Mr Sprayson's other hand, the left, seemed to have been welded at shoulder height to the lapel of the black, pleated and lightly chalk-dusted gown in which he was draped, so there couldn't have been a bag of nuts held in that one.

He gripped at the gown with such white-knuckled determination that those of us whose attention was all-too riveted on his imposing presence feared that if he were to relax his hold, the gown might well subside and collapse in folds around his feet.

Proceeding undaunted, as if he was unaware that to use the word "nuts" in a First Form lesson was to play to the gallery, Mr Sprayson read on.

"The number of nuts contained in the bag is n".

N?

Was *n* a number?

It hadn't been a number that I ever heard of at Port Isaac County Primary School, but I was now a pupil at Sir James Smith's Grammar School up in Camelford, and I had to expect that things would be different there. Most of us in the First Form were certain that if Mr Sprayson told us that *n* was a number, then *n* must be a number, even though each of us secretly thought it wasn't.

We had all recently acceded to the grammar school from our home village primary schools, awarded places in the former as a consequence of having achieved better results than a majority of our local fellows in the National Grammar School entry examination, known as the "eleven-plus" in homage to the average age of entrants.

We were all rather self-consciously decked out in a school uniform that we were still a long way off being accustomed to. The apparel hung sparingly on us, everything generally fitting where it touched. Trousers were the common bugbear, "tight under the armpits", as the popular expression went, and holding on by a wing and a prayer, but since we had been assured that one day we would "grow into them", the evil that they brought to us had to be sufficient unto the day.

Mr Sprayson, Headmaster, greatness personified and revered throughout the school, up, down, left, right and centre, was nick-named "Boss" or "KA". He could have told us that black was white and we would have been duty-bound to believe him.

He looked up from the textbook and gave each of us in turn a glance that was as inquisitive as it was imperious. It was as if he was on the hunt for a victim, laying out the threat, and considering pouncing without warning. He wrinkled his nose to demonstrate a certain disdain for the type of rural oafs we undoubtedly were.

His first question to us was, therefore, if not simple, then at least straightforward. "Who among you can tell me", he enquired, "how many nuts there would be in my bag of *n* nuts if I took one out and ate it?"

His left hand released the lapel of the gown and instantaneously extended in our direction, his index finger pointing at a pupil sitting at a desk up in front.

"You!" he said. His gown, deprived of its manual support, did not fall, although some of its pleats appeared to sag a little anxiously.

"Please, sir, dun't knaw, sir!"

"You then!" He indicated another pupil.

"Please, sir, where be the bag, sir!"

His pointing finger moved on. "You!"

"Please, sir, what kind of nuts be they, sir? Do 'em need some nutcrackers like me Gran 'ev to git rids of the shells, sir?"

"Please, sir, how many be *n*, sir?"

"No, no, no!" exclaimed Mr Sprayson. "There is no actual bag — the bag is hypothetical. The type of nuts that are in this hypothetical bag isn't important, and nor for the sake of this exercise is the value of *n*! N can be any number you like! If I take one of the *n* nuts out of the bag, I want you to tell me how many nuts are left in the bag! Surely that is an easy enough question to answer?"

"Please, sir, what do 'hypothetical' mean, sir?"

"Look, just use your imagination! I have a bag, a paper bag, containing *n* nuts. I take one nut out. How many nuts are left in the bag?"

"Please, sir, did ee eat the nut this time, sir?"

"Yes, yes, boy! I ate it. I ate it! Now, how many more nuts have I still got that can be eaten?"

"Dun't knaw, sir, some of 'em might be bad, sir".

"For heaven's sake! Look here!" said the Great Man with ill-disguised exasperation. "The answer to the question is that having removed one nut from *n* nuts in the bag, then what remains in the

3

bag is n minus one nuts. If the value of n was, let us say, fifty, then what I now have with one nut taken away would be forty-nine nuts".

"It must be a brave and big bag, sir, if it can hold fifty nuts, 'specially if they was Brazils, sir", a pupil observed.

"'Tis hard to open they even with a nutcracker", advised another to all in the classroom.

"Maybe they'm hazelnuts", came the opinion of a third.

And thus commenced the First Form's first lesson at Sir James Smith's Grammar School in a subject that Mr Sprayson had called something that sounded like Aljebber, although we later learned that it was pronounced Al-geb-ra. It was evidently a strange way of doing sums by substituting letters for numbers.

The consensus of pupil opinion, once these mysteries had been aired, with rational understanding left pending, was that the whole thing would have been greatly simplified if a proper number for all the nuts had been used in the first place.

We normally only ever came into first-hand contact with nuts at and around Christmas time. When Mr Sprayson told us about his hypothetical (whatever that meant) bag of the rare commodity, the calendar indicated that we had only just reached mid-September. There were three long months of travel to reach the promised land of Yuletide carols. It was impossible therefore not to be favourably impressed by the easy and early access to nuts that Mr Sprayson had demonstrated, and with this the Headmaster's stature did not fail to become instantly enhanced.

I wondered if he did own a set of nutcrackers, or if perhaps he shelled a nut as most of the rest of us did, by placing the nut on the ground, taking off one of our shoes, and whacking the nut with the heel of the shoe in a delicate balance of weight and timing for optimum results.

A bag of n nuts.

"There's richness!"

Later on, Mr Sprayson (and others of the teaching staff) would tell us that Algebra wasn't only about n, but could also call on a and b, and even more importantly x and y. Any one of these letters could either be numerically equal or unequal to any or all of the rest, not least if one was squared and the other wasn't.

In fairness to a baffled group of First Formers setting out on the long haul onwards and upwards through the academic strata of the school, in the course of which the sun of comprehension might well rise for some and be forever set on others, Mr Sprayson did his level best to make his Algebra lessons consistently dull. It seemed to be a fair bet, conveyed by his air of weary resignation, that he had been roped in to teach the subject against his better judgement, that he didn't like it and didn't care who knew that he didn't like it.

The textbook was his tool of the trade. During the lessons he read to us from it, line by line, setting it aside only now and then to emphasise a point he considered salient. He chalked various letters posing as numbers on a large blackboard which leaned on a heavy wooden easel erected not too far to the right of where he stood. His efforts on the blackboard were punctuated by the sporadic screeching of the chalk in action — a sound designed to send a frisson of nervous recoil around the assembled class.

2

The Primary Break

In his academic antecedents, Mr Sprayson was a graduate of the Faculty of Chemistry at the University of Birmingham. Chemistry was his prioritised teaching subject, and he was good at it — good enough to be an inspiration to his pupils. He encouraged star pupils — those survivors, that is, who made it all the way through to the Upper Sixth Form and the externally set General Certificate of Secondary Education Advanced Level (or A Level) examinations — to specialise in science subjects and to continue onwards, post A Level, to study the same at his Midland-based alma mater. His pursuit of this endeavour had met with not inconsiderable success.

Back in his salad days, Mr Sprayson had at some juncture played First Class Gentlemen's cricket for Worcestershire — to what extent was never really clear, but the experience was profound enough to mark his preferences. Pupils with an aptitude for the willow and the leather in combination soon discovered that their indiscretions in the context of school life were apt to be forgiven or ignored by him if they could score runs and/or take wickets in inter-school matches.

For me as a First Former to think of Mr Sprayson in terms of the nickname "Boss" came as no easy matter, since the Headmaster of Port Isaac County Primary School, the legendary Mr C. Victor

Richards, to whom my mind and sole school allegiance were still so closely conditioned, was also nicknamed Boss.

Boss Richards was likewise a highly respected figure, yet whereas Mr Sprayson favoured resolving situations by virtue of an affirmatively diplomatic iron fist in a velvet glove, Boss Richards customarily covered his velvet touch with a gauntlet of pure steel.

It was only as my familiarity with Sir James Smith's improved that I managed to feel more comfortable in thinking of Mr Sprayson as Boss. And then, beyond that, the nickname seemed to come to me as second nature.

Mr Sprayson was of average height, neither noticeably tall nor obviously short. He was broad of shoulder and sternly imperious of countenance. His hair was his most distinguishing feature, so severely parted in the middle that it put on display a line of pink scalp as sharp and true as a plough furrow. On either flank of this precise divide, waves of darkly greying hair rolled laterally outwards on a perfect right-angled vector, the one side a mirror image of the other. It was in a style to gladden the heart of Miss Violet M. Jones, who taught Geometry when she wasn't getting stuck into her principal teaching subject of Geography.

Miss Jones, who was blessed with the nickname" Jonesie", was a model of consistency in that both of her assigned subjects carried the prefix "Geo". That was a lot easier for me to rationalise than was a hypothetical bag containing n nuts.

Mr Sprayson's hair was admired as a work of great distinction when set against barbering qualities vested in a styling climate limited to a "short back and sides and some off the top". It provided him with an enhanced stamp of authority instantly recognisable at even long distance.

Mr Sprayson wore his gown of office with such dignity that you felt senatorial purple, rather than black, ought to have been its colour. It barely billowed as he strode through the school corridors, and it was rare indeed that anything other than the inevitable chalk dust was seen to mar its sable elegance.

The same consideration of near-pristine appearance could not have been alleged in respect of the gowns of most other members of the Sir James Smith's teaching staff, some of which, and in particular that pertaining to our History master Mr Menadue, gave an impression of being chalk-dust magnets. Mr Menadue, who went under the nickname of "Mena", rubbed out his chalk inscriptions on blackboards with a wooden-backed felt eraser using a sufficient level of fervour to generate a cloud of chalky motes in the eraser's wake. When Mr Menadue took the blackboard eraser in his hand we kept precautionary eyes on its movements, in order to avoid surprise and have the opportunity of ducking if he chose to throw it at one or other of us as an anti-misdemeanour missile.

None of our teachers, inclusive of Mr Sprayson, was ever seen to don a mortar board to complete the academic investiture of office in conjunction with the ubiquitous gown. The absence of such diagnostic headgear was regretted by many of us, not least myself, as we all knew it to be closely associated with the accounts of teaching practice which appeared on the pages of such authoritative weekly publications as *Adventure, The Wizard, The Rover, The Hotspur* and *Champion*, as well as *The Beano, The Dandy* and *Knockout*, among others.

We read avidly of teaching standards and stereotypes in the tales of Red Circle School in the *Hotspur* (my personal favourite); "Smith of the Lower Third" (later of the Fourth Form) in the *Wizard* and "Ginger Nutt — the boy who takes the biscuit" in *Champion*.

Yarns like these also featured an obligatory cane of thin bamboo as a teacher's essential accessory — although in my seven years at Sir James Smith's I never once saw a cane of any shape or form, either being carried, or left lying around, or hung from a nail hammered into a wall. Mr Sprayson's policy could be assumed to have defined the running of his scholastic empire as a cane-free zone.

It was inevitably rumoured that the Headmaster must have had a cane hidden away in the sanctum that was his Study, from whence, one day, it might be produced to deal with circumstances which permitted no alternative to its use. The rumour was never disproved, but few among us were bold enough to dismiss it out of hand.

I was required to present myself in Mr Sprayson's study on a number of occasions, some of which were for good and some of which were not. I looked around surreptitiously each time, but my eyes never encountered any form of instrument of punishment outside of the Headmaster's admonitory tongue.

Gowns were not worn by the teachers back at Port Isaac County Primary School, where there were four classes and four teachers, each of whom was fully dedicated to one of the classes, and it was only in the hands of Boss Richards that a cane ever made an appearance.

As far as Boss Richards was concerned, the function of a cane was that of deterrent. He wielded his as a sort of swagger stick to impress the masses. Since the mere sight of Boss Richards approaching guaranteed the existence of as much deterrent against misbehaviour as would ever be necessary, Boss's cane was, in principle, surplus to requirements, although its presence was not entirely for cosmetic purposes.

I felt the bite of that cane only once, when Boss flicked it at the back of my hand at an after-playtime assembly line-up at which I must not have been standing precisely where I should have been. The deep purple welt made by the cane took weeks to fade. I accepted that I had got what I deserved, as did everyone else who took a look at the result. One of the accepted golden rules of school was that whatever action a teacher took against your person must be right, and if what he or she did to you felt unjust, well, it was simply because you were guilty until proved innocent and there was nothing to be done about it.

The four classes at Port Isaac County Primary School were graduated in terms of pupil age. I commenced at the age of four in the infants' class, remaining there until I was almost seven. I then served two years in the second class until I was nine, and afterwards, following only a year in the third class, I was placed for a further year in Boss Richards' class, in with the big boys and girls who ranged up to the age of fifteen.

The extraordinary move for me to be taught by Boss Richards was not of my choosing, but stemmed rather from an entirely kind and supportive consideration by Boss himself to provide me with a substantive preparation for the so-called "eleven-plus" examination intended to gain entry to grammar school.

As it worked out, I had very much enjoyed my year in the third class under a charismatic teacher named Mr Perry, and would gladly have undertaken a second year with him. Leaving Mr Perry's cheery warmth for allocation to Boss Richards' class initially brought me cold comfort. It was not by any means easy to be a small boy in the society of a class of big boys. We were as immiscible as water and oil. However, since the big boys required someone to serve as the butt not only of their jokes but of their contempt as well, I was immediately compelled to assume that mantle. It is said that in reality nothing is ever as bad as you imagine it is going to be, but whoever said that never experienced what it was to be a small boy thrust against his will into the company of mature peers.

I overheard two of the big boys, Richard Couch and Brian Orchard by name, conversing on the subject of me — "Have you seen what we've got coming in with us next term?" — as if my presence among them piled a grave insult on their burgeoning manhood. Richard and Brian, known as "Rich" and "Otch", were a hard-edged double act that I knew the likes of me could never aspire to emulate.

One incidental stroke of good fortune did attend me in my year in Boss's class, as during it the much admired Mr Perry left the school to be replaced by a Mr Henry Pam, whose technique of teaching, nothing if not heavy-handed, quickly earned him the nickname of "Henry the Eighth". I was grateful that I never had to sit in a class under his mock-Tudor excesses.

For all that, a year in Boss Richards' class was a relatively short sentence to serve in the school scheme of things, not least since it was additionally focused on preparing me for the eleven-plus, also referred to as the grammar school exam, the Camelford exam or the scholarship exam. Sir James Smith didn't even get a mention at that stage. I was several months away from achieving the age of eleven-plus when I took the exam, but the rules didn't insist on candidates being in precise compliance with a minimum age of eleven.

The exam came along, I took it and it was behind me.

Whether or not my year with Rich and Otch and their strong-willed fellows improved my eleven-plus chance of success remained a matter for debate, not that debate ever mattered, then or now. In sitting the eleven-plus exam I was not unique, being merely one among a great host of primary school children all over the entire country, every one of us up for the same thing at the same time. It was one of the sad truths of the eleven-plus that many were called but few were chosen.

The line separating those who passed the eleven-plus and achieved grammar school selection and those who didn't was as fragile as it was fine. The side of the line that a winner stood on to some extent took account of merit and righteousness, but primarily it depended on the luck of the day, the influence of mentors, and a measure in some cases, naturally enough, of who rather than what you were.

Port Isaac County Primary School fell into the catchment area of Sir James Smith's Grammar School, located in Camelford, eleven miles away. Other town and village primary school centres in the same catchment area, incorporating a host of outlying farms and hamlets, were Boscastle, Tintagel, Delabole, Davidstow, St Kew, St Teath and of course Camelford itself.

Each primary school could be expected to send between three and five (it varied) of its eleven-plus candidates to enter the First Form at Sir James Smith's at the September commencement of an academic year, the overall annual First Form intake being a minimum of twenty-five and a maximum of thirty pupils.

In my Sir James Smith's entry year of 1950, Port Isaac County Primary School submitted five pupils to the First Form. Apart from me there were two other boys, Gordon Keat and Michael Vagges, and two girls, Mollie Hooke and Ann Thomas.

Those who, for whatever spurious reason, were deemed to be unsuccessful at the eleven-plus challenge, were faced with the prospect of continuing in primary school education up to the statutory leaving age of fourteen or fifteen. The eleven-plus offered few if any second chances.

I was neither inwardly conscious nor outwardly transformed in any way that I can recall as a result of my passing the eleven-plus. One immediate (and wholly unexpected) benefit of success, however, was that I received a gift in the form of a pound note from my revered and much-loved family doctor, Dr Donald MacDougal Sproull. One pound was more money than I had ever previously held in my hand as my very own, and it gave me a sense of wellbeing overladen with great unease, all of which dissipated entirely when I handed the quid over to my mother.

Dr Sproull was a medical man for all seasons, dedicated to his patients and forever kind and sympathetic in the face of adversity. He reserved the prickly side of his professional manner for dealing with malingerers.

Once the dreadful reality that I had to leave the safe and familiar haven of Port Isaac County Primary School in order to attend a far-off grammar school began to sink in, however, I sank into a despondent sense of great loss, of forced daily separation from all that I held dear, and barren exile from the circle of hitherto inseparable friends who would not be coming with me.

They were the almost painfully close friends of boyhood, the like of which only got made once. We had grown up together, had shared so much, knew one another's innermost minds and secrets, and were welded as one against every adversity that Port Isaac's wide range of miserable old buggers could throw at us. The eleven-plus was a true watershed, from the cusp of which we all were, with the best will in the world, destined to drift apart.

There seemed to be such iniquity vested in the process of grammar school selection, but yet, the tide flowed, and those of us who were caught up by it could do no more than either sink or swim in the unknown currents.

Within the scope of the eleven-plus exam that I sat, there were tests on arithmetic and English usage and grammar, and a requirement to write a composition on "Where I went for my summer holidays". The composition gave me some nervous moments at the outset — too much truth in pen and ink about my summer exploits could well have had the Port Isaac policeman calling at the door as a consequence, not that he was a stranger to our back door as a bringer of admonition. I had to fall back on subterfuge, but since I had never ever been away from home on holiday, I couldn't cast my net to a location any further abroad than Rock on the east side of the River Camel estuary, not too far from Port Isaac down the coast towards Padstow. I had been to Rock once on a Sunday School outing. It was an humble experience, but it was mine own. And so my composition dealt with my holiday at Rock.

I was fortunate that the examiners accepted the composition despite my unstylish handwriting. I knew that my handwriting was not of the best, as every teacher at Port Isaac County Primary never seemed to tire of pointing out to me.

On the subject of friends, I was told that at Sir James Smith's I was likely to make a new set of friends quite rapidly, although the assumption that this was the way it would be brought me little cheer. Those new friends would be natives of other villages, and any proper Port Isaac boy knew that natives of other villages weren't in any way like us in Port Isaac. They didn't even talk or think like us. Some of them might also be posh types, and I for one wasn't socially equipped to relate to the likes of those.

Although I knew the four other Port Isaac County Primary School classmates who acceded with me to Sir James Smith's very well, none of them was a member of my deep inner circle of friends, which meant that there was no immediately protective glue to bind us together against the strangeness of our first feet-finding days in Camelford.

I knew the two girls best of all, but as it would have been unthinkable for an eleven-year-old boy to hang around with girls of the same age, there was no available option to get itself off the ground where they were concerned.

Mollie was two weeks younger than me, and as pre-war (just) contemporary babies whose fathers were both serving in the Royal Navy, we had been wheeled together around the streets of wartime Port Isaac by our mothers. That gave us a strong early bond.

Ann lived two doors down from me in the row of new council

houses along Hartland Road. I went along to her house every Saturday evening for an hour or so to read her copies of "Film Fun" and "Girl's Crystal", as I didn't have a weekly order in for either of those down at Mrs Rowe's newsagents shop in Lower Fore Street.

Gordon was the only son of Mr and Mrs Samuel Keat. His father was tragically lost in the early part of the war, and his mother was famed for running a chip shop down near the bottom of the village. The Keat family were substantial property owners, and could be looked on as comparatively well-off by the standards of the time and in comparison to so many of the rest of us.

Mike Vagges was the younger son of a Port Isaac coastguard, Mr "Taffy" Vagges. Both Taffy and his wife were, unsurprisingly, of Welsh origin. Mike was the one among Port Isaac's other four First Form hopefuls who I knew the least well, and I could have wished to have known him better. In matters intellectual I thought he was some distance ahead of all of us.

3

The Legacy of Sir James

Sir James Smith's Grammar School in Camelford was one of a prominent number of grammar schools spread around the county of Cornwall, each one serving as a district centre for secondary education, and sourcing pupils from its own formally designated catchment area containing a broad scattering of local primary schools.

Camelford was a dour looking town situated on the upper reaches of the River Camel at a place where the river was presumably fordable in those far off days of old, when knights were bold. It was still quite feasible to wade across the river where the ford must have held sway, but the necessity to do so was long since obviated thanks to the provision of a road bridge.

Camelford was undoubtedly a unique town, in respect of which, at the risk of flogging an old gag, the word "unique" was derived from the Latin "unus equus". Whether or not Camelford was truly appropriate as a centre in which a district-serving grammar school might be founded, and where it might thereafter flourish, no longer mattered since the said school was an established fact. There it was, Camelford and its grammar school, well-supported by a distinguished history on which to hang an abundance of laurels.

An account of the school's history was expertly researched and written by Mr Sprayson's elder daughter Jennifer. The distillation of the school's historical record which now follows is acknowledged in its entirety as having being drawn from Jennifer's impeccable compilation, as without reference to her researches I would have been sufficiently lost for words to have justified a blackboard eraser, or at least a stick of chalk, being thrown at me by Mr Menadue.

Dutiful reference to Jennifer makes me sad to relate that, when some of us thought we could get away with it, we pronounced her name at school in the high falsetto tone of Ted Ray's creation in "Ray's a Laugh" — "Jenn-nee-fer!"

Sir James Smith's Grammar School, Camelford, or alternatively Camelford Grammar School (since a rose by any other name would be sure to smell as sweet), was founded by the good Sir James in the year of our Lord 1679. This key date was commemorated on the school uniform badge of my day. The badge's features were picked out in red on a green background. Red and green were the official school colours, shown perhaps to best effect in the alternating stripes of the school tie.

The badge displayed a static red camel posing on a dead flat footing that was perhaps intended to represent the ship of the desert ironically picking its way across a shallow river bed. As in the case of which twin had the Toni, only the designer of the badge knew what the camel was doing for sure. Three of the camel's hooves, the two at the back and the left one at the front, appeared to be barely submerged, if submerged at all. The camel's right front leg, however, was bent and slightly elevated, and since not a single drop of water appeared to be falling from it, either the fording concept was invalid, or the river had run dry when the badge's design was dreamed up.

Sir James Smith, the founder himself, was reputed to own property both in the Chelsea area of London and at Trehannick in Cornwall near to St Teath (a hole-in-the-wall village which in some other village communities, and not least in Port Isaac, was known as St Death). Sir James commenced his career as educational benefactor to certain select youth of the Camelford district as early on as 1671, when he purchased, and subsequently donated to the Town Corporation, a parcel of twenty-eight acres of land at Great Tregoth near Slaughter Bridge. The latter was situated a few miles outside of the town.

Slaughter Bridge stood in a drearily remote setting, marking the alleged site of the last battle fought by the legendary King Arthur. It therefore must accept its fair share of responsibility for the trials of Mallory's "Morte D'Arthur", and Tennyson's "Idylls of the King" in latter-day English Literature classes.

The motivation behind Sir James' donation of land set in such a wild location was reportedly his "goodwill and respect for Camelford". Such feelings of benevolence towards the town might not always have sprung so readily to the fore in the more introspective climate of the mid-twentieth century.

As a consequence of his largesse Sir James was not unsurprisingly "elected" as one of a pair of members of Parliament for Camelford in the shining year of 1679 when the school he founded was presumably just beginning to get up and run.

One of the key conditions underpinning Sir James' gift of the land to Camelford was that a school should be built and maintained on it, and funded by income received from renting the land out. There appears to be no record of a school having been constructed in the vicinity of Slaughter Bridge (for which now thank we all our God, with hearts and hands and voices), and the establishment was more properly inducted within the precincts of Camelford's Town Hall.

The then mayor of Camelford, together with certain of his civic acolytes, was subsequently reported to have used the rental income from Sir James Smith's land grant for personal benefit, all consistent with a great political tradition of under-the-counter trading which has stood the test of centuries.

The eighteenth century was reported to have brought along ever-declining standards of education at Sir James Smith's School, although the decline as such was obviously not a fatal factor. At one period in that far-off era, the school was, to its credit, enabled to publicise the particular asset of having a Writing and Grammar Schoolmaster in attendance, named Mr Nydhope Wallis. He must have had something substantial to contribute outside of his Christian name, as his fair surname eventually became enshrined as the name of one of the two competitive "Houses" into which the school's pupil complement was subdivided.

The second House was named "Drake". There were no prizes for guessing the derivation of that name. Its owner was sleeping down below, a thousand miles away in a hammock slung between the round shot.

By 1764 the Writing and Grammar Schoolmaster's position was being specified in terms of "Writing" only. Whether or not it could be assumed from this amendment that Grammar had suffered some form of academic relegation is not known.

Sir James Smith's School held its location in Camelford Town Hall until 1806, in which enlightened year it was evicted for reasons unknown, and its pupils were compelled thereafter to assemble in the Writing Schoolmaster's house.

Eight years later, a new Sir James Smith's School was built at an undefined location in Camelford, where it functioned as an independent establishment until about 1860, at which time it was amalgamated with the local National School. However, within the space of only a few years more, the local Charity Commissioners called for an improved building to be constructed to house the school, and with that its previous building fell into the hands of the Church, which may have been the intention all along.

In 1870, the Sir James Smith's School, then reportedly existing under the auspices of the Duke of Cleveland, was carrying out such teaching as it could in a single room near the King's Arms public house, located about half way up the steep incline of Fore Street on the Delabole approach side of Camelford.

There was to be at least one more relocation undertaken before the school reached its ultimate location on the far flank of town alongside College Road, where it opened in 1892 as a day school for boys, although, at the discretion of the Board of Governors, there might have been a possibility that girls could also be admitted. One could but imagine the Victorian stereotypes who must have sat on that Board of Governors, although as far as any details went it was probably better not to think too hard or too long about it.

For this late nineteenth-century resurrection of Sir James Smith's creation, the aforesaid Charity Commissioners reportedly laid down no fewer than forty-seven Articles of Administration, including the regulation of circumstances controlling the dismissal of the Headmaster; the nature and quality of the residence to be assigned to him; his terms of reference regarding powers to both engage and dismiss other teaching staff; and the fact that a good teacher's qualifications need not necessarily require the support of Holy Orders. There was no doubt, however, that a would-be teacher in possession of Holy Orders would not have been regarded disadvantageously by the Governors when it came to deciding whether or not to engage the former's services.

The ages of pupils in 1892 ranged from eight to fifteen. The school's mandatory entry examination covered the three good old Rs — reading, writing from dictation, and basic arithmetic with a knowledge of the multiplication tables.

Once a pupil was accepted for entry into Sir James Smith's School, the syllabus on offer to him (and her) was one of impressive academic rigour. It included religious instruction; reading; writing; arithmetic; geography; history; English grammar, composition and literature; algebra (shades of *n* nuts); geometry; Latin; a minimum of one foreign language; natural science; drawing; drilling (most likely a precursor of PT); and vocal music.

With the best will in the world, the Sir James Smith's School prior to 1892 gave the impression of having drifted through time on the seat of its pants. Its greatest achievement was most probably its survival as a distinctive institution for over two centuries. The date of 1892 could be held to mark its arrival as a true grammar school, very much alive and well, and, deservedly or not, representing as fine an asset as could be desired for placing the town of Camelford squarely on the map.

That grand syllabus of 1892 was not radically different from its counterpart in place at Sir James Smith's Grammar School when I took it up fifty-eight years later.

The school became formally co-educational when girls were freely admitted for the first time in 1905. By 1909 the proportion of boy to girl pupils was three to one. The intake net was cast wide, as pupils came from places as far away as Bude, St Austell and Plymouth. During term time they took room and board in the town. The school assuredly bore the hallmark of a distinctive centre of learning. Those seeds planted by Sir James Smith in 1679 had given rise to a tree of life bearing fair fruit.

There were sixty-six pupils on the school register in 1907, of whom one was described as a "free scholar"; fifty-two as "ordinary pupils"; three as "county scholars"; and ten as "pupil teachers". The latter were in all likelihood monitors or perhaps the Edwardian equivalent of prefects.

In 1913 the school was formally designated "The Sir James Smith's Grammar School", and so it remained thereafter. Concurrently, cookery instruction, the forerunner of domestic science, entered the curriculum.

By 1918, in a reflection of the exigencies of the Great War, pupil numbers at the school had fallen to a total of thirty-two, of whom nineteen were boys and thirteen were girls. However, although the numbers might have fallen, the boy/girl balance had improved. There was a teaching staff establishment of only two to take care of all subjects, and they were the Headmaster, Mr C. E. Leese, and a First Class Assistant Mistress named Miss Dale.

Mr Leese went on to become a fixed institution at the school. He was set as firmly in his position as Excalibur was in stone until he got drawn out to be succeeded by the new King, Mr K. A. Sprayson, in 1949. It was remarkable to reflect that during the full half century prior to 1949 the school had had only two headmasters, Mr Leese's predecessor having been a certain Captain D. B. Hart, who might have come from a military or naval background — unless it was derived from the mining industry, since Captain was a much honoured authoritative title at the operational end of Cornish mining practice. At least the good captain was unlikely to have emerged from the Holy Orders side of things, may blessings be counted.

Between the end of the Great War and the start of the Second World War Sir James Smith's Grammar School appears to have been constantly struggling to survive. Working funds were scarce to non-existent, and as a consequence, little or nothing seems to have been ceded free to pupils. True, there was dedicated school transport to bring pupils to the school, but there were no formal school dinners provided (by my lights not necessarily a bad thing). On the other hand it went on record that if all else should fail, fish cakes were available for purchase at tuppence each, with tea to accompany them at a ha'penny a cup. According to convention, pupils normally tended to bring their dinners to school from home and heat them up on the school's boiler. Furthermore, pupils were required to buy their own books and were assessed for school fees at a cost of three pounds five shillings per term.

Sir James Smith's Grammar School was in such parlous financial straits in 1939 that the Cornwall County Council proposed to close it down. Fortunately the Council authorities were induced to change their minds and grant a reprieve thanks to the intervention of one Mr Tucker, the Chairman of the Board of Governors, who had the backing of a celebrated gentleman destined to hold the Chairmanship in post-war years, the landed aristocrat Sir John Molesworth St Aubyn, Bart, of the Pencarrow estate near Bodmin.

As a result of Mr Tucker's timely intervention a policy defraying the cost of school fees to assist the poorer families of the district, as well as instituting subsidised school dinners, was adopted. Its success could be measured by pupil numbers having risen to one hundred and fifty when Mr Sprayson took over the headmastership from Mr Leese, and the number of teaching staff had increased to twelve.

With Mr Sprayson in charge, the school underwent a significant renaissance, and a golden decade beckoned. The pupils who attended Sir James Smith's Grammar School in the nineteen-fifties were privileged to experience the quality of the school at its best.

Mr Leese stood as a genuine pillar, both figuratively and literally, of all that the school was during the inter-war years. He had a reputation, as I heard it described, of having his ways set in concrete. He would not have been a man well able to manage the rapid sweep of post-war change and meet the constant challenges it imposed on matters both educational and social.

In 1949 Mr Leese might well have been taken out of the school, but the school could not be taken out of him, as he continued to stick his foot in the door as often as he was permitted, in order perhaps to draw sustenance for his inner soul. I saw him a few times around the corridors, cutting a lonely figure whose welcome was lacking in warmth, and who knew, with sadness, that his presence was not really wanted. Retirement after a lifetime of service performed entirely to his own satisfaction must have been like a small death in waiting for him.

After the war, all school fees were paid by Cornwall County Council, which meant that any sense of unfair elitism for pupils' parents could cease to be. Any boy or girl, no matter how humble their background might be, was subject only to success at the eleven-plus to gain entry to Sir James Smith's.

Who a pupil's parents were mattered less than what the pupil was capable of, and that fed fully into Mr Sprayson's credo. He was a man "without side", as the local expression went, a man of consummate benevolence, with or without a bag of n nuts in his hand.

4

In Uniform

And lo, it came to pass that by virtue of just directing my feet on the sunny side of the eleven-plus street, I came, thanks to the stern guidance of Boss Richards, to the end of my final term at Port Isaac County Primary School in July 1950. And behold, all that then faced me was a prospect of crossing the eternal bridge of six weeks of summer holidays prior to a place in the First Form at Sir James Smith's Grammar School in Camelford getting thrust upon me.

In keeping with the great remembered tradition of school summer holidays, it seemed that during the summer of 1950 the sun shone without let through glorious days and balmy evenings. Material things were set at nothing, which was just as well as there weren't many of them. All that mattered was to live for each moment of the day in hand on the assumption that the morrow would take care of itself.

One unavoidable priority reared up its unwelcome head to disrupt the placid flow of the summer, however. This was the ever-pressing necessity of getting me sartorially outfitted in time for the start of the autumn term at Sir James Smith's, since the school mandated a policy of strict uniform dress code to which there were no exceptions other than for Sixth Formers, who were permitted to turn up in smart casual attire.

I possessed little in the way of clothes that might fit any part of the conventional Sir James Smith's uniform — actually, come to think of it, I didn't have much in the way of clothes of any kind. I was one of those of whom it was said (usually after death) that all he owned was the clothes that he stood up in.

The standard of garb that the majority of Port Isaac boys like me wore was moulded by the fact that, although our families weren't completely poverty stricken, they were assuredly poor, and hence such coins of the realm as were available to them were essentially directed towards the provision of food for the table.

It was as Mr Walter "Ido" Glover said of his children, "Their clothes is shabby, but their bellies is full". Various mothers, not least my own, might be heard to observe of their offspring's tattered garb that it was "out to hass and out to helbow". Hand-me-downs and cast offs were the order of the day, on some of which even the patches were patched.

Down at Mr William John Honey's barber shop in Port Isaac's Fore Street one Saturday night I heard myself described by one of his invariable host of customers as looking like "a sack of shit tied up ugly". This felt to be a curiously appropriate description of my darned, patched and pulled together shirt, jumper, trousers and jerkin. I didn't take it personally as I was merely one of many in a similar state of disrepair.

On the other hand it would be unfair for me not to admit to owning what could, with a good stretch of imagination, be seen as a "best" shirt and a "best" pair of trousers. Although by no means elegant, these were more or less intact, and strictly reserved for wearing to Church, to Sunday School and again on festive occasions. It was only when I joined the optimistically named choir of St Peter's Church in Port Isaac and was assigned a cassock, surplice and ruff for service wear, that the donning of best clothes on Sunday became less of a strain. What the eye couldn't see under the cassock, the heart couldn't grieve over.

With regard to footwear, I owned one impressively threadbare pair of plimsolls that had been white when new (and were sometimes white again when touched up with Blanco), together with a pair of hobnailed boots to wear to school. When they needed to be repaired, my boots were taken to Mr Harry Morman, the Port Isaac cobbler, and Harry was more than equal to turning them around in a timely manner so that missing school on the excuse of a temporary absence of boots was a rare event indeed.

The uniform code set by Sir James Smith's was designed to set all pupils at a non-discriminatory level of appearance. Whether one's family was wealthy or impoverished, all pupils were as one in school uniform. In the prevailing climate of an utterly class-ridden society, a school uniform made a wonderful equaliser.

The school uniform wardrobe requirement for boys is shown on page 28. The uniform list for girls, although I never saw it, must have contained many items in common with the boys' list — badge, blazer, shirt, shoes, PT gear, satchel, footwear, socks (although white and shorter) and maybe even (at least to begin with) underwear. In the place of a cap, however, the girls wore a floppy beret-like device. Trousers were out — if a girl had ever turned up wearing pants it would have caused a sensation among teachers and fellow-pupils alike. The garment of key identity for the girls, under which all else resided in mystery, was a rather loosely hanging green gymslip. It came, I think, in both a heavier winter drape, and a lighter summer version.

However, that was all for them, and the boys' list was what concerned me. What I possessed of that impressive inventory of boys' scholastic elegance in the early summer of 1950 was almost precisely no part of bugger all. Therefore, all of it had to be obtained,

Boys' Uniform

1. A green cap with the school badge affixed centre front.
2. A white vest and a pair of white underpants.
3. A long-sleeved white (or grey) shirt (grey being preferred as it was less obvious at showing the dirt).
4. A school tie (alternate red and green sloping stripes).
5. A green blazer with the school badge displayed on the front left breast pocket.
6. A pair of grey flannel trousers (long or short, depending on which side of the adolescent divide you found yourself).
7. A pair of long grey socks with either elastic or garter support (or both to be on the safe side).
8. A pair of black leather lace-up shoes (to be polished each day please).
9. A pair of shorts for PT together with a pair of white plimsolls, the latter to be blancoed regularly.
10. A pair of football boots.
11. A drawstring bag (usually home-made) for carrying PT and sports gear.
12. A leather satchel fitted with a shoulder strap, used (ostensibly) to carry books and homework.

and that was no mean task for my parents to undertake, since they themselves were the owners of a little of not very much in the way of money.

Then fate took a small hand in our favour, as my mother had a noble stroke of luck thanks to the good will of Mrs Ellen Brown of the house known as "Carlenice" in Port Isaac. Ellen's son Maurice was a pupil of standing at Sir James Smith's, and at the time of my arrival as a First Former, he was for his part about to step into the Upper Sixth. Mrs Brown gave us a school blazer (minus its badge which had been co-opted to lie down in newer green blazer pastures) that Maurice had long since grown out of. We also got from her an old school cap of Maurice's, equally badge deprived. Not only had it ceased to fit Maurice's learned head, but also someone of his Sixth Form seniority was no longer obliged to wear it. Whenever anyone had a valid opportunity to avoid wearing a cap, the opportunity was seized without hesitation.

A feeling shared by almost all the Sir James Smith's boys, not least by myself, was an aversion to wearing a school cap. It didn't have to be worn on the school premises, but once you were among the public on the outside, to have a cap on your head was mandatory during school hours, and it was a punishable offence to be caught bare-headed. Doffing your cap on meeting elders and betters, including teachers, was a firm rule.

As a Sir James Smith's pupil, I encountered a teacher only once in a public arena without a cap on my head to raise to her. It wasn't really my fault, but pleading that form of an excuse at Sir James Smith's never did anyone any good that I ever knew of. I was as dead in the water as, rather coincidentally at the time, my school cap also was.

It so happened that one day I had been walking in the park adjacent to the river after dinner time when a rather beefy local boy whose appearance was as imposing as it was genuinely ugly — making him a model for one of Lord Snooty's Gasworks Gang arch foes — ran towards me and, without even introducing himself, pushed me over, seized my cap, ripped off the button at the crown, and sent the cap spinning out into the river. He then turned to me and informed me that should I report the incident, he would treat me "chronic". That was a big word for him to have come up with. He must have heard it somewhere in a similar context and thought it would be a good idea to use it himself, although I doubt that he would have been able to spell it if pressed. I didn't know what chronic meant either, but the tone in which it was voiced was threatening enough to suggest it didn't mean anything pleasant.

I said nothing, then and subsequently, and as a result was not treated chronic by him. My button-liberated cap was eventually retrieved from the Camel's shallows a short distance downstream, but not before I was spotted by a teacher, the cap's absence from my head being most conspicuous to one like her whose eyes were attuned to look out for such things. To meet up with any teacher in town was an unusual enough event to invite comment, but she lived locally and that probably explained her presence in the right place at the right time to pile detention on top of my injured feelings.

Not to look a gift horse in the mouth, Maurice's old blazer fitted me like a glove, although it would perhaps have been better if it had fitted me more like a blazer. It hung in the sort of folds that a set of curtains in the House of Usher might have exhibited in the moments before they fell. Nevertheless the blazer did me a signal service after being rendered truly utilitarian by the sewing of an oval-shaped leather patch at the back of each sleeve centred on my elbows, or where my elbows ought to have been when I set them on my desk top, cupped my chin in my hands, and held my head upright to give the impression in class that my mind wasn't elsewhere.

Loose badges for sewing on to blazers and caps could be purchased from Mr Moyse, the Camelford tailor, whose establishment was located on the left-hand side of the descent of Fore Street, down which steep incline incoming school buses entered Camelford. Mr Moyse's shop was the one and only officially designated distribution outlet for Sir James Smith's Grammar School uniforms and accessories.

My hard leather satchel was obtained at the shop of Mr Wesley Blake in Wadebridge. Vendors in Port Isaac were unequal to the challenge of providing such an item, although since Wesley was a Port Isaac man, the satchel was close enough to being a home purchase.

My mother made a PT bag for me out of an old piece of blackout curtain left over from the war and carefully stored away at the back of a cupboard on the grounds that you never knew when it might come in useful. An adequate length of thin rope to make the PT bag's drawstring was provided by my grandfather, Jim Creighton.

Boss Richards then gave me a pair of cracked leather football boots of uncertain vintage which were fortuitously discovered in a cubby hole used for storage at Port Isaac County Primary School and had found no one other than me willing to accept them. That alone spoke volumes as to the condition of the boots. They didn't fit my feet especially well, but since I was no shakes at all as a footballer, the perfection of fit was immaterial and so that was that. It was nominally a pair of football boots, and therefore capable of satisfying the needs of the school uniform list. Once a good application of Dubbin (the smell of which I loved) had been worked into the uppers, and a few of the old studs had been replaced with new ones by Harry Morman, Stanley Matthews himself could not have been better kitted out with his Blackpool boots than I was with mine.

To acquire the remaining items on the school uniform list so as to ensure that all protocols were followed to the letter, a visit by us to Mr Moyse's shop was called for. The great imponderable of the shopping expedition lay in just how we were going to get to Camelford. My mother planned to make the journey with me on a day late in August 1950. Although it wasn't quite a last-minute excursion, it came perilously close to being one.

In practice, the date of buying my items of uniform was governed by my mother's deep-rooted abhorrence of entering into debt. What she couldn't pay for in full in the here and now would have to wait until she could.

For anyone who owned or had ready access to a car, travelling from Port Isaac to Camelford was straightforward enough. Unfortunately, Port Isaac was unable to boast of too many car owners, which meant that public transport was in most cases the only option open to a would-be traveller. As it was, public transport, while reliable when it wished to be, tended to fall short in the qualities of either directness or frequency. There were in fact no scheduled direct bus services to Camelford from Port Isaac for the benefit of the general public. On the other hand, who in Port Isaac would want to go to Camelford anyway unless they had to?

The regular bus services out of Port Isaac went only to Wadebridge and back. Passengers had a choice of taking a bus belonging to the National Bus Company, known more simply as the "National", or one pertaining to the fleet of the brothers Prout. The latter were two in number, bearing the great Gospel-derived Christian names of John and Mark, John being the elder. They were Port Isaac men to the core.

Their transport company, under the title of "Prout Bros", or "Prout's" for short, was so established in the mastery of public transport from its Trelawney Garage nerve centre on New Road that the brothers could justifiably be referred to as true legends in their own lifetimes.

Prout's ran a daily school bus service from Port Isaac to Camelford in term time, picking up Sir James Smith's pupils all along the way. Occasionally a non-school passenger or two might be taken along if there was space available. My mother could have fallen into that category, but then again, August did not fall under term time, and she and I clearly couldn't wait until September to go up to

Camelford with Prout's to fulfil my uniform requirements.

Rail transport was a possibility to consider, as a regular Southern Railway train, serving selected stations between the fishing port of Padstow on the River Camel estuary and Waterloo in London, made stops at Wadebridge, Port Isaac Road, Delabole and Camelford railway stations and many points beyond for those bold enough to venture that far. The train looked attractive in principle, with the only drawback perhaps being that both Port Isaac Road and Camelford stations were located some miles from the communities for which they were named. They were, quite literally, neither here nor there. In contrast, Delabole station was situated close to the heart of its grey town namesake. The railway track skirted the rim of the gigantic slate quarry for which, difficult though it was to say anything complimentary about Delabole, the town was famed locally, nationally and internationally for the quality of the quarried product.

Fate then took a hand, as it did so happen that my father came into possession of a small Austin Seven car that I think he had been more or less given by someone who was relieved to have it taken off his hands. With the expert assistance of Mr Charlie Lobb, proprietor of Port Isaac's North Cornwall Transport Garage, and the addition of a bit of luck, my father managed to get the engine of the Austin Seven working well enough to permit the car to be driven around over modest distances. He spruced the bodywork up with two coats of royal blue paint, and considering that he applied the paint using only a paintbrush, did a very creditable job. The Austin Seven's appearance was better than its reliability, but it did get around and that was what counted.

It was in this little car then, driven by my father, that my mother and I were taken on a rattling trip to Camelford, along much of the very route pioneered and followed by Prout's school bus service. We travelled out of Port Isaac along Trewetha Lane; climbed Poltre-worgey Hill to the main (B3314) road junction; turned left along the main road to Pendoggett; went onwards to the China Downs crossroads (where the road up from Port Gaverne crossed on its way to St Teath); took the relatively straight and lengthy climb up to and through Delabole; and then drove on to Camelford Station, where a hard right turn was made to greet the long straight road into Camelford.

From China Downs onwards the road was exposed to the harsh vagaries and exigencies of Atlantic-hosted weather. I told myself that if my father's Austin Seven could make it to Camelford and back without breaking down, it would stand as a favourable augury for my looming grammar school career. The vehicle got there, but my part of the deal had no foregone conclusion.

And so it was that my mother and I on a certain day in the latter half of August 1950 stood outside a shop door in Camelford's Fore Street, on the inside of which the tailoring business of Mr Moyse lurked in a tantalising gloaming of cloth-bolted fastness. The door was modest in appearance. It opened to the jangle of a bell, spring mounted on the inner frame.

We stepped into a scene which would have had Charles Dickens reaching at once for his writing slope, quill and ink. There was an almost solid smell of new textiles to wade through; in no way unpleasant, but rather warmly inviting and even exciting. We were flanked all about by shelves piled high with great rolls of material of a quantity that seemed well able to provide the wherewithal to clothe Sir James Smith's pupils in perpetuity without any need to restock.

A gentleman emerged from the dimness of the inner fastness of the establishment to greet us. He glided towards us in the manner of Marley's ghost unencumbered by cashboxes. Mr Moyse — for it was he — was small, plump and balding, clad in a beautifully cut although slightly rumpled three-piece suit. About his collar a tape measure dangled as a symbol of office. In one hand he grasped a big chunk of a white substance, probably chalk, which had the shape and form of a Neolithic hand axe. In his other hand he brandished a large and fearsome looking pair of tailor's shears. He conveyed the impression that he was masking a keen business acumen with stereotype, seemingly imbued with all the professional confidence and self-importance of one who knew full well that his customers needed him much more than he needed them. He gave me my first faint inkling of what a monopoly might be all about.

Once he had set down the intimidating implements of his trade, Mr Moyse received us with much dry-washing of hands. He was, he said, ready to serve and to fulfil our every need. That our every need involved, at my mother's insistence, only one each of just a few of the items on the official school Uniform list led to Mr Moyse exhibiting definite discontent. My mother bought from him only what she could afford and refused to be persuaded otherwise — her purchases being, namely, one pair of short grey flannel trousers, one white shirt, one pair of school socks, one school tie, one blazer badge and one cap badge.

The trousers and shirt came off the peg, which meant that I didn't get measured for fit by Mr Moyse in anything other than a eyeballing manner. I needed to try them on, however, to ensure that they were of a size that I would, sometime, grow into, and then, once clad, I was compelled to parade around the tight confines of the shop until my mother was ready to express a satisfaction about my appearance that I didn't feel.

Mr Moyse was adamant that the purchase of two of everything was a must, but my mother leant on the consideration that one uniform ensemble worn through one school week could be washed at the weekend ready for the next week. I was used to that and would have been surprised had it been any different.

We parted company with Mr Moyse and left his theatre of operations with our purchases neatly contained in a brown paper package, expertly tied up with string. I am not sure that it was one of my favourite things, but with its contents I knew that I was as ready as I could ever be to perform the role of a well turned out lamb in sheep's clothing fit to be a pupil at Sir James Smith's Grammar School come September.

5

The Open Day

The bell signalling the end of the preliminaries had yet to be rung, however. One essential bout still needed to be fought prior to the dawning of the first day of my first term in the First Form. The advice came in the form of a letter of invitation to attend a First Formers' Open Day at Sir James Smith's, with each soon-to-be pupil to be accompanied by one (or even two, but no more than that) of his or her respective parents.

This stellar event presented members of the new First Form with an opportunity to obtain a first-hand impression of the grammar school and its buildings and facilities, which presumably was intended to be a Good Thing — or so ran the general idea. In addition, the Open Day would give the impending classmates the chance to take a cautious look at one another, become absolute strangers no more, and perhaps get started on smoothing out some of the rougher and keener edges alike prior to the start of term.

To me, the Open Day was tinged with faint hope and the feeling of a red-sky-in-the-morning prognosis. Although the school's layout should in principle have been quite simple to assimilate, by comparison with Port Isaac County Primary it looked at first sight to be a sprawling agglomeration of buildings, and rather difficult to take in with just one go.

A feature for all Open Day attendees was a guided tour through what seemed to be miles and miles of corridors and a multiplicity of adjoining rooms, some of which were impressively huge in dimension. We feasted our wondering eyes on rarities such as a chemistry laboratory; an out-building dedicated to the teaching of art; a sawdust-fragrant annex where woodwork classes were held; a library lined with shelves groaning under the weight of unread books and stratified dust; and a basically appointed gymnasium in which PT sessions could be conducted, if (as turned out to be not infrequently the case) the weather in the yard outside was inclement.

Under normal circumstances, we were told, the gym was used as the Third Form classroom. As to where the Third Form went for lessons when their sanctuary was commandeered for PT, I assumed I would find that out when (or if) I became a Third Former.

It was standard practice for boys and girls originating from any one village to be highly suspicious, even fearful, of their counterparts from any other village in North Cornwall. The differences between communities were all too clear in terms of looks, culture, dialect and manner of speaking. As a consequence, that Open Day objective of promoting social intercourse amongst incoming First Formers was inevitably destined to meet with little success, as we all formed up into village-specific clusters and defended them as if we were under siege.

These tribal groupings stood firm throughout the Open Day like rocks resisting the River of Change. Those among us who hailed from remote rural outposts, and had little in the way of familiars to latch on to, drifted around on the outside like pieces of wave-buffeted flotsam.

It was the character of the guides that we were assigned which made the greatest impression on me at the Open Day. They were Sixth Formers who may have been willing volunteers but who were more probably press-ganged for duty by the Headmaster. All of them sported a small shield-shaped green enamelled badge pinned more or less to a left lapel, and bearing the inscription PREFECT picked out on it in bright letters of fine brass.

Each Prefect seemed to have the aura of a god, and the type of bearing and elegance that I had yet to dream of. I was no stranger to great big boys like Rich and Otch at Port Isaac County Primary School, not to mention strapping girls like Harriet and Joyce and Thelma, but as far as they were concerned, for all their size and superior age, they were still just boys and girls. The Sir James Smith's Sixth Formers by contrast seemed to be young men and young women. I couldn't credit that they were still attending school.

Neatly turned out in sports jackets, grey flannel trousers and the obligatory white shirt and school tie, the young men of the Sixth who guided us were entirely charming and helpful. As I would find out when term time came along, however, such wholesome qualities as they exhibited then would be rare commodities indeed for a First Former to encounter again.

Was being like them what was to become of me? Looking ahead a week into the future was usually more than I could manage. Gazing down a long tunnel of years disclosed no light to mark its end.

The most authoritative of the Sixth Form guides wore a second and much bigger shield in place on his lapel, this one in red enamel with the words HEAD BOY glittering on it. He was Preston Hicks, a native of Camelford. Preston moved with what I saw as feline grace. His hair hung with studied casualness over his right eye. I took to him instantly.

As Preston was in the Upper Sixth when I was in my First Form year, our overlap was short-lived, but then, since the Sixth Form and the First Form were akin to east being east and west being west with the twain only meeting by accident, I could only look on and admire Preston from afar.

There was only a single occasion in my first year at Sir James Smith's when I saw Preston behave less than generously — he was milk monitor of the day at the time, and one of his Second Form customers was heard by him (and me) to remark on how "Pissy Press fell down a precipice". This inventive statement was rewarded with a clip around the wit's ear by Preston's hand.

The ascendancy of Forms from the First through the Second, Third, Fourth, Fifth, Lower Sixth and Upper Sixth was structured on rather feudal lines. The happy understanding was that, with the exception of those in the First Form, every other pupil had the ability to a greater or lesser extent to look down and drop shit on underlings and inferiors.

As a postscript to my association with Preston, on a certain Saturday afternoon late in 1959, when I was two years out of Sir James Smith's and just into my third student year at the Royal School of Mines, Imperial College, in London, I chanced to be standing in north London with a friend from my college year in a long queue for the Underground, following on our having attended a home match of the Arsenal FC. I don't remember the match result, or the name of the away team — it wasn't Chelsea for sure, as I was then a die-hard Chelsea supporter and a game involving them would never slip my mind.

From my place in the creeping queue of cloth-capped humanity I spotted a familiar face on a passer-by, and it was that of none other than Preston Hicks. One of the many limitations on my attributes was (and is) that I tended to instantly forget names as soon as I heard them, although the balance was (and is) to some extent addressed by my having a sharp memory for faces. If a needle placed in a haystack had on it a face that I had previously seen I would have had no trouble in finding it.

Without hesitation I stepped out of the queue for the Tube and ran to greet and embrace Preston. It was a golden moment, and such a pleasure to be able to exchange a few short words with him, again prior to us once more heading on to our respective destinations.

I returned to take up the recently vacated place in the queue alongside my friend, only to be hauled out instantly and unceremoniously by a heavy-handed policeman. I learned quite rapidly, as the copper frogmarched me by the scruff of the neck all the way back to the rear end of the queue, that protest counted for less than nothing with custodians of the law when it came from a queue jumper caught in the act. It seemed altogether fateful that, on both the first and last occasions when I saw Preston, a form of queuing was a common feature.

A key item of the Open Day's agenda was a General Assembly of all present for the purpose of listening to a homily-laden pep-talk given by Mr Sprayson. In his pursuit of this vital duty, he was seen to be at his most avuncular. It was a state of being in him to savour while it lasted, for holding in the heart to cherish and resurrect should a feel-good moment prove elusive at any time in the future. In his teaching of the rudiments of algebra, which was to mark my subsequent encounter with him, Mr Sprayson's bag of n nuts would generate a somewhat reduced level of avuncular cheer.

Flanked by an entourage of Sixth Form disciples and one or two of his teaching staff who presumably had drawn the short straws, Mr Sprayson made an impressive figure in a business-like suit and black scholastic gown as he swept regally into the classroom in which were gathered the Open Day congregation, and stood there before us. His hands grasped his lapels comfortably, providing him with all the security from pressure that he needed in order to avoid having to worry about just what he might do with his hands otherwise.

His subsequent discourse covered a range of themes and topics — the spirit and tradition of the school; the wonderful rewards and opportunities that were about to open for the new pupils; the great fortune that had befallen them already with their eleven-plus selection; the importance of maintaining sound harmony, good manners, acceptable behaviour, healthy exercise, hard work and respectful cooperation with both peers and teachers alike.

We were exhorted by Mr Sprayson to play with a straight bat, to set our feet on the straight and narrow, and always to take pride in the school and our membership of it. He didn't make reference to "wearing the Old School Tie", or tell us to "play the game you cads, play the game", but apart from that, a goodly portion of what he said ran parallel with the stage routine of Kenneth and George, the Western Brothers.

Nevertheless, Mr Sprayson's exhortations were both kindly and inspiring. As he made his key points, the members of the teaching staff by his side nodded sagely at one another in a knowing way that seemed to suggest that if any pupil was prepared to play ball with them, then it was just possible that they might not give him or her a hard time. I was familiar enough with the mores of teachers to know that truces between them and their pupils would always be of short duration.

The real substance of Mr Sprayson's address, once the diplomatic platitudes and thickly-strewn clichés had been stripped away, was designed to promote pupil compliance with teacher-driven discipline and so pave the way towards our living with the shape of things to come throughout the next seven years.

This was of course a tried and true technique regularly employed by politicians, institutions of learning and organised religious bodies to hold the waverers in line. It all amounted to an acceptance of suffering in silence now in order to reap rewards at a future date that was as vague as it was unspecified. A similar theme would be routinely presented by every luminary guest speaker at each annual school Speech and Prizegiving Day that I attended.

There would be, I supposed, plenty of time available for First Formers to get to know one another when the actual term broke out in September. Awareness of who and what we were and how we might best comply with Mr Sprayson's rallying cry was one of many bridges which would need to be crossed in the months and years ahead, provided any of us was up to it.

With reference to spanning gaps, the aforementioned Miss Jones told us in one of her Geometry lessons – I was then a Third Former – that mastering the proof of the theorem of Pythagoras was a vital member of that same fellowship of challenging bridges. This theorem declared (and I knew it must be right as Danny Kaye sang a song about it) that the square on the hypotenuse of a right-angled triangle was equal to the sum of the squares on the two adjacent sides. The theorem was known in Latin, she said, as the *Pons Asinorum* which meant the "Bridge of Donkeys", although given the average hesitancy to cross it, it could equally have meant "the bridge of the uncomprehending".

In fact, over on the far side of the *Pons Asinorum* lay great satisfaction, and the assurance of a tool learned, understood and available for lifetime application. Compared, however, to the massively scary task of bridging the abyss between Primary and Grammar schools, conquering the theorem of Pythagoras (or "Pythag" as he was fondly referred to) was a mere bagatelle.

I was reasonably confident that some of my new First Form classmates would be easy to bond with and some wouldn't. There would be those who would tolerate me and those who might find it a strain to give me the time of day. There would certainly be a number, hopefully very few, that I wouldn't like and most probably never would like.

That was the way of all schools everywhere.

The way it went as you rose up through the various academic levels of a school was that you needed to fight that little bit less with each year that passed. On the other hand, although the capacity for conflict faded with time, its presence was immutable. As long as there was a class that was more senior than the one you were in, you were always likely to find a bully peering down on you. Mostly, all you needed to get a bully off your back was the ability to stand up to him, and that got easier as you got bigger—that is, unless a teacher was the bully. There was no satisfactory way to stop one of them.

As was commonplace, I took persecution as my due, never speaking of it or complaining about it. The Golden Rule of primary schools—that a teacher was always in the right even when he or she was plainly in the wrong, and its consequence that a pupil was always in the wrong without exception—applied equally at a grammar school. There was a comforting familiarity in knowing this, and I think that had the Golden Rule not applied to Sir James Smith's it would have brought me disappointment.

What the theorem-loving Miss Jones might have described as the Golden Rule's corollary also found general favour at Sir James Smith's — this being, namely, that anything less than pleasant that happened to you at school was a matter kept between you and its perpetrator; that you didn't tell tales; that you didn't name names; and (of critical importance this) that you didn't go home and inform your parents about anything untoward that might have happened. It didn't matter anyway in the latter instance, as you wouldn't have been believed, and even if you were given a hearing, the blame would be placed entirely on your shoulders, and would bring with it the minimum expectation of a clip around the ear by your father to encourage you not to do again what you hadn't yet done in the first place.

And when all of this was said and done, the great truth that came out of such waves of oppression as occasionally darkened the largely placid waters of school life was that the existence of a shared enemy was a great motivator for unity.

Mr Sprayson didn't tell us anything about this at the Open Day.

6

The School Bus

I travelled to Sir James Smith's Grammar School from Port Isaac on an officially sanctioned school bus. The bus was one of a number operating under contract to the Cornish Education Authorities to transport pupils to the school and back from each of the main village centres of its catchment district. My bus therefore originated in Port Isaac, and went up to Camelford in the mornings and from Camelford back home again in the evenings. It was an indelibly familiar vehicle to me, being one of the (admittedly numerically not large) Trelawney Garage fleet of the Prout Bros. In the course of its daily duties it followed an optimised route in order to best maximise pupil pickups all along the way.

Both the Prout Bros bus route and its tightly adhered to timetable were entities held to be as sacrosanct as if they had been written on tablets of stone. No deviations, unplanned detours or even delays were to be tolerated, assuming that they had ever been contemplated in the first place. A similar mandate presumably governed the conduct of all other school buses of the district as well. They plied the north Cornish roads and lanes in exhaust-belching splendour, never hesitating to shoulder aside the invasive bursts of nettles and blackthorn springing from the ancient roadside hedges, which so often gave the impression that no amount of organised trimming could ever succeed in holding such audacious growth in check.

Unless, that is, road verge maintenance was vested in the brilliantly capable hands of Mr Frank Gilbert of Port Isaac. Armed with only a scythe, a billhook and a short length of hazel stick, Frank had turned hedge trimming into a fine art. He created an order of neatness of which not only man but also nature could be truly proud. The outer boundaries of Frank's zone of hedge responsibility were easy to spot thanks to the immediate welter of uncontrolled growth thereafter.

The school bus from Port Isaac departed promptly from the near vicinity of Trelawney Garage at eight sharp each school day morning, in order to reach its pupil disembarkation point at the foot of College Road just down below Sir James Smith's at ten minutes to nine precisely. Thus were all school-bound passengers present and available, if not wholly willing, to join the morning Assembly line-up before it moved off to the Assembly Room at nine o'clock. There was a ponderous quality about Assembly which often meant that the subsequent first lesson of the school day could come along and feel like light relief.

At ten minutes past four in the afternoon, exactly ten minutes after the last lesson of the day had ended, the buses would be standing at the foot of College Road waiting to carry their respective charges of pupils away again.

The Prout Bros themselves were two in number, and were named John and Mark, John being the elder by what appeared to be a reasonable number of years. He drove the school bus regularly, but it was something of a rare event to come across Mark sitting in the driver's seat. In so many respects, this being merely one of them, John and Mark were in nature like chalk and cheese.

The pair of them were so well known for the personal qualities of their professional public and commercial transport services in North Cornwall that they had achieved the local status of becoming household names. I liked them both, but I was especially fond of John, and so it was in the balm of such heartfelt affection that I went so far as to commit an act of defacing (or maybe improving), certain India paper pages of the Bible I used in Religious Instruction classes at Sir James Smith's. It was my own Bible anyway, won as a St Peter's Church Sunday School attendance prize, and so I had no compunction in writing "Prout" in large inked letters at the end of the respective title headings of the Gospel according to St John and the Gospel according to St Mark.

The public transport business of the Prout Bros was a thriving concern. It was founded back at a time when locomotion by horse and cart was in vogue. Since those halcyon days the Prout family had moved into motorised transport, specialising in buses, but with some diversification into goods haulage and occasional taxi services. The great business constraint on taxi usage was that there were few Port Isaac residents who could afford to avail themselves of it.

Prout's bus fleet was four or five strong, each bus being capable of seating around forty passengers. Each bus was clad in a distinctive cream and grey/green trim with the legend "Prout Bros" prominently displayed at strategic locations on the bodywork, thereby relieving the casual observer of harbouring any doubts regarding the bus's ownership.

The Sir James Smith's school bus contract was far from being the only string in the Prout Bros' bow, however, as they additionally operated a scheduled bus service travelling the full nine miles between Port Isaac and Wadebridge for the benefit of the fare-paying public. Furthermore, one or another of the Prout's buses was always on hand for the convenience of organised outings (as for example for the elderly, the Sunday School, the County Primary School, the Church, the Chapel, the Mothers' Union and the Women's Institute); for group shopping trips to wondrous places like Plymouth and Truro; for a wide range of day excursions in the holiday season to destinations of both scenic and historic interest in much of Cornwall as well as in north and west Devon; and furthermore for the conveyance of working men down to the moonscape-like china clay works near St Austell, or the great grey slate quarry up at Delabole.

The Prout Bros were Chapel people. They bore the Chapel stamp on them as firmly as if it had been created just for them. I was of the Church, and in common with the good and the not so good of both grand institutions of combative piety, could recognise the cut of a member of our opposition even in the dark. However, the rivalry between Church and Chapel, which so often fell only just short of outright antagonism, was fortunately devoted largely to matters spiritual. In matters secular we normally managed to tolerate one another very well.

As if to cast their Chapel credentials in concrete, John and Mark were noted choristers, prominent members at one time of an excellent Port Isaac community choir in which my mother also sang. John was even more involved as a member of a vocal quartet which went under the truly descriptive name of "The Four in Harmony". The Four appeared often on the stage of Port Isaac's Temperance Hall, and were equally in demand to perform in concerts at many venues in North Cornwall and beyond. Their repertoire focused on sweet, low and slow numbers of which "Silver Threads Among the Gold" was a perennial favourite, and they drew profound applause for their renditions of certain of The Inkspots' popular classics.

In support of the chalk and cheese allegation levelled at Mark and John, the latter was slight of figure, stooped of shoulder, thin of hair, jerky, bird-like and nervous in mannerisms, and exceedingly dithering in conduct. In sharp contrast, Mark was tall, straight and handsome, with darkly saturnine looks. He carried a full head of perfectly Brylcreemed hair; his eyebrows beetled; and was seldom seen to be lacking in the accessories of collar and tie. He was, in short, a seriously imposing character, a Tyrone Power to set against John's similarities to Bert Lahr's Cowardly Lion in *The Wizard of Oz*.

The thing was, however, that it was far too easy to underestimate John, as so many did to their detriment. John never underestimated himself, as a result of which he never seemed to realise just how erratic his driving skills were. He drove his bus with aplomb coupled with sublime disregard for the fortunes of pedestrians, ambulating farm livestock, road verges and hedges, parked and passing traffic, and any other potential obstacles that presented themselves to his line of advance.

A bus journey with John at the wheel consisted of a steady sequence of near misses that he took absolutely in his stride, while his passengers shuddered and trusted that they were not being held as hostages to fate.

Mrs Joe Knight, whose husband owned and operated the Port Isaac Central Garage, located on the opposite side of New Road to Trelawney Garage, once took the part of Mr Wilfred Pickles in a Temperance Hall pastiche of Wilfred's famous wireless programme, "Have a Go". "We came here", said Mrs Knight, opening the show in what was an uncannily accurate impression of Wilfred, "in a bus driven by a Mr John Prout". That got a huge laugh from the audience right away. "We know now", Mrs Knight went on, "why they call him 'Hellfire' John."

As well as bringing the house down in mirth, that last gag enshrined John forever as "Hellfire John" in my eyes. I hastened to return to my Sunday School prize Bible and its New Testament to amend the title of the fourth of the gospels to read "The Gospel according to St Hellfire John Prout".

As well as John, there were two other regular school bus drivers employed by the Prout Bros. These were both men that it was a pleasure to ride along with. One of them was Mr Maurice Renowden who had driven a National bus previously. Maurice personified perkiness. He was a cheeky chappie with an infectious cheerfulness. Kipling's "If—" could have been written with Maurice in mind. He was never short of a quip, and sarcastic repartee came to him as readily as if he had been to the manner borne. It was only now and then, perhaps, that his stream of patter could become too much of a good thing, but no one got on or off Maurice's bus without a shaft of Maurice's keen-edged wit coming their way.

My favourite driver, however, was the other, Mr Garfield Gilbert. Garfield was incidentally a nephew of Mr Frank Gilbert, that road verge maintenance man *par excellence*. Garfield, brim full of character and equanimity, drove for the Prout Bros for several years,. He was young and so essentially good humoured that his popularity with the pupils he drove was assured from his first day. Garfield treated us as equals and we greatly respected him for it.

During my two Sixth Form years at Sir James Smith's, I had the pleasure and privilege of travelling in the front seat of the bus alongside Garfield, with Gordon Keat seated on my left. Gordon was nicknamed "Arker" (sometimes shortened to "Ark") after Mr Gordon Harker, a celebrated character actor and star of the cinema, one of whose films, *Phantom Light*, allegedly included location scenes shot in Port Isaac back in the mid-1930s.

Every bus trip with Garfield was to be savoured. His banter was pure milk and honey. We felt relaxed and at home in his good company, which gave us no small boost towards coping with the daily exigencies of Sixth Form work.

Garfield was blessed with a line in yarns and observational wit that no Port Isaac Pawlyn's Fish Cellars *habitué* other than Mr Tom Brown could ever emulate, and that was saying something. He was pure quality, exuding kindness, gentle consideration, and the great sincerity of never talking down to us.

It was Garfield who came up with an exchange ensuring his name would live in fond memory forever within the pantheon of worthy associates of Sir James Smith's, and it came about thus.

One morning when Gordon and I were in our seats and the bus was rolling on the road to Camelford, Garfield said to us, "Here, he's looking for you!"

"Who is He?" I asked.

"Chunky", replied Garfield.

"Who is Chunky?" was our rejoinder.

"He's the man with pineapple balls", responded Garfield.

We had probably heard funnier things, but I for one couldn't remember when. It was absolutely hilarious.

The "Chunky" exchange was immediately shared around, and swept through Sir James Smith's like wildfire. First of all it enlivened the boys all the way up to and even beyond the time when everyone knew not to get caught out, but let themselves get caught out anyway. Then, with the boys' pool of capacity for surprise drying up, Chunky was shunted into the ranks of the girls. The great joke in directing it at the girls was that Chunky's claim to fame was never to be divulged, which only served to make the guessing-game *dénouement* even funnier for the boys.

The girls were suitably mystified at the outset, but later, as Chunky Phase Two was getting close to having run its natural course, many of them showed signs of becoming fed-up with it, perhaps not unjustifiably. Yet for all that, it was good while it lasted.

As indeed was Garfield. When he told us one day that he was leaving the Prout Bros to take up another job elsewhere, it was as if he had dropped a bombshell. We could barely bring ourselves to contemplate the loss of such a bright highlight of the school day. In our capacity not only of being his passengers but also of being his friends, all who travelled with him on the bus contributed to a collection, with the proceeds of which we bought Garfield a farewell present of a book, which we all signed on the fly leaves.

The book was entitled, *The One that Got Away*, a true story of a German POW in England who escaped and made his way back home. A film based on the book was subsequently made, starring the excellent German actor Hardy Kruger. I didn't realise the significance of the book's title to Garfield's departure until sometime afterwards.

Garfield was sorely missed. Time in his company was, to quote Robert Burns (in "The Cotter's Saturday Night"), "one cordial in this melancholy vale". He was a precious and gracious man.

Thereafter, the wonderfully mild, benign and frighteningly erratic Hellfire John was back more often at the wheel of the bus, and our journeys of ultimate relaxation from Port Isaac to Camelford and back were but a memory.

From Hartland Road to College Road

From where I lived on Hartland Road in Port Isaac at the inner end of a stark row of New Council Houses, I had three feasible options for being picked up by the school bus each morning. One of the three, the least attractive to me and hence the one never taken, was that I should board the bus at its point of departure just outside the Church Rooms on the New Road bend at the top of Back Hill. Most pupils who took the school bus from there came up from the lower regions of the village and so walking down to it wasn't highly regarded by those who lived higher up.

I could in any case catch the bus much more easily at the triple junction of Hartland Road with New Road and Trewetha Lane. From the Church Rooms, the bus came up along New Road and made its first stop at that junction before proceeding onwards up along Trewetha Lane.

What I normally did, however, was board the bus at its second regular stop, located on Trewetha Lane a couple of hundred yards further on. From the bottom of the back garden of our council house I could access a short cut to reach that stop by taking an unpaved track which was rather optimistically named Lundy Road. I then waited for the bus alongside the garden wall of the last house but one on the left at the outer edge of the village. On the opposite side of the road the post-war prefab estate sprawled in all its glory.

That last house but one was occupied by the family of Mr Jack Short Jr, a mobile fishmonger by trade, otherwise known colloquially as a "fish jouder". His elder son, David, was a Third Form pupil at Sir James Smith's when I joined the First Form.

David, nicknamed Shorty, was Short in name, short in stature, and quite often even shorter in temper. He was physically strong and was gifted both academically and in sports, particularly football; a boy clearly equipped with the potential to be a leader. Unfortunately Shorty's positive attributes didn't always show themselves in an especially pleasant way in my experience. I would not have wanted to serve anywhere or in any capacity under his supervision.

I came into direct contact with Shorty's *modus operandi* at first hand (and his other hand as well) when I was an underling in the St Peter's church choir. It would not be unfair to describe the choir as occupying the choir stalls at Sunday services for cosmetic purposes. Shorty was a senior member and appointed by the vicar as processional cross bearer. His favourite trick in the vestry, before and after services and out of sight of the vicar, was to knuckle certain of the younger boys like me in the ribs to cause us pain for no good reason that I could judge other than that he liked doing it.

Shorty had a second nickname, which was "Minnow". Perhaps Minnow took its origins from "small man" syndrome. On the other hand, Shorty's father was closely connected with fish, and his grandfather, the imposingly sanctimonious Mr Jack Short Sr, a bitterly intolerant man who some boys thought of as Jack Shite, was himself a retired fisherman. Fishiness was obviously a family trait.

To address Shorty as Minnow, as I found out to my cost, was to trigger in him a release of blind and violent rage. Hence few if any called him by that name twice.

One day, during a training session of the St Peter's PT Club in the Port Isaac Church Rooms, I was sent to look for an item of equipment in the adjoining ante-room. The Vicar at the time, the utterly gung-ho Revd F. B. Soady, was in the ante-room attending something or other, and while I was looking around for what I needed, he unexpectedly raised the subject of nicknames with me. It seemed that having heard one or two such sobriquets called out during the current PT Club session, his curiosity had been aroused. I gave him the benefit of my inside knowledge — he then pressed me on his cross bearer's nickname and succeeded in getting me to mention the dreaded "M" word.

Shorty, although not a member of the PT Club, was for some reason also present in the Church Rooms at the time. Perhaps he was assisting the Vicar in whatever that Reverend gentleman was doing in the ante-room. The Vicar, immortalised in ink on the fly leaf of my Prout Bros-defaced Bible as "Good Old Soady", immediately strode over to the open ante-room door and shouted, "Hey Minnow!" His words brought an instant reaction. Shorty stormed into the ante-room from without, ran past the Vicar, punched me hard in the stomach and rushed out again without further ado. In the great tradition of Hoagy Carmichael's "Old Music Master", the Vicar simply sat there amazed, as wide-eyed and open-mouthed he gazed, and he gazed at me gasping on the floor.

That was Shorty, and that also by the way was Good Old Soady.

In his Upper Sixth Form year at Sir James Smith's, Shorty was appointed to the position of Head Boy, with Richard Blake as his deputy. We of the school electorate puzzled mightily when the result was announced at Assembly — finding anyone who claimed to have voted for Shorty was not easy, but finding anyone at all who would admit to voting for Richard was an impossibility. Richard came directly to Sir James Smith's as a Senior from a prior public school background, which placed him instantly beyond the pale for us.

It was suspected that the Head Boy's "election" was ever a purely fictitious exercise, as, correctly or not, Mr Sprayson was widely believed to appoint the Head Boy he wanted, irrespective of the voting results. The problem for Mr Sprayson was that the school's electorate tended to vote for the softest option, whereas he preferred something rather more flinty. To be fair, Shorty did not do too badly as Head Boy, and he never let the courting of popularity get in the way of his personal ambition.

He graduated from Sir James Smith's to study at the Camborne School of Mines. Following his first year at the CSM, for which he was awarded the year prize for excellence, he undertook course-related vacation work in the Copperbelt of Northern Rhodesia, where he tragically lost his life in a weekend road accident. Such greatness as might have come to him, given time and an infusion of humility, was to be forever denied.

For a full four years of travelling to Camelford and back on Prout's school bus, I boarded outside Shorty's house, together with Shorty of course, on each and every day. We exchanged greetings naturally enough, but not a lot more than that.

For the duration of an academic year, all pupils of the more senior calibre of Shorty and a few of less senior but not especially junior rank, which essentially meant from the Third Form upwards, generally tended to always sit in the same seat, as if it had been reserved for them. The right to such dedicated seats was considered inviolate, and no one would have thought or dared to transgress this unwritten rule.

At the start of a new school year, the seating plan adjusted in accordance with everyone other than newcomers moving up the scale a bit. In principle, this shift of seating was a sort of ripple effect spreading from the back to the front of the bus. The jockeying for seats on the first day of the autumn term was consistent with Darwin's law of natural selection. Might was right, and ultimate seniority conferred ultimate power. The most coveted seats were the two up alongside the driver.

First and Second Formers were left to fight it out between themselves and fare as best they could back at the rear end of the conveyance.

The route taken by the school bus never varied from day to day by as much as a jot, a tittle or an iota. The way led along the full length of Trewetha Lane via Colstanton Corner to Poltreworgy Hill, and then onwards a little further to take a left turn at a T junction with the main Delabole to Wadebridge road, (formally designated the B3314). In the local sense, a main road was distinguished from its secondary and tertiary relatives by the more limited amount of grass that flourished along its crown.

The T junction was located two miles out of Port Isaac, and the immediate approach to it, after Poltreworgey Hill, commanded a wonderful panorama of a huge expanse of Cornwall. There ahead, the shadows of clouds drifted like a vast Armada over an endlessly undulating landscape of fields and woodlands, with purple moors out to the east lifting all the way to the peaks of Roughtor and Brown Willy, Cornwall's famous pair of granite "tors". Far away to the south, white saw-toothed waste tips of St Austell's china clay district were spread out in surreally haphazard grandeur.

Of the two tors, Brown Willy was the higher, although since Roughtor was the nearer, it was the one that looked the more sub-stantial. It was a matter of perspective, said Miss Holloway, the Sir James Smith's Art teacher. Both tors stood sharp against the distant horizon when they weren't either enveloped in rain or shrouded by fog.

If you took a quick glance to the right at the T junction you could spot the square bell tower of the ancient church at St Endellion, (which had been Port Isaac's parish church prior to the construction of St Peter's in the second half of the nineteenth century), standing proud and blunt a couple of miles distant on the height of land, backed by a black, wind-wracked grove of Scots pine trees.

Now and then, and always by arrangement with the driver, the bus would halt for a moment at the T junction to permit Tony Blake, a form contemporary of Shorty, to disembark briefly in order to release, from a wicker basket he had brought with him, a number of homing pigeons that he said he was in the process of training.

Tony, or Blakey as he was best known, was a wild and woolly character, an extrovert with a well-developed penchant for raucous behaviour. He was up for anything that didn't involve studying or putting in an appearance at a Methodist chapel. Blakey was the antithesis of his father, the impeccable Mr Wesley Blake, that well-known Port Isaac Methodist local preacher and true gentleman (in every sense of the word) who sold me my leather satchel.

In fact, Blakey was much more of a chip off the old block of his uncle, Mr Jack Hicks, himself the Son in the sum of J. N. Hicks and Son, Family Butchers of Port Isaac. Jack was a fine butcher, but when off on his own, and especially if a pub entered the equation, could be, as the expression went, as rough as Roughtor. Blakey, in his capacity as a Sir James Smith's pupil, was very much a boy of the moment, undistinguished in class, but a self-assured focus of attention out of it, an early master perhaps of the triumph of style over substance.

His homing pigeons, whose return destination may have been one or other of the rickety slate-roofed barns at Mr Jack Chapman's

Bodannon farm back near Trewetha and where Blakey spent a lot of his free time, must have made it home at every release if their repetitious appearances on the school bus were anything to go by. On the other hand, individual pigeon recognition was a skill possessed by almost no one, and the pigeons that Blakey released at the T junction could very well have had different identities on each occasion.

Having reached the T junction then, the bus turned left to proceed along the B3314 and make a gradual yet steady ascent for the next six miles or so to where Delabole hunched in bleak slate-shrouded austerity, open to the unfettered force of wind and weather, sheltered by neither tree nor goodwill. For a while, the road ran gully-like between hedges as impressively high as they were, being outside Frank Gilbert's demesne, hopelessly overgrown. Every now and then the hedges were perforated by a farm entry track, or an occasional stile or a wooden five-bar gate.

No more than half a mile up the road from the T junction, the bus passed through an overtly modest hamlet named Pendoggett, which certain of the less mature of its passengers liked to refer to as "Penny Dog Shit". That fair place consisted of a motor repair garage, a widely favoured public house named "The Cornish Arms", a small chapel, a post office facility and a few cottages. It wasn't much, although for those who lived there perhaps it was enough. The garage, owned by Mr Ned Mewton, was an asset that many places much bigger than Pendoggett might have been proud to call their own.

Ned's garage served to ensure that the pub never really lacked for customers of the itinerant variety. The pub, a free house, was by reputation one of the best of its kind in North Cornwall, blessed as it was (or so I was told) with a blend of charm, style and atmosphere at a time when such qualities in the beer-vending trade were indeed rare.

Pendoggett was located right at the head of the valley that ran down to meet the sea at Port Gaverne, a quarter of a mile along the coast to the east of Port Isaac. When you stood on the shingle at the top of Port Gaverne's beach you could cast your eye up along the trough of the valley and see the dark outline of Pendoggett's few buildings up there on the skyline, two miles inland.

Shortly before Pendoggett a subsidiary road came in from the right to join the B3314 — it offered a means of access out to Port Isaac Road railway station as well as to the small local communities of Trelill and St Kew. The school bus took a short detour into this rustic territory to collect two pupils, both of whom were memorable for the sort of well-defined individuality that was most likely a product of the solitude that surrounded their homes.

From Trelill came Rita Cutler, a slim girl who was a year ahead of me at Sir James Smith's. Rita was fair of hair and fleet of foot, an accomplished athlete who was not only a regular star at Sports Day, but also a key member of the school's hockey and netball teams. She was articulate of speech and accent-free — all in all a superior cut above the common herd that so many of the rest of us formed part of.

Rita additionally had a talent for the stage, as was evidenced at the Christmas Concerts, produced by the pupils for the pupils (not forgetting the teaching staff). Her tour de force in one memorable Concert was to give an impression of both Peter Brough and Archie Andrews of radio's "Educating Archie" fame. Peter was a ventriloquist and Archie was his dummy, unless it was the other way around, since Archie always seemed to be the member of the double act who showed the most verve and personality.

Also on its little pre-Pendoggett detour the bus picked up David Pierce, a St Kew resident who was in the First Form intake with me. David, like Rita, was also fair haired, although his locks were induced to appear artificially darker thanks to an unstinting application of Brylcreem. We addressed him by his surname — somewhat unusually, as it never seemed to get softened by the traditionally diminutive suffix.

In this regard my widely applied nickname at Port Isaac County Primary was "Platty". Surnames were always easier to bend into nicknames than were Christian names. In Port Isaac I was universally known by the full version of my Christian name James, but at Sir James Smith's this rapidly got shortened to Jim, and I had to admit that it was Jim that I preferred. Jim of course was no nickname, but in the best way it was how my grandfather was named, and that was more than good enough for me.

To the limited extent that I was aware, as boys tended not to talk to girls too much in the confines of the school, girls didn't appear to have nicknames, although perhaps within their own society such things may well have been in full play. Boys, however, were not reticent to assign covert nicknames to girls, all too often related to either perceived personal defects or endowed physical attributes.

David Pierce seemed to be a relatively secretive boy, which meant that although he was likeable, he wasn't easy to get to like. As it was, he made his exit from Sir James Smith's without notice when he was a Third Former, taking with him in the mild wake of his passage any option for us to get to know him properly. The direct contacts that I had with him were mostly on the school bus, since in the theatre of the classroom and school yard he was not a member of the close-knit group that I adhered to. School society was in principle a single force, but within its well-defined outer boundaries milled a host of clans and cliques, each seeking the main chance to assert its superiority over as many of the others as it could. It was just fortunate that by and large these turbulent undercurrents tended to cancel themselves out into an equation of mutually tolerated neutrality.

In the later stages of the autumn term David often boarded the bus in the morning with a large yellow apple in his hand, which, once seated, he proceeded to consume. He was oblivious to the covetous eyes of his fellow travellers. For most of them, apples looking as nice as that came only to hand as the spoils of a scrumping expedition into an unguarded orchard of choice. Food of any kind was their passion, not for its own sake, but because what it was when it came along was never enough to satisfy.

Each bite of the apple that David took was accompanied by entreaties from various of his almost slavering spectators that they might be permitted to have a bite of it themselves. He knew only too well that if he was to accede to any such request he would see at least half of the apple vanish down the recipient's throat at one fell swoop of jaws. So he didn't give the apple up and the tantalising sight of him munching it did little to enhance his popularity.

He was, however, much more amenable to handing over the core of the apple to one or other of us when little of the flesh remained. I was the beneficiary of the core on more than one occasion, never being reticent to act where a bite to eat was concerned, and I was happy to consume it all apart from the stalk. As long as they were edible, receiving crumbs from a rich man's table could never offend my pride.

On the far side of Pendoggett, the subsequent feature of note encountered by the onward journey of the school bus was, after a couple of miles more, a crossroads at a locality known as China Downs. To make the four-way junction, a narrow roadway coming up from Port Gaverne crossed the B3314 and continued on to St Teath, a village that had so little going for it (according to a consensus opinion of everyone who didn't live there and some of those who did) that it was not infrequently spoken of as St Death.

Although to be fair, St Teath was a pleasant enough little village, clustered around a pub and a fine old granite church set in a well-tended graveyard that was entered via a quaint lichgate. St Teath's quota of Sir James Smith's pupils travelled to the school on its own dedicated bus.

The visual qualities of China Downs were either graced or marred, depending on your point of view, by a couple of cottages, one standing on each corner of the junction on the St Teath flank. For an extended period of time, my great and much admired friend Mr William "Gaggy" Hosking (actually a contemporary of my mother) lived in the right-hand cottage in the sense of looking along the road to St Teath. I was always alert to try and spot Gaggy when the school bus came to China Downs, although he was rarely to be seen. He was then working at a new cheese factory situated near Davidstow on the edge of the moors above Camelford, naturally enough to the extent that a man of Gaggy's flamboyant talents ever worked at anything at all. Nevertheless, there was no doubt in my mind but that the origins of Davidstow cheddar owed Gaggy a debt of gratitude.

Gaggy was a gift-of-the-gab man of supreme quality, full of promises ripe with sincere intent in the instant before he forgot them. In the luxuriance of his hair and the set of his jaw there was more than a suggestion of Spencer Tracy, who was incidentally my mother's favourite film star. Gaggy was the quintessential manifestation of a loveable rogue. It was impossible not to like him. I found his company to be as irresistible as it was memorable.

From China Downs the B3314 ran for a further two miles on an unusually straight and only modestly rising course trajectory through open farmland which dropped gently away towards the coast of Port Isaac Bay on the left. Mr Ted Robinson, a Port Isaac resident, and the father of my good friend Tony (one Form in front of me at Sir James Smith's), owned a sleek, fawn-coloured Jaguar car which he allegedly once drove at eighty miles per hour along that stretch.

The straight section ran out of rectitude amidst an untidy conglomeration of farm buildings, beyond which the road soared into a steep up-and-over hump of a hill. At the hill's crest, Delabole could be seen emerging a mile ahead, like a grey wraith out of an even greyer coffin. The awesome celebrity of Delabole's slate production aside, the town occupied what many thought to be the bleakest location in North Cornwall, if not in the whole of Cornwall, or for that matter in all of Christendom.

At the farm buildings the bus made an accredited stop alongside a signpost pointing down a rutted track and offering the unheeded advice that if anyone should wish to head down the track, then the Tynes slate quarry was there to be discovered.

Tynes Quarry was defunct, and had by no means been as prodigious in size as its mighty, still operating counterpart which gave Delabole its *raison d'être*, as Mr Turner, the Sir James Smith's French teacher, might have put it.

Another substantial quarry down below Tynes had been cut into the Port Isaac Bay cliff face at a location formally known as Tregardock, but thought of more affectionately as "Donkey's Hole". Its rectilinear outline could be seen clearly from the more elevated easterly parts of Port Isaac, not least among which were the front bedroom windows of the new council houses along Hartland Road, where I lived.

Port Gaverne was at one time commercially very active in shipping out cargoes of split and trimmed roofing and ornamental slate produced by various local quarries including Tynes and Donkey's Hole. At Port Isaac County Primary School we were told that Port Gaverne translated from the old Cornish language as "Slate Port", and in keeping with many others who heard this, I had as little reason to doubt the truth of the assertion as I had the motivation to follow it up.

An impressive range of slate-related products emerged from the local quarries to fulfil a host of industrial and consumer-driven needs. These included various fractions of screened aggregate used both in road metalling and in concrete blocks; natural building stones; great flooring flags; roofing slates; and high-quality ornamental stone for public buildings, monuments, tombs and memorials. Examples of the latter in the churchyard at St Endellion bore inscriptions which were as true to the long-term remembrance of those they honoured as they were crisply resistant to the sharp-edged teeth of centuries of North Cornish weather. The slate protected the living and held the dead inviolate.

Miss Jones, in her geographical capacity, informed us in class that finely powdered Delabole slate, marketed under the brand name "Delafila", was the basic material used in the manufacture of gramophone recordings designed to turn at a speed of seventy-eight revolutions per minute. Such records were highly brittle items. They shattered satisfactorily by intent, and disappointingly by accident. There was a popular programme entitled "Smash Hits" on Radio Luxemburg (otherwise known as "two-oh-eight" thanks to its position on the tuning dial) which immortalised the ready breakability of seventy-eights — the presenter played, at the written-in requests of listeners, records that the listeners loved to hate, and as each record played out he ceremonially smashed it (or so he said he did) with great glee and a suitable sound effect.

Where the Tynes Quarry access track met the main road, the school bus picked up half a dozen local children, all of whom were pupils of Delabole County Primary School. They were all from the same family, and if looks weren't enough to go on to establish the family commonality, the gradual deterioration from eldest to youngest of the shabby hand-me-downs in which they were clad made it distressingly obvious.

The children were all of unkempt appearance and not particularly clean of skin. I had no trouble in recognising and empathising with such characteristics, as I had had some personal association with the conditions and qualities on display. Yet in the Tynes children, any manifestation of the pride of honest poverty appeared to be absent. Snot ran free, thick and yellow (when it wasn't green), from the noses of the younger element. One small boy had a pair of curious protuberances like incipient horns sticking out in front of his ears. They were all very much a sad sight and tended to be given ample space on the bus.

I once told a friend I was with about their nasal fluidity when we were standing in line in the chip shop in Port Isaac's Lower Fore Street owned and run by Gordon Keat's mother. Mrs Keat got rather short-tempered with me for what she declared was my sullying the thoughts of others among her waiting customers through sowing appetite-destroying images. But really, it would have taken a description of a lot more than a grandly running nose to put the average Port Isaac native off his or her chips, and Mrs Keat's chips were always of a quality to easily override visions of varicoloured snot in all its glory.

Once the Tynes Quarry children had boarded, the school bus proceeded up and over the crest of the hill immediately ahead, then down and up again on the ascent along Atlantic Road, flanked by a row of innocuous-looking cottages on its right-hand side, and so into Delabole.

A few of these cottages produced Sir James Smith's pupils for the bus. One I came to know well, as she was in my class, was a girl named Carole Isles. There were also a couple of likely lads two forms ahead of Carole and me — namely Oswald (Ossie) Martyn and Mike (Screwer) Moore. Oswald was as intensely imbued with nervous energy as Mike was blessed with placid resolve. The latter's leanings were into science, which perhaps explained the derivation of his nickname. He and Oswald were always a pleasure to encounter. Where the inscrutable Oswald was concerned, however, I always felt that latent pressures held deep within him had the potential to be too easily released to disadvantage anyone addressing him with a wrong word, inadvertent or otherwise.

The stature, experience and survival qualities of Third Formers were so far beyond anything that any First Former could appreciate, aspire to, or even hope to aspire to, that those older stagers were to be cautiously respected, if not fawningly revered.

It was the work of but a moment to have Carole thought of as "Missiles". She viewed the world through spectacles fitted with lenses as thick as the base of a Vimto bottle. She was a good-tempered, pleasant-mannered girl who muddied no waters.

And so the bus plunged into the heart of Delabole itself, a town made by slate, but offering little or no expression of gratitude for the happy convergence of those various accidents of geology which served to create the slate's unique and world-class quality.

The town of Delabole seemed to be as graceless as it was thankless, in no way aided to be otherwise owing to its being subjected to every excess of weather that the Atlantic Ocean chose to throw in its direction across Port Isaac Bay. On a reasonably normal day in Delabole, rain, wind and fog all liked to vie for precedence.

In every sense of the traditional litany, on any tree that dared to root itself in and around Delabole there was no branch high enough to hang a man from, no trunk broad enough to provide the timber for his coffin, and no bough thick enough to fashion a stake to drive through his heart and properly finish him off. There might also not have been sufficient soil cover on the slated fastness in which to bury him — however, the availability of a tombstone for him could never be in doubt, and the pit of the great quarry was more than adequate in its immensity to have his body cast into and be lost for ever.

Delabole slate quarry was — and I knew it for a fact because Miss Jones said so — the biggest man-made hole (or excavation) in the world at the time. Miss Jones' use of the word "hole" was possibly less than well judged, since it invited the observation that in the North Cornish context of holes, the town of Delabole ran its quarry a close second.

When I was in the Third Form, a class field trip to the quarry under the supervision of Miss Jones was undertaken. The extent of the quarry workings and excavations and the multitudinous men, many hundreds in number, who toiled there, were a breath-taking sight. Men and machines swarmed like ants in the dust-roiling depths beneath a spider-web tracery of thrumming hawsers and wires. Rail and haulage tracks plumbed the vertiginous walls seemingly without rhyme or reason, yet they served in full measure to hoist massive chunks of raw slate from the maw of the pit to its crest, where further hordes of men could set about refining the commercial product. The men at the top sorted and controlled the quality of ornamental and monumental blocks, cut flags for flooring, trimmed and split roofing slate, crushed and screened the residue down to a range of aggregate fractions and prepared raw screenings for incorporation in building blocks.

We watched a shed full of craftsmen splitting roofing slates down to wafer thinness. The tools of their craft were no more than a broad, sharp-bladed masonry chisel and a wooden mallet technically known as a "bettle". On the road that the school bus took through Delabole, the town's one and only public house, opposite the Co-op, and appropriately slate-bedecked, was named "The Bettle and Chisel".

That particular little sector of Delabole commerce was additionally enhanced by the presence of the austere-of-aspect County

Primary School and a small butcher's shop, although if the truth be told it was made especially memorable for non-natives by a cinema, ironically named "The Regal"—performances nightly (excluding Sundays) with a change of programme in mid-week.

One of the men who plied his instruments of steel in the butcher's shop, my mother told me, was a gentleman surnamed Rowe, whose Christian name had long since been supplanted by the nickname "Boxer". It was by that nickname that he was universally known and admired. His celebrity was widespread, not so much for his purveyance of what the French text on the side of an HP Sauce bottle referred to as "viandes", as for his alternative persona able to deliver a comic presence to the public second to none. Boxer was thereby a Cornish stage artist of enormous popularity. My mother knew him well, swore by him, and gave me rave reviews of his set piece monologue, "The vicar and I will be there". As with so many gems of North Cornwall's culture, that one deserved better than it got from me.

My attraction to Delabole's Regal Cinema was enjoined on a number of specific occasions, however, drawn by there being two programmes screened each week and a tendency now and then for the Regal to show (relatively) recent film releases in a way that Port Isaac's once weekly Friday-night "Cinema at the Rivoli" was unable to emulate. Prout's ran a regular bus service from Port Isaac to the Delabole Regal and back on two evenings per week to ensure that all changes of programme were covered for Port Isaac cinemagoers who wished to attend.

Of course, nothing was ever allowed to stand in the way of Friday night's attendance at the Rivoli, for to miss the weekly serial instalment was unthinkable.

My first serious encounter with the Delabole Regal took place at a time around the end of the war, when, aged five, I accompanied my mother and Gran on Prout's cinema bus to see the epic film *King Kong*, the script for which was incidentally written by the great Edgar Wallace. Sadly there was no room at the Regal's inn for me, owing to the British Board of Film Censors having furnished *King Kong* with an "X" certificate. I was therefore refused entry at the portal.

Gran went in, but my mother and I had to wander around the dismal streets of Delabole until the cinemagoers who failed to escape before the end of the first drum roll of "God Save The King" had done their full penance to His Majesty, and the bus was ready to take us all home. With or without a blackout, Delabole was endowed with the kind of well-disguised charm and joyless atmosphere characterised in the film *It Always Rains on Sunday*.

As a consolation for missing *King Kong*, I was taken along to the Regal again some little time later to see the Walt Disney film production of *Song of the South*, starring Brer Rabbit and Uncle Remus. Zip-a-dee-doo-dah! I didn't care for it very much.

The first film I enjoyed to a supreme degree at the Regal, a few years later, when flight from "God save the Queen" was then the final objective, was *Lucky Me*, a Doris Day musical. I went to see it again (twice) at the cinema in Wadebridge, coincidentally also named The Regal, and held the opinion for a very long while that in *Lucky Me* cinema had reached hitherto unequalled heights of greatness.

Then, in my Fifth Form days, it came to pass that I found myself once more at the Delabole Regal, this time to see a John Wayne film, *The Searchers*. I had read and been enthralled with the novel written by Alan Le May on which the film was based. The book was lent me by my grandfather, who was a totally dedicated aficionado of westerns, and indeed read little or nothing outside that genre other than the pages of the *Daily Mail* and *News of the World*. The film of *The Searchers* was every bit as good as the book had been, if not better, and to this day it remains my favourite movie.

Unfortunately, thanks to a surfeit of enthusiasm to discuss the merits of *The Searchers* immediately afterwards with Dave Richards from Tintagel, a pupil one year below me at Sir James Smith's who had also been in attendance, I lost track of time and so missed Prout's bus back to Port Isaac. The moment was not such a happy one, my sole available option being that I must proceed home on foot at a time of night when traffic of any kind was rarely known to mar the sombre tranquillity of the B3341.

But, walk it was, and for the first mile or so, I found myself in the company of Mary Hicks, a St Teath girl. Mary was a Sir James Smith's classmate of mine and for reasons which were entirely her own had also been placed in a position of having to return home on Shanks' Pony. We walked together as far as the foot of the inclined approach to Delabole where an adjoining road to St Teath veered away to the left, and there our ways parted.

I didn't know what concerned me the more, going on foot to Port Isaac from Delabole in the deep black of night, or of my being observed in the company of Mary on a lonely road by someone who knew us both and who might use the intelligence thus gleaned in a way that could only be both embarrassing and detrimental to us. It was therefore a relief to me, and perhaps to Mary as well, when we went our separate ways. I liked Mary, who was cast in a firm mould of rural stolidity. She could probably have felled me at a stroke, but she was kind hearted, and not every one of the girls of our class was blessed with her even temperament.

Leaving the "Bettle and Chisel" to appreciate the constituents of its exhaust fumes, the school bus carried on along Delabole's one artery of significance, threading through the sectors of town known as Pengelly and Rock Head, or "Rockaid" as those unfortunate enough to live locally were wont to refer to it in the prevailing argot.

Pengelly seemed to consist of rows of stout yet gloomily stark-looking buildings. These were chiefly dwelling houses, extending all the way down to the boundary of the quarry property on the right. Most of the houses owed much, if not practically everything, to the ubiquitous use of slate as both building and roofing material. In their own modest way, and with the exhibition of an air of nonchalant decrepitude, they were, in their totality, a monument to celebrate the quarry. Together they formed an exclusive grey ghetto established to accommodate quarrymen and their shades, and to hold them in thrall literally within a stone's throw of their place of work.

It was at the Pengelly stop, counting from when I was a Second Former, that a pupil named Derek Trewin caught the school bus. Derek's appearance was striking, as he seemed to embody all the dark, well-formed and handsome elegance of a young Dirk Bogarde. He was an accomplished pianist as well as being a very good footballer who played regularly on the school's first team while he was still a junior.

Derek's prowess on the piano keyboard was put to optimum use at Christmas Concerts. He served up fine renditions of numbers that were, no doubt at the insistence of Mr Sprayson and at least a few members of the teaching staff, drawn entirely from the works of classical composers. Such a style of music did not sit too well with the cultural philistinism of the majority of a typical Sir James Smith's audience, but there was nothing that could be done about it since one of the understood rules governing the Concerts was that no strain of a popular tune (i.e. one that might find air time on two-oh-eight) or of any other kind of melody that swung in any way, was permitted to offend the audience's ears.

As Cyril Fletcher liked to instruct his listeners, prior to delivering one of his "odd odes" on the radio, it was decreed that we must "pin back our lugholes" for the benefit of composers who had been long in the grave.

Similar considerations of musical blandness also applied to vocal offerings, with or without accompaniment. Most of the singers gracing the school's stage were drawn from the ranks of the girls. Choral pieces were presented by preference, but an occasional duet got thrown in to add variety. The safety provided by the combined voices of many was very effective in cloaking any individual discords which lay among them.

Modern lyrics expressing feelings of love in any shape, size or form were also banned outright, although all that such censorship tended to do was limit the available repertoire. In terms of the evolution of music, time had seemingly stopped for Sir James Smith's at a point when the Luton Girls Choir made their recording of "Nymphs and Shepherds Come Away" and thereby advised us that in this grove we should sport and play, sport and play, sport and play, it being not only Flora's holiday, but also Flora's ho-ho-ho-li-day. Progress was equally arrested once Mr Peter Dawson had informed his public as to just what it was like on the Road to Mandalay, not to mention being Down among the Dead Men.

A classmate of Derek's caught the school bus at the Rock Head stop at the far end of Delabole. He was Graham Dungey, owner of a surname that was no more or no less than a gift to nickname artists. Graham as a pupil was small and bustling. His footballing skills went beyond mere excellence and reached into the realms of star quality. As one whose credentials for football could only be found in the bottom scrapings of a barrel, I looked on admiringly at Graham in action.

Yet, however impressive Graham was with a football at his feet, he and all lesser mortals stood in the footballing shadow of Charles "Chips" Stapleton from Tintagel. Chips was my senior by two forms and supreme enough with the ball to have been scouted at one time by Wolverhampton Wanderers FC at the behest of the then legendary manager of the club, Mr Stan Cullis.

Delabole was surely a town designed for non-residents to travel through without alighting from their conveyance — unless of course they were going to a showing at the Regal — but the town undoubtedly produced a goodly array of talent in its time.

After Rockhead the bus route wove its way uphill past fields and hedges that looked impoverished enough to be not many stages removed from reverting to scrubby moorland. A few isolated farmhouses and stone barns stood out in the bleakness, few of them in any more than half-decent repair. Even in summertime the living up there would not have been easy. The farmers of North Cornwall were in any event very well-practised in pleading the case of poverty, although it was all much to the disbelief of the general public whose penance was to have to listen. My father often claimed that there was "no such thing as a poor farmer!" Although he was, perhaps, a man holding tightly on to more than a few deeply held prejudices, in this one he was probably not far off the mark.

On one particular winter's day the school bus was obliged to discontinue its journey on the road linking these lonely upland farmhouses when the driver most uncharacteristically lost a battle to force the vehicle through two to three feet of still deepening snow.

Although this was a sad defeat for the bus — since in the Prout Bros book of rules nothing took on a greater importance than getting the bus to its intended destination no matter what — for the passengers, the thick deposit of snow was accepted as if it was manna fallen from heaven. Snow and manna were, we believed, each blessed with equally restorative qualities. Against the driver's entreaties we all abandoned ship in a cheerfully united exodus, formed up into a ragged column and took off on foot over the two miles of snow-choked road which still separated us from Camelford and Sir James Smith's. The drifts did not yield easily, but neither did they succeed in holding us back. There was no thought of retreat. Forward was the only plan.

On the way through the snow I slipped and fell quite heavily, sustaining a gash on my right knee, but I had the fortune to be insulated from any sense of pain and saved from much loss of blood by the cold. It was always understood that, come what may, we all had a duty to attend school and so we went on willingly.

Camelford Railway Station, in the neighbourhood of a significant right-angled crossroads junction was the first marker of the snow-bound march. In keeping with many of its counterparts on the North Cornwall section of the Southern Railway line, the Station was not elaborate, its facilities consisting of little more than a cold waiting room, a ticket office, a space for freight storage, a cubby hole for the stationmaster, perhaps a toilet, and two platforms facing one another across the twin tracks of the up and down lines. When a train came, you got on or you got off. There were no creature comforts.

At the crossroads, the road up from Tintagel and Boscastle came in from the left, and the long, straight way into Camelford, flanked by open fields, headed off to the right. Directly ahead, the road went past the back of the station, and was thereafter destined to shrink in stature and continue on to link upwith the main Camelford to Launceston road in the general vicinity of Davidstow. The principal feature met with on the way through was the previously cited locality in Arthurian legend known as Slaughter Bridge.

Everyone knew that the ruins of King Arthur's Castle were located out at Tintagel Head, and it was also no great secret that the King's sword, Excalibur, was being held by a hand on a disembodied arm, "clothed in white samite, mystic, wonderful," somewhere (allegedly) deep down in the cold waters of Dozmary Pool on Bodmin Moor. These geographical associations had little of a credible cluster about them, although in the context of a legend, perhaps all things were possible.

Camelford, as the name suggested, was founded to take advantage of a readily fordable stretch of the River Camel, and had presumably been induced to spread out around the ford thereafter. The River Camel coursed through the town and flowed on down to the sea. Once it had passed beneath the mediaeval Bridge-on-Wool at Wadebridge, it widened gradually but famously into a broad, scenic and sandy estuary anchored by Padstow on the left bank and by Rock and Daymer Bay on the right.

Constrained by the Camel valley, the town of Camelford seemed to have taken the line of least resistance in its occupation of the valley slopes. Hence to reach the heart of the town required a descent irrespective of the direction of approach. By the same token, eventual extrication required an equal ascent. The steeper gradient occurred on Fore Street on the way in from Delabole — the gentler climb was on Victoria Road leading out towards Davidstow.

This convergence of urban development and up and down physical geography did not add up to a particularly attractive picture, although the wooded valley to the south of Camelford was not without a certain sylvan charm when seen from a distance.

On entering Camelford the school bus initially descended to where the Co-op shop skulked like a commercial behemoth awaiting, with some eagerness, the arrival of customers bearing ration books ready for scissoring at its grocery counter. It then made a sharp left turn to proceed down Fore Street flanked by pubs, shops, the chapel and the offices of various local administrative institutions.

Right at the bottom, where the road crossed the River Camel on a low stone bridge, Camelford's nicely appointed park drew away upriver on the left. And finally, no more than a hundred yards after the bridge, the school bus turned right into the lower narrows of College Road, where, at its appointed moment, it halted, its outward duty done.

All pupils travelling on the bus had to disembark in College Road whether they liked it or not, and then proceed to trudge onwards and upwards to reach Sir James Smith's Grammar School, which stood there, proudly poised in elevated grandeur, ever-ready to receive their homage and once more struggle to live up to the faint hopes of more than a few.

I suppose it wasn't much of a climb from the bus up to the school really, but for all that, it was steep enough to allow the descent at the end of each day to be taken at a relief-ridden easy run.

8

A Janitorial Interlude

A few cottages stood in a row on either side of the foot of College Road. The uppermost of these on the right was home to a gentleman named Mr Samuel Coombes. Mr Coombes was well known to all Sir James Smith's pupils and was referred to, when he was spoken of, as Sammy. During the first three years or so that I spent at Sir James Smith's, Sammy was employed as the school's janitor cum general factotum.

He was by no means young, and gave an impression that any youthful sentiments that his heart had ever felt had long since been swallowed by a marked degree of barely contained pent-up rage. Sammy made no secret of the fact that he possessed a well-developed sense of ill humour. As if these perfect qualifications for his school janitorial position were not enough, he spread a keen dislike of boys as the cream on his stale jam-free splitter of life, and chose never to hide his spite under a bucket.

He seemed to bear the cares of the world on his shoulders, not that this prevented him from carrying out his duties reasonably well, but it did ensure that whatever he did never managed to demonstrate any form of grace. Sammy, in short, invariably appeared to be highly pissed off about something or other, if not over practically everything in general. In fairness to him, he might have been weighed down by personal circumstances which, had they been known to us, could well have mitigated the general consensus that he was a miserable old bugger, but in sad hindsight, we only ever came into contact with his professional side and our judgement was invariably based on what we knew of that.

As a consequence, most of Sir James Smith's boys tried to give Sammy as wide a berth as was possible, but it was all to no avail. Sammy had a masterful nose for smelling out misdemeanours, and at break times he lurked at corners of the yard and hovered around in the vicinity of the boys' lavatories in the hope of spotting someone misbehaving, smoking, fighting, swearing or, best of all, dropping a piece of litter.

We believed that Sammy served as an extension of Mr Sprayson's eyes and ears, being well enabled to sneak around and spy in a way that for Mr Sprayson would have been impossible to achieve personally if the dignity of his office was to be preserved. Sammy's forte was the gathering of incidental intelligence and its presentation to the Headmaster with added embellishments. He allegedly told his tales to Mr Sprayson, and the latter might or might not then be motivated to follow them up and hand out penalties.

No-one loved an informer.

Mr Sprayson's pet hate was the sight of litter on the ground. A discarded toffee paper was a particular *bête noire* of his, and engendered in him the kind of reaction that a red rag was traditionally supposed to bring out in a bull. He would pounce on an offending scrap of wrapping, pick it up between thumb and forefinger and wave it about wildly above his head while exclaiming, "A toffee paper? A toffee paper?" He delivered the repetitive query to all of the instantly nervous audience within earshot using the full inflexion of tremulous disbelief as exercised by Lady Bracknell in respect of a handbag.

It was perhaps only fortunate for the sake of Mr Sprayson's blood-pressure stability, as much as for the wellbeing of those who were predisposed to the random discarding of litter, that toffees and other wrapped sweets were in short supply thanks to their being rationed. The two ounces of sweets per week that the ration prescribed to each of us were, during the very limited time that the sweets remained in hand, consumed surreptitiously, and kept well out of the sight of others, since others would show no reticence in demanding a share if the availability of sweets was as much as hinted at. The desire to give your sweets away was directly proportional to the extent to which your arm was being twisted at the time.

Sammy's janitorial duties on behalf of the school, of both the clandestine and the occupational variety, came to an end on the occasion of his formal retirement. If any pupil, or for that matter any member of the teaching staff, regretted Sammy's departure, they kept it to themselves.

The last roll of the dice had yet to be cast in Sammy's direction, however, as he continued afterwards to dwell in his little cottage at the bottom of College Road, from whence he could cast a baleful glare at his many non-admirers as they passed his ever-open back door on their way up and down from the school.

One day, Bob Pethick, a lively little redheaded boy from Camelford who was one form senior to me, exhibited a few stink bombs that he had obtained on a recent visit made to Plymouth. These noxious items took the form of tiny sealed spheres of thin glass filled with yellow liquid. They broke easily when thrown, or alternatively they could be left on the ground in a public (and preferably enclosed) space for someone to step on and crush unknowingly.

By whatever means such stink bombs were broken, the

consequence of breakage was the immediate release of an inescapably widespread miasma, redolent of the smell of rotten eggs. Bob and I regularly sat facing one another across an assigned table in the school canteen at dinner time, which appreciably cordial association led me to be gifted with one of his supply of stink bombs.

I would not have dared to activate the capsule on the school property for fear of the consequences, which meant that I had to decide on an alternative location for setting it off. My initial plan was to take it home and safeguard it pending the revelation of an optimum opportunity to use it purposefully.

Then, as I headed down College Road at the end of that very day on which Bob gave me the stink bomb to where the return school bus was waiting, I saw Sammy's ever-open back door, and on an impulse, without pausing for a single thought, I suddenly realised, almost with a feeling of horror, that I had impulsively pitched the little glass sphere through the open door onto the slate-flagged floor of Sammy's kitchen. Perhaps the chance to do it had been too inviting, or perhaps unhappy memories of Sammy had overruled any common sense. I regretted the action even as the stink bomb left my hand, but by then it was too late for me, and too late for Sammy as well.

The post-Sammy vacancy for School Janitor was filled by a Mr James Boundy, known to all pupils as Jim. In terms of age, Jim was already a good match for Sammy, although unlike Sammy, Jim bore his years with kindness of spirit. He was always a man worth passing the time of day with, ever ready with a smile and a dedication to both offer and accept a joke.

Only on one occasion did I see Jim get noticeably agitated to the point at which he might have been described as showing at least a trace of irascibility and certainly a ruffled air of being not quite enamoured with the prevailing run of events. This incident took place when I was in the Lower Sixth and followed hard on the heels of a prolonged spell of wintry chill that had resulted in all liquid products in the school's exterior freezing solid, not least those which existed in, and in the vicinity of, the boys' lavatory block. Irrespective of the possibility of toilet flushing being impossible under the grip of sub-32-degree temperatures, a number of boys — rather too many in fact — still elected to go on using the lavatory facilities for both number one and number two relief purposes. The inevitable result was that the bowls in the appointed cubicles quickly became as full of shit as one or two members of the teaching staff were popularly reckoned to be.

Although the boys' lavatory area was colloquially known as "the bog", under its frozen circumstances the great traditional name of "shithouse" seemed much more appropriate for filling the bill.

In order to prevent the process of shit being piled on shit from going too far, as the authorities seemed unwilling to do anything about it, I went up there at a quiet moment, locked the cubicle doors from the inside to prevent access from the outside, and climbed out through the small gap separating the roof from the top of the door frames. As a public service action I thought that this could not be faulted. The rationale behind it was that the doors could be reopened by climbing back in when a thaw had established itself and flushing was once more an option. In spite of the logic, Jim was not at all amused by what he saw as a blatant violation of his territorial rights.

Moving swiftly for once, Jim lost no time in informing the Headmaster of his disquiet. For his part, at the following day's morning Assembly, Mr Sprayson was at pains to announce his own most severe displeasure over the incident of the locked shithouse doors, although he didn't say it in quite those words of course. This outrage had, he thundered at the ranks and columns assembled before him, caused Mr Boundy, who was (in something of an understatement) not a young man, to be forced to break the locks on the cubicle doors to achieve access to what lay within. (Well, I thought, at least Jim didn't have to do any climbing.)

A vision of Jim breaking into a shithouse to some extent calmed my rising sense of guilt. This was fortuitous, as Mr Sprayson, in the ponderously Biblical tones that he normally used to read a lesson at the school's Christmas Festival of Nine Lessons and Carols, called on him who had committed the dreadful door-locking deed to come forth and confess his sins without delay. Should the culprit fail to own up, Mr Sprayson declared, it would then go all the more hard on him when the truth was finally out.

I hovered on the point of stepping out to own up, with my head hanging and a *mea culpa* on my lips, only to pull back. It wasn't an honourable course to take, but I was suddenly seized by a sense of feeling that discretion really was the better part of valour. What I had done, I did for what felt like a sterling motive and so I kept my own counsel. I had few regrets, although I was most upset about inconveniencing Jim.

Following an almost painful interlude bridging a silence so profound that if anyone had chosen to drop a pin the validity of the old adage about the ensuing sound would have been in no doubt, and in which eyes fixed and forward focused was universal, Mr Sprayson cleared his throat and expressed a bitter disappointment that whoever was responsible lacked the courage, moral fibre, integrity and several other what-have-you factors of that sort, to own up and play the game.

I fully intended to go afterwards and see Mr Sprayson in private and make my confession — it was a well-meant intention, but one of the kind that paved the road to hell.

Mr Sprayson thumped the cover of the Bible lying on the lectern behind which he stood. "When you go to the lavatories," he demanded of us all in a voice trembling with passion, "touch nothing that is not your own!" At this, more than a few boys appeared to be having difficulties in suppressing sniggers at the consequent image which Mr Sprayson had inadvertently conjured up for them.

And finally, that was that. In its execution, the locking of the lavatory doors was perhaps not one of my finer moments at Sir James Smith's, but in its aftermath it was assuredly an action that did good, unlike that of the stink bomb assault on Sammy's cottage.

School Photograph, 1951 (central portion)

Teaching Staff (*seated*), *from left to right* – Mrs Pearce (*Admin*); Miss Holloway; Miss Jones; Miss White; Mr Sprayson; Mr Menadue; Mr Hooper; Mr Jeal; Mr Turner and Mr Perry. **First Formers** (*front row, cross-legged on the ground*), *from right to left* – Pat Sleeman; Mike Ferret; Geoff Bourne; James Platt; Arthur Smeeth; –; Pauline Bigsby; Anne Bogle; Ann Thomas; Mollie Hooke; Jennifer Callaway; Mary Hicks; Glenis Cann. **Others mentioned in this book** – *Back row, sixth from left*: Jennifer Sprayson. *Back row, tenth from left*: Richard Blake. *Seated to the right of Mr Perry*: Preston Hicks. *Seated alongside Preston*: Hugh Menadue.

School Photograph, 1954 (central portion)

Teaching Staff (seated), from left to right – Mrs Pearce; Miss Lyons; Miss Quick; Miss Holloway; Miss Jones; Miss White; Mr Sprayson; Mr Menadue; Mr Hooper; Mr Jeal; Mr Turner; and Mr Perry. Third Formers (back row, standing), from left to right – Mary Hicks; Muriel Beard; —; —; Anne Thomas; Mollie Hooke; Sheila Bourne; —; Pauline Bigsby; James Platt; Mike Ferrett; Gordon Keat. Others mentioned in this book – Third row (standing), from left to right: Sally Burnett; —; —; Moira Sprayson; Rita Cutler; —; —; —; —; Arthur Smeeth; Ross Cobbledick; —; Dave Richards; Colin Mitchell; Mike Vagges; Bryan Teague. At far right on seated row: Richard Blake. Third from right, cross-legged on the ground: Duncan Andrew. Seated alongside Mrs Pearce: Jennifer Sprayson.

School Photograph 1957 (central portion)

Teaching Staff (*seated*), *from left to right* – Mr Perry; Mr Boothby; Mr Turner; Mr Williams; Mr Jeal; Mr Hooper; Mr Menadue; Mr Sprayson; Miss White; Miss Jones; —; Mrs Pearce; Mrs Perry. *Seated alongside Mr Perry*: James Platt (*Upper Sixth*). *Seated alongside Mrs Perry*: Sheila Oates *and then* Moira Sprayson *and* Angela Wingfield (*all Upper Sixth*). *Third Row* (*standing*) *sixth from left*: Duncan Andrew.

and while he opened to us the scriptures?

33 And they rose up the same hour, and returned to Jerusalem, and found the eleven gathered together, and them that were with them,

34 Saying, The Lord is risen indeed, and hath appeared to Simon.

35 And they told what things *were* *done* in the way, and how he was known of them in breaking of bread.

36 ¶ And as they thus spake, Jesus himself stood in the midst of them, and saith unto them, Peace *be* unto you.

37 But they were terrified and affrighted, and supposed that they had seen a spirit.

38 And he said unto them, Why are ye troubled? and why do thoughts arise in your hearts?

39 Behold my hands and my feet, that it is I myself: handle me, and see; for a spirit hath not flesh and bones, as ye see me have.

40 And when he had thus spoken, he shewed them *his* hands and *his* feet.

41 And while they yet believed not for joy, and wondered, he said unto them, Have ye here any meat?

42 And they gave him a piece of a broiled fish, and of an honeycomb.

43 And he took *it*, and did eat before them.

44 And he said unto them, These *are* the words which I spake unto you, while I was yet with you, that all things must be fulfilled, which were written in the law of Moses, and *in* the prophets, and *in* the psalms, concerning me.

45 Then opened he their understanding, that they might understand the scriptures,

46 And said unto them, Thus it is written, and thus it behoved Christ to suffer, and to rise from the dead the third day:

47 And that repentance and remission of sins should be preached in his name among all nations, beginning at Jerusalem.

48 And ye are witnesses of these things.

49 ¶ And, behold, I send the promise of my Father upon you: but tarry ye in the city of Jerusalem, until ye be endued with power from on high.

50 ¶ And he led them out as far as to Bethany, and he lifted up his hands, and blessed them.

51 And it came to pass, while he blessed them, he was parted from them, and carried up into heaven.

52 And they worshipped him, and returned to Jerusalem with great joy:

53 And were continually in the temple, praising and blessing God. Amen.

THE GOSPEL ACCORDING TO
HELLFIRE ST. JOHN. PROUT.

CHAPTER 1.

IN the beginning was the Word, and the Word was with God, and the Word was God.

2 The same was in the beginning with God.

3 All things were made by him; and without him was not any thing made that was made.

4 In him was life; and the life was the light of men.

5 And the light shineth in darkness; and the darkness comprehended it not.

6 ¶ There was a man sent from God, whose name *was* John.

7 The same came for a witness, to bear witness of the Light, that all *men* through him might believe.

1074

Personalisation of the Good Book in a tribute to a Legend in his own lifetime.

Upper photo: The redoubt of the School commanding the ascent from College Road. The face of the First Form classroom is on the left and that of the Second Form classroom (and Assembly hall) is on the right. In the right background can be seen the roof of the Chemistry Laboratory. *Lower photo*: Part of the Boys' Yard in 2005. Clockwise, the surrounds of the Yard show the main entry set proud into part of the Assembly corridor; the window to the Boys' Cloakroom; and the windows and exterior of the First Form classroom. The roof of the Library appears in the background. With the Grammar School defunct, the buildings as at this date housed local council employees. *Sic transit Gloria mundi.*

Maria Platt and Terry Graystone make a visit to the Boys' Yard in 2005.

9

A Matter of Form

Arriving to confront my very first day at Sir James Smith's, clad in an unaccustomed school uniform that felt a little less than comfortable on me, shaped up as a sink or swim experience in every one of its great unknowns. Sinking or swimming in the literal sense was an experience not altogether unfamiliar to me though, as in keeping with most other small boys of my generation I had learned to swim by virtue of being thrown into the sea by bigger boys who had been previous beneficiaries of the same lesson.

I knew that my first day at Sir James Smith's was going to be deep-end stuff.

All through the summer holidays preceding the start of term, I had been told so many times by certain of Port Isaac's more senior Sir James Smith's pupils that my days of playing at Cowboys and Indians were over that I had no alternative but to assume I would have to live with that unpleasant reality. But I still wasn't sure if I could. In any case, sinking or swimming would be the shared fate of every member of the new First Form — that is, all save one. The performance of this odd First Former out during the previous academic year had led to him being required to do it all over again — he therewith held an advantage over the rest of us as his classmates, in that he not only knew who was who and what was what around the school, but was also conversant with a range of well-established techniques designed to make life easier by pulling the wool over a teacher's eyes.

The name of this fount of wisdom in all things other than academic was Ross Cobbledick, known as "Rossy". He was much consulted by his new classmates in the manner of an elder statesman. Rossy's surname suggested a wide range of possibilities for the ribald field of playground humour to improvise on, but since he was large and beefy, tongues were usually held mute on that subject.

The Sir James Smith's First Form Class Register for September 1950 recorded the First Form members (in alphabetical order) as shown on page 96, boys first, and then girls. The Register was called by the designated form master or mistress prior to the commencement of lessons each morning when everyone was back from Assembly and all seated at their allocated desks.

The boys were called by their surnames and the girls by their Christian names. When there was duplication, or even triplication, of one or the other, as with those three girls named Ann(e), both Christian and surname were called. It was standard practice throughout the school for the teaching staff to address boys only by their surname. To begin with, this made me feel very uneasy, but it fairly soon became no more than a matter of fact thing.

My First Form group then, consisted of twenty-nine pupils of whom twelve were boys and seventeen were girls. These relative proportions were very probably an accurate representation of the girls being rather brighter than the boys. Sir James Smith's was proudly co-educational in every facet of its brilliant-cut philosophy under Mr Sprayson, yet by an almost tacit agreement there was very little fulsome interaction across the great gender line, not least in the junior ranks of the school.

First Form Register, September 1950

NAME	ADDRESS

BOYS

Geoffrey Bourne	Churchtown Farm; Lesnewth
Ross Cobbledick	Brunswick House; Valley Truckle
Michael Ferrett	Dunn Street; Boscastle
Brian Fisher	Delanuth; Delabole
Gordon Keat	Kealey; Fore Street; Port Isaac
David Pierce	Rose Cottage; Tregellist; St Kew
James Platt	9, Hartland Road; Port Isaac
Patrick Sleeman	16, The Butts; Bossinney Road; Tintagel
Arthur Smeeth	Cullodoon Farm; Camelford
Bryan Teague	Sunnyside; St Breward
Michael Vagges	HM Coastguard Station; Port Isaac
Leonard White	1, Delaview Terrace; Camelford

GIRLS

June Arnold	Glenmore; Tintagel
Muriel Beard	3, Marine Terrace; Boscastle
Pauline Bigsby	Windyridge; Trenale; Tintagel
Ann Bogle	Roughtor View; Camelford
Glenis Cann	Rose Cottage; Tintagel
Jennifer Callaway	Palm Cottage; St Teath
Celia Dennis	Manor House; Camelford
Mary Hicks	Trevilley Lane; St Teath
Mollie Hooke	2, Church Hill; Port Isaac
Carole Isles	4, Atlantic Road; Delabole
Margaret Jasper	Riverside House; Camelford
Kathleen Ladbrooke	Trevallen; Trevalga
Ann Mitchell	Hillside; Chapel Street; Camelford
Maureen Rush	Elm View; Trewaldon; Delabole
Anne Thomas	11, Hartland Road; Port Isaac
Jennifer Walke	Police Station; Camelford
Angela Wingfield	Sunnybrae; Tintagel

Of the twenty-nine named on the Register, which comprised the new intake of twenty-eight plus the second-time-around Rossy, nine related to Camelford; six to Tintagel; five to the finest location in North Cornwall, namely Port Isaac; three to Delabole; two each to Boscastle and St Teath; and one each to St Kew and St Breward. Sir James Smith's arms had opened wide to reap a random harvest from stony ground.

The Register of course was really no more than the opening gambit in what was to become very much a moveable feast. As the years went by and we moved up through the school, adjustments to the class register took place consequent on both arrivals and departures, all of which were not only usually unannounced but also rapidly adapted to with barely as much as a shrug of the shoulders from those who still remained. The school abhorred a vacuum.

As it happened, most of the pupils listed with me on that First Form Class Register stuck together as classmates all the way from the First up to the Fifth Form. It was only at the Fifth's monumental juncture that the bloody cull of external Ordinary (O) Level School Certificate Examinations resulted in a decimation of the ranks and therewith precipitated the parting of so many ways.

At the end of the Fifth Form academic year the average pupil age was sixteen. A consequence of reaching that age determined that in certain cases, irrespective of academic achievement and demonstrated potential to flourish onwards in the Sixth Form, a pupil could well be required under a parental ultimatum to 'git off yer bleddy backside, git a job and bring 'ome some money t' earn yer keep'. My father was vociferously insistent on my following that very route, but my mother was equally determined that I should go on to the Sixth Form, and her will prevailed, although it didn't stop my father from continuing to regard me as an idler for most of my two Sixth Form years.

Out of we twenty-nine First Formers who began together, only seven survived to sit the Advanced Level School Certificate examinations (A Levels) seven years later in the Upper Sixth. These seven stalwarts were Mike Ferrett; Gordon Keat; Bryan Teague; Celia Dennis; Angela Wingfield; Margaret Jasper and me. The intellectually gifted Michael Vagges, who left after the Fifth Form, would undoubtedly have made an excellent Sixth Former.

The pupils who, like Michael, fell away from the school dynamic simply seemed to be extinguished. They were gone in an instant, much like the flame of an England's Glory match struck in haste in order to light up an urgently needed Woodbine. They went unsung, without ceremony, vanished. There was no slowly fading away in the manner of old soldiers.

It would be unfair to say that our losses were not regretted, it was just that they were not regretted for very long. A gap would open only to be instantly closed, and Sir James Smith's rolled on. Most of the promises made to keep in touch were forgotten by the following week, overrun by more current priorities.

Way up in the senior echelons of the school's form hierarchy, the inevitable breakdown of the social boundaries separating boys and girls tended to be offset to some extent by academic specialisation. As a rule, although it was something of a force-fit, boys trod the route of scientific subjects while girls followed the pathway of the arts. The school timetable seemed almost to conspire that rarely the twain should meet.

The gender divide was also sharply defined in classroom seating arrangements. The desks were single and precisely lined up in front-facing columns. Boys sat in the columns on one side, and the girls sat over on the other.

With the ascending progression of seniority from the First Form up to the Sixth, it might have been expected that seating boundaries would become increasingly blurred, but if they did it wasn't noticeable.

96

10

Friendship's Path

The time available to us to properly get to know one another in the First Form had its limitations, since the greater part of the school day was devoted to lessons given by teachers who were experts at discouraging any form of communication in the ranks that was not related to the lesson in hand. As classmates, we were together only during school hours on five of the week's seven days and at the end of each of those five we all went on our separate-village ways home. We gave little thought to matters scholastic at weekends in term time, and, naturally enough during the school holidays, anything to do with the school and its range of associations was a lost cause from break-up day onwards.

We were, however, able to get together to cement burgeoning friendships at the morning Assembly line-up; in the two fifteen-minute breaks from lessons that we were granted each day; and also at dinner time, although where dinner time was concerned the priority was not so much to talk as to get stuck into the food on offer, or (just as likely) to devise a means of consuming as little as the prevailing no-food-to-be-left-on-plate mandate would allow itself to be stretched.

The basic rule of association was that like spirits were never slow to recognise one another and act to bond together in small clans within the framework of both the class and the school, but primarily the former. Therein lay the security of friendship.

Common ground for further social intercourse (a condition which was advised directly and without a touch of irony from the mouth of Miss Jones — it apparently had nothing at all to do with stories in the *News of the World*, as we were disappointed to learn) was found in the Wednesday afternoon playing field ordeal by either football or cricket in season; at the form's Christmas party in which the best highlight was the moment when the party was finally laid to rest; in the audience at the school's Christmas Concert; in the congregation at the Christmas Festival of Nine Lessons and Carols; on Sports Day and in that great battle to combat the onset of un-remitting boredom known as Speech Day.

In this communicative context, the occasional staging of dramatic performances, some light, others ponderous, yet all with hidden depths of quality, could be seen to present important extra-curricular meeting points ready to be taken advantage of. But then again, since such events happened in the evenings and were designed to attract the patronage of parents and members of the general public, the majority of pupils present tended to belong to either the cast or the back-stage crew and were therefore not out for a lark — at least not on opening night.

I gravitated naturally into becoming one of a small, appreciably closed coterie of classmates and felt comfortable in their like-minded company. These were four in number, namely Mike Ferrett (Bos-castle), Pat Sleeman (Tintagel), Bryan Teague (St Breward), and Arthur Smeeth (Camelford). Village rivalry was suspended for the duration and together we were more than the sum of our parts..

A few words about each of these worthy stalwarts will be appropriate.

Mike Ferrett was innately amiable, bright, cheerful and slow spoken like me. Mr Turner once referred to him in a French lesson as "Monsieur Le Furé", which provided one of the few occasions when I saw Mike uncharacteristically caught off guard.

My most striking contact with him took place at the school sports field one Wednesday afternoon during the cricket season. It came about in this way.

I lived in a state of truce with the generally placid ambience of cricket, although I never bothered to try to understand the rules of the game, dullness being too kind a word with which to describe them. Naturally enough, thanks to a dysfunctional hand to eye coordination, I had no prowess whatsoever as a cricketer, but, when the weather was warm and the formal level of activity expected from me was low enough to barely make it worthwhile for me to work at goofing-off, I was willing to summon up interest.

If my having to go in to bat ever became an unavoidable necessity, the span of an over marked the absolute limit for determining how long I would survive at the wicket. When my team was fielding, I could count on never being called upon to bowl, and was then content to take it easy in the long grass of the far outfield where I could stand in the sunshine watching grasshoppers, listening to the drone of bees and trusting that a ball would never get hit in my direction.

The best thing about cricket was the enjoyment to be had in helping to push the school's heavy granite roller up and down the cricket pitch. Rolling the pitch was a team effort, a recipe for pleasure with added spice thrown in as the roller's edge went over someone's toes.

Be that as it may, one of the then current stories in that comprehensively thrilling weekly publication *Adventure*, a copy of which was reserved for me each week at Rowe's Newsagent's shop in Port

Isaac, featured the exploits of a cricketer named Willie Wallop.

Willie Wallop's celebrity was derived from his affecting a unique batting stance akin to that adopted by baseball players, the cricket bat being held raised and slung over his right shoulder. Willie was thereby primed to deliver a full-bodied swing to any ball bowled at him, with the result that the ball invariably went for six, right up into the stands and sometimes even out into the mean streets that lay behind.

"Willie Wallop?" queried Otch back in Port Isaac, and then answered himself, "He will and all!"

In an attempt to emulate the said Willie Wallop, I picked up a cricket bat during a pause during a pitch-rolling session, and swung it back over my right shoulder in order to demonstrate Willie's classic stance to Pat Sleeman, who had not yet read of Willie's unique exploits. It was just unfortunate that I omitted to check into the possibility that someone might be standing behind me at the time, and it so came to pass that Mike Ferrett was that someone and his location was well within range of the bat's outer swing. The end of the blade contacted the side of Mike's head with a dull clunk.

Mike subsided gracefully and measured his length upon the ground. Mr Menadue, assigned to sports duty for that particular afternoon, then approached me with little or no grace in his step and a great deal of condemnation for me on his lips. He appeared singularly unimpressed by my exhibition of Willie's technique, and even more disenchanted with me. I don't recall his dismissing me from the field for reckless behaviour, as indeed he should have done, but I did discover what it was to be given an over-enthusiastic dressing-down by an expert in the art of heated invective.

Mike revived quickly, and apart from exhibiting a cranial lump that came to be much admired over the few days that it took to subside, was none the worse for wear.

As if a form of revenge for the Willie Wallop assault was decreed by fate, I received my Boscastle-inspired come-uppance one Saturday afternoon when I cycled up to that secluded village to meet Mike. My bike was a birthday present bought by my mother from Mr Joe Knight, the proprietor of Port Isaac's Central Garage. It was by no means a new bike — definitely second hand and for all I knew it could even have been, third, fourth or fifth hand. None of that mattered, as the bike was the first of its kind that I had ever owned. I liked it and gratitude for its possession was foremost in my mind.

I rode the bike often, journeying out of Port Isaac into foreign parts as remote as the far limits of places like Wadebridge, Tintagel, Polzeath, Camelford, and many points in between. My bike ride to Boscastle had me come along by way of Delabole, and it was all plain sailing until I reached the head of the hill descending into the deep valley that Boscastle and its rocky harbour lay at the narrow Atlantic mouth of.

A sign at the top of the hill warned road users that a sharp bend would intervene on the way down. I heeded the advice and so was fully alert to negotiating the anticipated bend as I descended with what for me was a marked degree of caution. There was indeed a bend of sorts at about the half-way mark, but it didn't look too arduous. I rounded it without a care in the world and continued with the descent, thinking that the warning sign up above had hardly been necessary. That this was wishful thinking dawned on me suddenly at the immediate foot of the hill, since there the road took an almighty twist to the right that neither I nor the speed of my bike could negotiate.

We collided head on with a low retaining wall on the outer left hand side of the bend. I soared over the handlebars and met the ground robustly, doing no favours to both my knees as well as the side of my left forearm. The bike's front wheel buckled, and its front fork bent. My Willie Wallop whack on the skull of one of Boscastle's finest sons was therewith appropriately avenged. A lesson learned there and then was that what went around, came around.

Pat Sleeman, my valued friend, hailed from Tintagel. He was nicknamed "Slim", which might have been held to bear a direct relationship to his surname, but which was primarily derived from a consideration of his wafer-thin physique on which clothes hung like tired curtains. Pat's appearance was elfish — his ears stuck out at an angle sufficient to gladden the heart of any teacher addicted to pupil appendage pulling; his eyes were bulgingly querulous, and his hair paid a slick tribute to the suppressive properties of plenty of Brylcreem,

Pat was always good company. He and I shared almost identical tastes in our evening listening on the radio, so that we were never short of things to discuss on the subsequent morrow. We compared notes on comedy programmes in particular, and analysed gags we had heard with far more relish than was contained in our approach to doing the same for the set works of English Literature.

The comedy series that we both regarded as forming the very crown of the radio pantheon, and for which failure by either of us to listen to either the original broadcast or its subsequent repeat would have counted as a major tragedy, was *Hancock's Half Hour*, or, as "the lad 'imself" put it at the commencement of each show, "H-H-H-H-H-H-'Ancock's 'Alf Hour".

So it came to pass that our conversation (and that of many others throughout the school), were larded with catch phrases made famous by Anthony Aloysius St John 'Ancock and his supporting cast, such as, "Stone me!"; "Shut your cake 'ole!"; "Are you looking for a punch up the bracket?"; "Another cup of tea, vicar?" and, last but not least, "Stop messing about!" We particularly enjoyed Hancock's vituperative exchanges with his principal co-star Sid James.

Hancock's Half Hour was enormously popular, and at a school Christmas Concert held when Pat and I were in the Fifth Form, the Fourth Form performed an excellent Hancock routine, with Derek Trewin taking the role of Sid, and Dave Richards as the Lad 'Imself.

We were very much enthralled with serial radio programmes which consisted of half an hour of exciting storyline with a cliff-hanger ending. With a week to wait for its outcome, the cliff hanger provided material for intense speculation as to how it might be resolved.

The mandatory-listening exploits of *Dick Barton — Special Agent* had been terminated by the BBC, to universal displeasure, prior to my starting at Sir James Smith's, thus depriving us of a basis for critical review that could have been second to none. Alas, the serial replacing Dick's adventures as an early evening institution, entitled *The Archers*, seemed to be as laden with manure as were the boots of the farming folk who featured in that turgid everyday story of country folk.

Recompense arrived, however, with *Journey into Space* by Charles Chilton. He was rumoured to be still writing the ending for each episode even as the first part of the episode was being broadcast. *Journey into Space* related the extra-terrestrial adventures of Jet Morgan, played with great aplomb by Andrew Faulds, and his chirpy sidekick Lemmy — a gift role for David Kossof. We were even more enthralled by its sequel, subtitled *The Red Planet*, which involved a trip to Mars. An especially memorable character in the crew of Jet's Red Planet spaceship was the sinister Whittaker whose catch phrase, "orders must be obeyed without question at all times", was delivered in a subservient monotone designed to gain the admiration of a teacher in an instant. It became another mainstay of our stock conversational gambits.

The great benefit of the week's break between serial episodes was that it kept us from realising how very thin some of the plots on offer were. The *Paul Temple* murder mysteries by Francis Durbridge were such a case in point, but for all that, they were totally gripping and gave us licence to mull over plot twists that didn't actually exist. The theme music for the *Paul Temple* series, the "Coronation Scot" will be forever evocative of that era.

Among the more popular variety programmes that we were steady listeners to, was *The Show Band Show*, featuring Cyril Stapelton leading the BBC Show Band. This wonderful orchestra played in many styles and catered for a broad range of musical tastes, accompanied by star vocalists such as Lita Roza, Julie Dawn, Dennis Lotis, and Dickie Valentine, the trombonist Don Lang and a close harmony group the Stargazers (who were on the air). Pat and I discussed respective performances in the greatest of detail, as if in doing so we were in touch by proxy with a world of good taste and sophistication that was almost diametrically opposed to the one we really inhabited.

Among the greenest radio comedy pastures that we were made to lie down in was a series scripted by the peerless partnership of Messrs Bob Monkhouse and Denis Goodwin, the best segment of which was devoted to the interactions of the duo themselves. Bob and Denis were masters of the quick-fire, spouting out jokes which would have smelt as sweet by any other name. One part of their show featured a rapid succession of one-line gags that brought along more laughs per square inch of radio time than any other comedy series could ever hope to emulate.

Pat and I tuned in to Bob and Denis at our separate homes, pencils in hand, school rough books open in front of us, and we scribbled down as much of the cascade of humour as we could manage. Then, at school the next day, we compared our notes and selected the best of what we had to enshrine in a definitively plagiarised compilation intended for a material airing in our form's contribution to the next Christmas Concert.

If a joke was good it could be worked into a Christmas Concert quite easily — all that we had to ensure that we kept clear of was anything that a member of the teaching staff might be inclined to view as suggestive, innuendo-laden, or verging towards any shade of blue in colour. I learned a keen lesson when I invoked a Bob and Denis line comparing a topical news story to a honeymoon at sea, both being a lot of bunk. Mr Sprayson pounced on that gag with all of the unerring take-no-prisoners ire that he normally reserved for wanton discarders of toffee papers.

On one certain red letter day, Pat opened the discussion session on highlights of the previous evening's listening with the comment that he had heard, on two-oh-eight, something that he described as "a good song". His encounter with this good song must have taken place at rather a late hour, as the good song's title, once he had announced it, was not one that any member of our little clan of then Fifth Form warriors could admit to having heard.

For most of us, the evening time frame for tuning in to two-oh-eight began with the adventures of *Dan Dare — Pilot of the Future*, which commenced at a quarter past seven, up to the ending at a quarter to ten of the instalment of the latest case being handled by Perry Mason. "It's half past nine, time for Perry Mason" was the famous announcement introducing the drama.

Never one to be outdone, Pat had written down the title of the good song that took his fancy, and he showed it to us. We were, at that momentous moment, gathered together in a side aisle of the Chemistry Laboratory. And there it stood in pencilled truth, "Rock Around the Clock", performed by an ensemble known as Bill Haley and his Comets. Our immediate reaction was to give way to a burst of incredulous laughter at the outlandish nature of such a title for

Pat's good song.

In fact, it materialised later, we had all heard that good song before, as it was featured a few years back in the soundtrack of a Glenn Ford film, *The Blackboard Jungle* which we had all seen. Glenn Ford played a school teacher in that film, and it was perhaps because it had been such an atypical role for a star of so many of the great cowboy films that met our preference that *The Blackboard Jungle* had not been memorable.

We were then, all completely unaware of quite how significant Pat's announcement was. He had divulged to us a concept in music on the opening edge of its time, although even Pat was oblivious to the grand nature of the revolutionary stone he had cast into the still waters of our bland culture. Yes, they had all laughed also at Christopher Columbus when he said the world was round — but, ho, ho, ho, Pat had the last laugh now.

Once our ears were opened to the chunky rhythms of "Rock Around the Clock", such was the imperative to repeat the experience over and over, that when it was reported in a daily newspaper that Pat's good song was to be played as an example of "barrel house blues" on the Third Programme, many of us were emboldened to sit through the turgidly intellectual musical gymnastics of the programming preceding its broadcast. We didn't know much, but we did know what we liked, and although the Third Programme wasn't what we liked in any shape or form, we learned that if you dug hard enough into the stodge of a figgy duff, you might come across at least one currant somewhere along the way.

A little later on, when I was in the Lower Sixth, a mixed Fifth/ Lower Sixth bus outing was undertaken to attend a showing at the Wadebridge Regal of a by then recently released film *Rock Around the Clock*, featuring the earth-shattering talents of Bill Haley and his Comets performing not only the title song but many other

106

wonderful pioneering numbers aided by a galaxy of supporting stars.

It was sad that Pat, a true original who had figuratively brought the good song news from Ghent to Aix, had already parted his ways with Sir James Smith's. Yet, although not present at the Wadebridge cinema in person, he was very much there in spirit.

Bryan Teague, known as "Tigger", or alternatively as "that boy Tigg", was at the Wadebridge Regal on that rocking outing. He was a quietly introspective boy from the remote, and appreciably wild and woolly, moorland village of St Breward. The name of St Breward, coupled with that of Blisland, a relatively near neighbour, was redolent of cold, wind-driven rain and weeping granite tors. Apart from a regrettably painful period of a few weeks, Bryan was an integral member of the inner circle of classmate friends to which I was so happy to belong.

Bryan, with a good head of wavy hair, a modest build and slightly pointed, sensitive features, was a passably handsome boy. His background was of the Chapel, which no doubt travelled outwards with the last trappings of civilisation as they all faded away into the foothills of the moors behind St Breward.

He regularly played the cornet in the St Breward Silver Band, an excellent musical institution known all over North Cornwall, always in great demand to perform as much in the open at fêtes and village carnivals as it was for hall-enclosed concerts and musical functions. In the summer, when holidaying visitors were thick on the ground in Cornwall, the St Breward Silver Band regularly travelled to coastal venues like Port Isaac, there to deliver a goodly selection of their repertoire to the acclaim of an *al fresco* public, and to conclude by leading their enthusiastic audience and hangers-on in procession through the village streets, leaping and tripping to the thumping strains of the Cornish Floral Dance, more popularly known as "the Flora".

In keeping with the ways of most of our group, Bryan took the line of least resistance in his dealings with school regulations, usually managing to skirt around the hidden pitfalls designed to identify and trap both the brash and the daring. The essential direction that we all followed was to ride with our backs to the prevailing winds of protocol in the best Vicar of Bray tradition, while at the same time unhesitatingly using group resources whenever the opportunity to put one over on our authority figures came along.

Circumstances could change of course but could always be adapted to. Yet for all of that, there were red lines drawn in the sand of classmate solidarity which ought never to be crossed if a perception of One and All was to be ensured. Almost anything could be both tolerated and accepted, provided we all pulled together in the same boat. As long as whatever happened to fall on any one of us, or all of us, was seen to be fair, it didn't matter what it was, as it always gave a boost to morale.

These ideals all fell apart dramatically one day when Bryan elected to step across a red line, and for far too long a time thereafter his action drove a bitter wedge into our company.

The stage for the single-act tragedy was the canteen, and its props were our school dinners. The canteen contained an arrangement of elongate, refectory-type trestle-mounted tables, each table seating nine pupils, four at either side and one at the head. The table head was normally a Sixth Former with Prefect status — not that there were many Sixth Formers who weren't Prefects. To have blotted your copy book sufficiently to have prefecture denied you if you made it to the Sixth would have called for a high level of effort, ingenuity and courage against the odds that had not yet been invented.

The head of the canteen table at which I was assigned to sit was none other than the aforementioned Shorty. As with all heads of table, it was Shorty's job to keep order among his flankers, in which task he was assisted by two acolytes of his own choice, one of whom sat at his left hand and the other at his right. Bryan, resulting perhaps from his having a compliant malleability, turned up on a certain day as one Shorty's two selected lieutenants.

The three thus constituted did not only suppose themselves to be in control of good order at the dinner table, but more importantly they knew they were officially responsible for the disbursement of equal portions of the bulk contents of the dishes and platters sent out from the kitchen containing the various items of the menu of the day onto nine plates.

The trouble was that their subdivision of the culinary offerings seemed to have little of fairness or equality about it, most certainly insofar as those of us who sat along the lower reaches of the table judged it. When the dinner was worth the eating, the three at the head of the table took unto themselves disproportionately large shares. When it wasn't worth eating, which was fairly often, they chose to pile excess amounts on the plates of the other six. There was a mandate, strongly enforced by the invigilating teacher and the dinner ladies in the kitchen, that all food sent out to the tables must be consumed. Only empty plates were acceptable for return to the kitchen for washing up. The War was over, but rationing was still in force, and waste-not want-not was a maxim to live by.

An unequal allocation of dinner was almost always accepted by the juniors when the dishing-out was done by seniors, if only because that was the way that it went in everyday life at home as well. However, it was felt to be moving well beyond the pale when a fellow classmate was complicit in unfair sharing, as Bryan came to do in the grip of Shorty. Food, and particularly the lack of the same, were subjects never far from our minds. We didn't starve, but there was never a time of day when most of us didn't feel a little bit hungry. We weren't greedy, but being granted what was our due was considered an absolute right.

Bryan threw in his lot with Shorty, and in spite of all entreaties directed at him, both in and out of the canteen, he either refused or failed to err on the side of fairness. Our reaction was that he should be sent to Coventry. We weren't really sure what sending someone to Coventry actually involved, but we had read about it working at Red Circle, and it sounded as if it could be done to order. Bryan was therefore sent to Coventry. It was hoped that the mere suggestion of such drastic action would have been enough to bring him back into the fold, but it wasn't, perhaps because he felt strengthened by Shorty's backing.

The longer Bryan's ostracism went on, the harder it became for any of us on either side of the dispute to compromise. I found it became very wearing to keep it going — I was as keen as anyone else to call it a day, but I didn't know how to, and so the situation was just allowed to drag on for far too long a time.

Bryan became thought of as Shorty's "asshole creeper", as a consequence of which he received a new nickname — "the Creep". Coincidentally at that self-same time, a dance craze known as "the Creep" was enjoying a short-lived period of fame, being derived from the tune to a popular song of the same name. Someone sent in a request to Pete Murray at two-oh-eight for the song to be played for Bryan, but the request fell on deaf ears (fortunately) as far as Pete was concerned.

Eventually the whole sorry saga ran out of steam and expired, leaving us all with gladdened hearts. Whatever form true justice took, or in whatever manner it was served, the means of getting there reflected no credit on anyone who was involved in seeking it out, and in this particular case there were no winners, other perhaps than Shorty, who, like Old Man River, just kept rolling along.

Arthur Smeeth, familiarly known as "Gaffer", or better yet as

"Gaff", was another prized member of our solid quintet. Arthur was a cheerful rustic for whom school was never going to be a priority as long as farmland beckoned and a fragrant odour of freshly spattered cow manure could hang in the air around him and dapple his hobnailed boots and leather gaiters

He secreted his undoubted intellectual capability behind a false front of hayseed mannerisms laced with gems of rural lore delivered in a local accent that in Port Isaac would have been awarded dimensions "s' broad ez 'twuz long". Indeed Arthur's Camelford-engendered accent was far broader than my Port Isaac version, although if pressed I would have had to confess to stretching mine to its outer limits in English lessons as a means of providing our English teacher Miss White with the direct evidence she always seemed to be searching for in order to shoot me down in flames. Arthur never seemed to be subjected to such predations, and it could well have been that I drew Miss White's heat away from him, as with what I gave her she didn't have to dream up spurious reasons to find fault in the accents of others and could focus her vituperative streak on a single target.

Arthur was the elder son of a Camelford farmer-cum-smallholder, although I couldn't swear to the smallholder part. Suffice it to say that Farmer Smeeth husbanded a small herd of dairy cattle that were milked once daily, if not twice, in a long barn occupying one side of a farmyard traditionally floored with good Cornish mud, cow manure and straw, all trampled by man, beast and time into a smooth slurry. Wherever he happened to be, Arthur peered at the world around him through narrowed eyes that seemed to be searching the near distance for signs of incoming cattle.

He could always be counted on to express himself with a bucolic aphorism drawn from home roots as tenacious as those of dandelions rising in meadow grass. He had much in common with that

111

noble order of rustic professionals exemplified by broadcasting celebrities like Ralph Wightman and A. G. Street, held in great affection by the listening public and respected for their homeliness and good humour rather than for their godliness and serious discourse.

There were obvious boundaries on the extent to which a grammar school career could be reliably followed by someone like Arthur, whose heart was wedded to the land, and whose daily schedule as the school years progressed was subjected to more and more inroads related to the requirements of his father's farm. He left us at the end of our Fifth Form year, having completed his O Level exams. Arthur was a boy without guile. What you saw was what you got with him, and there were not too many of us of whom that could be said.

Academic honours for the Smeeth farming dynasty were left to Arthur's younger brother George to pursue and achieve. George was also able to play the hayseed reasonably well, but his *modus operandi* was to merge with the madding crowd rather than to stand out like Arthur as a latter-day Walter Gabriel in his own right.

11

Subjectivity

The subjects covered in the curriculum that all we splendid First Form examples of North Cornish intellect were compelled to take up at Sir James Smith's were a far cry from the less rigorous strictures we had known at primary school.

In the case of primary school, proficiency in the "Three Rs" took pride of place, and warnings on the perils of having to deal with a bag containing n nuts didn't even exist in sufficient strength for their absence to be conspicuous.

On the following page is set out a list of not only the stimulating subject delights that were on offer to fill up our schooldays throughout seven years of tenure at Sir James Smith's, but also the names and nicknames of the guilty parties who strove to inflict the said delights upon the innocent, thus rendering the latter innocent no more.

The list is surely studded with the richness of fine diamonds, displayed in a setting as regal as it was impressive, opening up in its beauty and truth not only all that might be known on earth, but surely all that we needed to know.

School subjects

SUBJECT	TEACHER	NICKNAME
Art	Miss Holloway	Holloway
Biology (1)	Miss Lyons	Pam
Biology (2)	Mr Boothby	Boothby
Chemistry	Mr Sprayson	Boss (or KA)
Domestic Science	Miss Holloway	
Drama	Miss Jones	Jonesie
English, Language and Literature	Miss White	Polly
English, Language, Literature and General	Mr Williams	John
French	Mr Turner	Bert
Geography	Miss Jones	
Geometry	Miss Jones	
History	Mr Menadue	Mena
Latin (1)	Miss Battle	Battle
Latin (2)	Miss Quick	Quickie
Mathematics, Pure and Applied	Mr Hooper	Alfie
Music	Mr Turner	
Physical Training (PT)	Various	
Physics	Mr Jeal	Joe
Religious Instruction (RI)	Mr Hooper	
Religious Instruction (RI)	Miss Holloway	
Sports and Games	Various	
Woodwork	Mr Perry	

12

Around the School

For most of us in our new role as First Formers, Sir James Smith's academic style and sophistication were two words beginning with the letter S with which hitherto we had had little or no experience. Looking up the meanings of these words in a dictionary required a level of motivation that went beyond what passed as normal for First Formers. Nearly all of it was frighteningly new, and I for one was instinctively aware that such words bore little in common with my life outside the school perimeter. But the array of buildings which came together to juxtapose their elements in order to define the school's infrastructure gave a First Former like me something that could be related to immediately, and if it wasn't at first appreciated that in that relationship might lie a certain elusive style and a sophistication of form, then it was at least possible to sense that the substance of it all fell not far too short of being majestic.

As the years went by, and as the First Form went on to become the Second and then turned into the Third and proceeded to climb ever onwards and upwards to reach the pinnacle of the Sixth, all that there was of the essence of the school became utterly absorbed by all who made the journey. The ambiance surrounding the school buildings entered our souls, and the passage of time served only to make their instillation all the more complete. There was an ever-burgeoning feeling of ownership, so that there was not a panel in a corridor to bang into, a pothole in the school yard destined to turn an ankle, a desktop on which a set of initials could be carved, an item of Chemistry Lab equipment to misuse, or a plate of dinner in the canteen to be moaned over, in which an individual's personal stake was not vested.

There was a lot of love–hate to contend with, and I knew a little about that. For example, more than a few of the fishermen who gathered to yarn away the day on the Port Isaac Town Platt were undeniably miserable old buggers and were there to beware, and yet I knew in my heart, with affection, that they were "my" miserable old buggers. All of us belonged to one village society, which meant that although I could think whatever I liked about them, if a stranger should dare to direct criticism at them, I would be ready to leap in an instant to their defence.

Comfort and security lay in familiar surroundings, which were exactly what Sir James Smith's provided — a bastion of teaching, and hopefully learning, atop a not especially prominent piece of high ground, yet elevated enough to impress. The stone-faced solidity of the school's core buildings exuded timelessness and tradition.

In keeping with the spirit of a well-known Irish blessing, from the school bus disembarkation point at the foot of College Road, the road rose to meet Sir James Smith's and was ascended with ease when the wind was at your back. The rain, when it fell, which was often enough, did not always land especially softly on the surrounding fields, but the sun, when it shone in its infrequent way, cast both kindness and warmth on the school halls of academic virtue. And if God didn't choose to hold Sir James Smith's in the palm of his hand, then Mr Sprayson certainly did just that, and he was so close to being God in the eyes of his Assembly that a helping hand from any other theological entity would have been superfluous.

The school buildings consisted of a unified central core array surrounded by a scattering of ancillary, annex and satellite building afterthoughts. There was no great architectural uniformity to be seen, but for all that the construction fell together in a conglomeration that was not unpleasing to behold. It took no more than a short while for the general layout and its internal geography to fit into the second nature of an initiate.

If the central core could be said to have had a hub around which all the rest of it fell into place, then that point of prime function was the Headmaster's Study. From the common-purpose hall outside the study's rarely open portal, corridors seamed away like healthy arteries studded with doors opening to classrooms, cloakrooms, a library, a laboratory and the free and open air beyond.

It mattered not that a commonly held first impression tended to suggest that the design had been carried out by a self-important committee, the members of which had not a thing to lose, and who furthermore were not averse to taking risks. Once you had negotiated your way through the labyrinth, and had discovered the secret of getting from here to there either as expeditiously as possible or with as much delay as could be reliably wrung from a prevailing situation, the feel of the school fell very little short of being perfect.

And that was not all, for there also remained the outbuildings to be taken into account. These, at an educated guess (the one kind of guess permitted at Sir James Smith's without reservation), were dropped into place at various junctures of the school's more recent history in support of the aspirations of a steadily expanding teaching regime. Their style (or more properly their lack of the same) encroached on modernity — a fair amount of pre-fabrication was naturally in evidence, unintended for use in perpetuity, yet more than fit for purpose.

The grand spread of the school buildings stood, dark faced and imposing, on a prominent if not quite dominant set of terraces cut into the front of a flattening crest of rising ground. At the rear, a border of well-established hedges sealed off direct access to open farmland. The terraces were four in number, stretching perhaps to five for purists who chose to include the extra cutting and levelling arrangement on which the boys' lavatory block stood. On the other hand, since that essential facility was erected in such close proximity to an annex sometimes used for woodwork or physics classes which stood on the smallest terrace of the four, the defining of a fifth was probably unrealistic.

Gently inclined pathways, assisted by flights of stone-shod steps where steepness made a mere path impracticable, were the links binding each and every building that made the school the sum of its parts. Depending on the direction which you took or from whence you came, the walkways went either up or down — in practice it was mostly up where walking was concerned, as descents more often than not involved a slide, a run or a few hops and jumps down an embankment. As a result, the embankments had become appreciably rutted and worn, and were apt to get a lot more muddy than was reasonable in wet weather.

From where the buses stopped, it needed an ascent of about a hundred yards up College Road on a modest gradient to reach the entrance to Sir James Smith's Grammar School on the left. A firm hedge holding a few ribbons of allotments at bay marked the left-hand side of the climb. At the right there was also a hedge, over which the topography slid down across an expanse of fallow land to where the River Camel trundled easily over slippery brown stones, between which tiny fishes darted in the eddies.

The entrance to the school grounds, which might have been described as the school gates had there been any gates in place, was ever open for access. The rising gradient of College Road actually peaked not much further on, and hilly pretensions then came mercifully to an end. Upon levelling out, College Road proceeded between those constraining hedges for a couple of hundred yards more, where, having left Sir James Smith's in its wake, it terminated abruptly against a five-bar gate.

On the far side of the gate, irrespective of whether or not you opened it to pass through or simply elected to climb over it, a public (or bridle) footpath conducted you onwards at your leisure down to the river. This was a very popular walk, there for the taking before or after dinner time. Anyone whose tastes ran to close-cropped grass, sporadic trees, the hum of bees and a wealth of rabbit drop-pings, might well have found it idyllic. The fleshpots of downtown Camelford on the far side of the river were barely able to compete with its tranquillity. That was indeed a walk to conjure with, used frequently by boy and girl pairings, who in all probability liked one another but were reluctant to give any impression that they did to surreptitious observers, of whom there were many. Such couples walked slowly, separated by more than enough distance not only to kill off the art of conversation, but also to deny any possibility of its resurrection. Nevertheless, they were as one, and their comportment spoke louder than words.

Standing at the gateless entrance to the school, you had to lift up your eyes unto the school buildings, which stared back, redoubt-like, from atop a risen bank, only partially screened off by some scrubby bushes and a few branch-trailing conifers. At first sight the prospect of the bank did not offer assurance that this was a hill from whence would come any help, even under the full knowledge that up there, Mr Sprayson, he who kept us, neither slumbered nor slept.

To the immediate right as you stepped through the entrance, a lengthy, low-slung building of prefabricated construction stretched parallel to the edge of College Road. Anyone looking to find an aura of grandness in it would not succeed. All in all, it was not much to look at — it was in what took place within its flimsy walls that transcended the lack of promise suggested by its exterior and gave it nobility.

This prefabricated edifice was subdivided thrice laterally. The smallest of the subdivisions, at the end nearest the entry, contained what could be referred to without a single degree of intended irony, as the cook-house, or kitchen. The central subdivision housed the canteen where the school dinners produced in the kitchen were consumed with varying degrees of reluctance. The culinary offerings which landed on the canteen tables were usually as long on promise as they were short on hope that the promise would ever be fulfilled. It needed the rare occasions on which kitchen output did live up to expectation to keep any hope alive at all.

The motto of the canteen might well have been, "Ah well, there's always tomorrow", and its kitchen version could have done no better than to adopt Mr Wackford Squeers' "Here's richness!" The harried ladies who toiled at the kitchen stoves undoubtedly did their very best with the austerely basic ingredients available to them, and were not to be faulted at all on that score, even if what they turned out was more often barely edible than appetising. In the context of a time when getting enough food was a constant preoccupation for all, that was surely saying something.

The canteen tables, eight in number and covered in oilcloth, were lined up in geometric rectitude at right angles to the walls. A mere wipe with a kitchen cloth, hopefully clean, and any spillage, prolific or not, would be but a memory. A chair at the head of the table and a flanking bench on each side made up the seating arrangements.

The members of the teaching staff ate elsewhere, perhaps in the smoky atmosphere of their Staff Room in the main body of the school up above. It was not known if they dined on the daily canteen offerings or not — theirs was a free choice so it was assumed they gave the kitchen's menu a miss. Had they partaken of it an upgrade in quality for all would probably not have been long in coming. All that was seen of teachers at dinner time was the single designated member of staff strolling up and down the canteen's central aisle to invigilate, nip horseplay in the bud, attempt to hold the noise level down, evict the innocent and guilty alike, and ensure that only cleaned-off plates were returned from the tables to the kitchen.

With two dinner sittings, both time and speed of consumption were of the essence. You developed a technique of being well into your afters before the reverberations of first-course slurping, burping, grumbling and griping had faded from the conscious. All too often the best moment was when the last bite had been hastily swallowed and all recriminations put to rest — or at least put to rest until the next day's dinner time.

The third, and final, subdivision at the far end of the prefabricated unit could boast of approximately equivalent dimensions to the adjoining canteen. It was the Fourth Form classroom. The wall partitioning it off from the canteen bore witness to the fact that, on whichever of its sides you stood, soundproofing had never been a serious objective of the designer. Noises-off from the kitchen and canteen, consisting mainly of cooks' voices trained to adopt the Peggy Mount model of both volume and stridency, assaulted the partition, penetrated it and arrived with ease inside the ears of Fourth Formers. Although it was disturbing when first encountered, after a week or so it became merely part of the background, and could sometimes be a welcome distraction to punctuate the mind-numbing drone of certain lessons.

Insulation of the walls and ceilings appeared to be another facet of design that builders had overlooked. This was reflected in the fact that the prevailing climate within the Fourth Form room was much the same as the prevailing climate without. Hence, depending on the time of year, Fourth Formers sat at lessons feeling either soporifically warm or inordinately cold. To battle against the latter, a cast iron stove, fed with coke, did its best when called upon to generate heat, and invariably met with success over a radius of a few feet from its incandescent core.

A form of incandescence was a feature of certain of the teachers as well, but in their case the radius of maximum effect was not subject to restriction. On the other hand, no self-respecting Fourth Former ever chose to care much about the incendiary quality of his or her teachers, and so most of it was wasted effort.

It was possible to enter the Fourth Form room from the canteen through a door set into the partition, but the normal entry was through a door to the exterior at the far end of the building. From the main body of the school buildings on its terrace above, you came down to the Fourth Form room via a pathway coated in cracked tarmacadam, the inclination of which was ameliorated by the insertion of a couple of short flights of steps, one at the top and the other at the bottom, the latter ending directly in front of the entry door.

On opening the door, you found yourself faced by a broad panel, or baffle, which served to screen off that which awaited in the classroom beyond. You turned left or right to step around this panel so as to enter the classroom proper in behind the blackboard and teacher's desk. A few columns of skeletal, skid-mounted pupils desks faced you, stretching away into a distance which fell remarkably short of infinity.

Such was the Fourth Form room, a theatre ready for jolly japes and corking wheezes, even if dedicated somnolence reigned supreme more often than not. Cripes! Yarooh! The jokefulness was terrific!

And so — to quote Spike Jones and his City Slickers; as the sun sails gently across the sea, and our boat sinks slowly in the west — we must unwillingly leave the Fourth Form to its own devices in order to return to the entrance to Sir James Smith's on College Road, there to commence our ascent to the Elysian plateau on which most of the rest of the school buildings were located, and where setting foot on the yard at the top would bring respite from the climb. The particular part of the yard thus encountered was designated exclusively for the use of boys at both break time and, on occasions of clement weather, for PT lessons.

The girls' area of yard was away to the right, around and past the proudly jutting school walls on the heights looking down on the united dining facilities and Fourth Form sanctuary.

The surface of the yard was neither very smooth nor very flat, but then, a little irregularity didn't hurt anyone, or at least didn't hurt anyone very much. Unless, that is, you were in one of Mr Perry's woodwork classes attempting to plane a piece of wood against the grain, or endeavouring to make a dovetail or mortise and tenon joint that you knew was going to fit only where and if it touched. Fortunately, the golden rule of giving way to invective required Mr Perry to be actually present to express his frustration in no uncertain terms, since he was more normally somewhere out at the back going through the motions of appreciating yet another not so very rapidly smoked fag.

The boys' section of yard was ample enough in size to permit boisterous games of handball to be played during PT lessons taken under the direction of Mr Jeal. A PT session consisted of a rigid sequence of calisthenics, which always seemed to rely on cold weather as a motivator for keeping moving. Should the weather be really poor, PT was transferred to the school's grandly named gymnasium — which was in fact the Third Form classroom in an *alter ego.*

Mr Jeal, for reasons best known to himself, was an aggressive promoter of games of handball using a football as the instrument of play, and he pushed it at his classes as much in the arena of the gym as he did in the school yard. As was always the case for me in a game involving a ball and a need for eye, foot or hand coordination with it, my lack of skills did not place me in the ranks of Mr Jeal's favoured few. Since, however, the one sure thing attending to handball in the gym was that at least one of the more active players would get a splinter from the worn wooden floor deeply embedded somewhere or other on his person, it seemed that taking a back seat in handball was not altogether a disadvantage.

Although its dimensions were suitable for staging handball contests, the boys' yard was too restricted in size to permit balls to be kicked about, randomly or otherwise. There were too many windows too closely surrounding the field of forbidden play.

A short distance off to the left from where the way up from the entrance met with the yard was a moderately large building set on a very slightly less elevated terrace. It served comfortably as the school's theatre, being long, broad and well able to seat a couple of hundred or more if chairs could be found for them all. Within its airy auditorium, a stage backed by some cramped utility and changing facilities was set up at the far end.

It was indeed a fine venue, playing host as it did to various special occasions, some of genuine jollity, some of jollity eventually achieved through no fault of those present, and some of which had jollity thrust upon them. Included were the forms' Christmas parties, the school's Christmas Concert, dramatic presentations, and other specifically ticketed events open to members of the general public — the inference being that the general public consisted of the parents, relatives and friends of pupils, plus the usual handful of chancers and hangers-on who might not have realised what they were getting themselves into.

During my first year or two at Sir James Smith's, woodwork classes were held in the school's theatre, thus creating a boon for Mr Perry, who could thrive in its relative remoteness from the school's core and smoke contentedly out of sight of both God and mammon. Later on, the ham-handed use of timber under his guidance took place in the much smaller annex located up within virtual sniffing distance of the boys' lavatory block. That annex was also commandeered to function as a physics laboratory when needed, but since from the Fourth Form onwards I would drop Physics as a subject, and with that action release myself from the disparaging clutches of Mr Jeal, I didn't have to dwell overlong on its physics lab function.

Suffice it to say that for those who would work, either of the two woodwork venues satisfied woodwork's needs, and more importantly perhaps, those of Mr Perry himself, whose penchant for a quiet life was his most redeeming feature.

The boys' lavatory block, otherwise known as the "bog" or better still and not without good reason as the "shithouse", looked the part, smelled the part, and therefore was what it was. The facilities within were compact rather than roomy. There were three covered stalls fitted with chain flushing toilets and possessing doors able to be locked from inside if engaged, and able to be opened at will from the outside either when vacant or if the user inside had forgotten to engage the lock. There was no charge for entry — spending a penny at that venue was figurative rather than literal. Janitorial inspections were frequent, and the heavy hand of authority fell so heavily on anyone who chose to write on the walls that the sort of gems of poetic art which were known to grace the walls of public lavatories elsewhere were sadly conspicuous by their absence.

125

The front of the trio of stalls was separated by an aisle as narrow as it was noisome from a slate-faced trough urinal, capable of accommodating as many as four boys standing shoulder to shoulder to pee in a row. There was not a scrap of vitreous china against which to direct the flow. It remained a mystery as to whether or not the girls' lavatories on the far side of the school surpassed the boys' in standards of appointment, yet one could speculate that, minus the urinal of course, they would have done. As to the girls' lavatories possessing a girl-given nickname, that also rested with the unknown, but it would have been fair to suspect that "shithouse" was an unlikely candidate, thereby allowing the boys to rest easy in their uniqueness.

The time-honoured tradition of the boys' lavatories being a favoured location for loose banter and clandestine smoking sessions may very well have found favour at Sir James Smith's. Loose banter apart — and where would any such institution have been without it — I cannot admit to ever having noticed anything of the latter activity taking place on any shithouse visit I made, although that ought not to be taken to mean it didn't happen when I wasn't there. Anyone caught smoking faced an irate dressing-down by Mr Sprayson, with substantial detention to follow. The practice of smoking was evidently for the teaching staff only, and it took no keen powers of observation to recognise that they made the most of every opportunity that presented itself to indulge themselves in the joys of the "hateful weed".

My personal use of the boys' lavatory block, in line with that of so many others among the Sir James Smith's pupils, was, other than on rare occasions when urgent need begged no alternative but that one should go for a number two, otherwise confined to the issue of number one. We didn't have a lot going for us in the way of social protocols, etiquette, decorum — call it what you will — but such as we did have we adhered to zealously. A number two behind a bush up in the valleys, or within a cave on the beach at low tide was never to be ruled out of course, but outside of such eventualities, the emission of a number two was a function exclusively confined to the privacy of home.

Perhaps that was how the teaching staff managed it as well. We as pupils had no awareness of just where and when the teachers went to creep in, crap, and creep out again. It wouldn't have surprised any of us to have had it confirmed that teachers didn't go in for that kind of thing. And even if they did, it was a well-known fact that they reckoned to have only fragrance following in their wakes.

In times past, prior to the more recent extensions and expansions of the school buildings and annexes, the school yard must have wrapped itself in a smooth and unbroken arc all the way around the school's outer walls, lapping at their feet like Tennyson's mere in "Morte d'Arthur" when the wailing fell away. But that was then, and in the nineteen-fifties the yard was broken up by the promontories and piers of a few newer constructions, which had the effect of turning it into a sequence of linked patches.

At the mid-morning and mid-afternoon breaks, when irrespective of the state of the weather we were directed to the yard to partake of air that was quite often much fresher and more rapidly moving than we wished it to be, we tended to huddle around in groups for the fifteen minutes' duration, our shoulders hunched, our heads down. It took no great stretch of the imagination to recognise that in the tableau thus displayed were many of the essential elements of "Big House" exercise yards as seen in a host of the sort of B films which graced the screen at the Rivoli Cinema on Friday nights.

The boys' sector of yard was split in two owing to its bisection by a chunky, glass-bound walkway corridor linking the older and original body of the school to the newer Fifth Form classroom, which squared up at the top end of the corridor like a magnificent blockhouse.

The cross-sectional dimensions of this striking corridor were more or less eight feet by eight feet. A glassed-in porch, set into the middle of the corridor's front-facing wall, served as the school's principal point of entry. Within the corridor, shortly before the commencement of lessons on each and every school day, all pupils came together in a decorous line-up arranged in precedence of class seniority, boys standing along the left wall with girls on the right, everyone ready at a given signal to march unhurriedly into morning Assembly.

The morning Assembly was held in the Second Form classroom. After all, that was the room where the school's piano was kept, since without piano accompaniment the singing of the day's chosen hymn might just not get off the ground. Musical accompaniment, delivering note-perfect chords, was coaxed from the instrument under the virtuoso hands of Mr Turner. Some sang along to it, some tried to sing along, others moved their lips in a pretence of singing along, and the rest just couldn't be bothered one way or the other. It was reckoned to be a good day if everyone reached the last note of the final verse of a hymn at about the same time as Mr Turner played it.

The pupils at Assembly filled about two thirds of the classroom floor space from back to front in perfect order. Shoving and other forms of mild horseplay were activities usually confined to the line-up. Once again, the boys occupied the space on the left and girls on the right, with a gap left between the two bodies to make a narrow central aisle. Along the aisle, the prefects stood in a self-conscious column, girls at the front and boys at the back, with the Head Boy and Head Girl at the ultimate rear of their respective set of troops.

The teaching staff sat in a row at the front on chairs backed against the classroom's front wall. They stood up only to comply with the norms of religious etiquette. Central to their array, a tall, heavy and venerable lectern dominated the foreground and on its sloping top took the weight of a rather grand Bible bound in black leather. The piano was over at the far left, just inside the entry door. When we were all in place at Assembly we endeavoured to stand easy — it wasn't quite the Charlie Chester Show, although many a popular hymn did get murdered at the piano.

The section of school yard to the rear of the line-up corridor was small and dank in nature. It abutted on one flank against the library wall and was hemmed in by a steep embankment on the other side, into which a flight of steps was set to assist those who might wish to ascend to the boys' lavatory block or to the woodwork-cum-physics lab annex on the heights at the top.

The inner corner of this portion of the yard, wedged hard up against the embankment, was occupied by an open-sided, wooden-framed lean-to, fitted with a well-weathered roof of corrugated sheet metal, commonly referred to locally as "galvanise". The galvanise was fairly impervious to meteorological attack but it didn't refuse ready entry to the rain if the rain pushed hard enough. The intensity of Camelford's wind and rain might not have been comparable to the stinging onslaughts of the same around Delabole, but in combination the two elements possessed the means of exploiting chinks in armour with great skill, and in that regard they viewed the lean-to opportunistically. The lean-to's rudiments of shelter weren't entirely defeated, but gaining them involved beating the rush of others to get in under, since normally when shelter was called for the demand greatly exceeded the supply.

The ultimate negative pertaining to the lean-to, however, was associated with the mid-morning break, since beneath the flawed canopy of galvanise the daily ration of free milk was delivered in crates crammed with capped bottles, each of which contained half a pint by volume, one bottle per pupil. We were, in every sense of the words, forced imbibers — each of us under decree to receive a bottle and swallow its contents. Straws were available to assist the over-squeamish. Whether you drank your milk willingly or reluctantly mattered not — the rule said that drink it you must. The distribution procedure was carried out under the command of duty monitors, mostly Prefects, who worked from a prescribed list of names. Armed with the list, the monitors ticked recipients off with a great show of self-importance as they handed the bottles over, and then went hunting for those who sought to evade the milk-drinking mandate.

School milk was a gift horse whose unfortunate mouth was always being subjected to detailed scrutiny. All through the year, the milk invariably seemed bleak and cold, and in winter it could often get so cold as to be painful to drink. There were many days on which the milk was frozen to mush in the bottles by the time we got it. Refusing to knock the milk back was not an open option — once the half pint bottle was in your hands the deal was done. The return of bottles to the monitors for re-crating was only acceptable when the bottles were empty.

Back in Hartland Road, we obtained our daily milk supply from a well-known Port Isaac farmer, Mr Hillson. He walked his milk round, carrying the day's milk for his customers in a big, shiny, lidded pail slung over the crook of his right arm. His farm was located only a little way up Trewetha Lane from where Shorty lived, and so his milk, when it came, was as fresh as any milk could ever be, still warmly steaming from the cows which provided it. According to how much milk my mother wanted, Mr Hillson measured it out from his bucket into her large enamelled basin using a one-pint or a half-pint capacity dipper — or both, in the case of irregular measures being called for. My mother then placed the basin of fresh milk over heat to be "scalded"— in other words heated to near boiling point before being taken off the heat to cool. As the milk cooled, its cream fraction rose in clots to float on the surface, from whence it could be scooped out with a spoon and placed as an accumulation in a small dish.

Mr Hillson's milk I understood and appreciated. School milk for me was as incomprehensible as it was unloved. I didn't like its taste, besides which the bottles were cold to the hand and almost mortifying to the tongue. School milk was described as being "pasteurised", having been subjected to a treatment process which allegedly homogenised and sterilised the liquid, thereby succeeding in eliminating all elements of taste, not least among which was the undefined bit of "goodness" which my Gran reliably told me was possessed by all food products, even if it wasn't always easy to find. Goodness was a prime casualty of Mr Louis Pasteur's epic discovery.

It was felt imperative by many of us that the compulsory milk-drinking order had to be circumvented, and the much-loathed liquid disposed of by some means other than casting it down the throat. The steep embankment adjacent to the lean-to whence the delivered milk bottles were handed out thereby became an absorbent haven for the clandestine upending and discharge of the contents of countless bottles. That was the best of times — the worst of times came when the embankment was waterlogged by rain. After a sustained period of rain, for example, the yard below ran as white with spilled milk as did a certain Parisian thoroughfare run blood-red with wine in A Tale of Two Cities.

Milk was spilt, and few who spilt it sought to cry over it. But then again, and in fairness, there was no gainsaying but that the hand-out of the daily half pint of milk was well intended, and whether specific individuals liked it or not, it did bring a profound benefit to many.

The girls no doubt had a similar milk-issuing facility in their area of the yard on the other side of the main body of school buildings. It was mildly curious that few boys, including me, ever chose to investigate the girls' sector, or for that matter, bothered to give it a second thought or even wondered why they weren't interested.

The Assembly line-up corridor was a virtual Hadrian's Wall that could be entered, but which could not be crossed over. It could be climbed perhaps to provide a direct route from the main yard, but the penalty for being caught in the act of clambering up school property always loomed up as an ultra-strong deterrent for any would-be adventurer.

Climbing over the corridor was also unnecessary, as it was simple enough to walk around the back of the Fifth Form redoubt and, like the chicken who crossed the road, so get to the corridor's other side, forgetting for the moment that in one version of the chicken's journey story, the bird was alleged to have crossed the road in order to see Gregory peck. The route behind the Fifth's sanctuary could be either along the top of the backing embankment or through an exceedingly tight gully separating the muddy base of the embankment from the foot of the classroom's outer wall.

As might be expected, with a total of six forms, Sir James Smith's was able to boast of having no fewer than six accommodating classrooms. Classroom dimensions varied, but the internal furnishings and their general arrangement were standardised and kept more or less uniform. The Fifth Form room was actually the largest in size, which was assumed to be an accident of planning, since few if any crumbs of comfort were ever thrown to the Fifth.

The First and Second Form classrooms were also both rather well proportioned. These two rooms stood side by side, the one a virtual mirror image of the other about a common dividing wall. The classroom for the Third Form was most probably of a similar size to its junior counterparts, although its occasional use as a wet weather gymnasium served to add to its stature and thereby enhance the impression of grandeur that was vested in a fixed array of smoothly finished and reliably varnished wall bars, as well as in four thick climbing ropes strategically suspended from the eaves. The single drawback to the Third Form room's magnificence was the palpable odour of tobacco smoke which seeped and swirled through the doorway of the adjoining Staff Room each time it opened, which bore all the redolence of a gateway to unspeakable horrors.

The haven of the Fourth Form, slapped up against the canteen, was several sizes narrower than that of the Third, and for that matter at least a size or two shorter. The available space, however, was wholly adequate for the containment of its devil-may-care complement.

And indeed, that very sentiment of fulsome adequacy could un-questionably have been levelled at the Sixth Form room, although as the Sixth could only claim a limited number of hopefuls to accom-modate, any struggle for breathing space was obviated. Additionally, it helped that Sixth Form horseplay generally lacked the good quality of boisterousness. With that said, that the Sixth Form room was quite small needed to be accepted. With its brown-panelled walls and the restricted light filtering in through a single window affording a close-up glimpse of the milk distribution lean-to at the back, the sense of presence within was almost gothic.

From the lowliest to the most exalted, anyone who sat behind a desk in any of the school's six classrooms was an ephemeral object in a timelessly traditional, simple configuration. The desks were set up in forward-facing orderly columns, each desk accessorised with either a built-in seat or a loose chair in the absence of the former. A much larger desk, for the teacher, was centrally placed at the front, facing towards the desk columns.

To the left of the teacher's desk, an easel-mounted blackboard completed the classroom's inventory of removable furnishings. The blackboard leaned against its easel, with its base supported on a narrow shelf, adjusted for height, level and inclination through the judicious insertion of a matched pair of supporting wooden pegs into holes in the easel's legs drilled for just that purpose. On the shelf, a few sticks of chalk and a blackboard eraser found their natural home. The eraser, approximately six inches long by two inches wide by an inch or more thick, consisted of a thin layer of tightly woven felt adhering to a thicker backing of wood.

Without exception, the school's blackboards were held to be instruments of trial, a feeling not entirely unrelated to the inscriptions that the teachers chalked on their dusty surfaces in that never-ending battle to din knowledge into pupil consciousness. A sense of torment was motivated by the edge-of-teeth-setting, reverie-disturbing screech made far too often when contact between chalk and blackboard turned antipathetic.

The normal hue of the chalk was, as its name suggested, white. On rare occasions a stick of blue or red chalk might be impressed into service to alleviate the monotone, but such appearances occurred purely by chance, and the use of colour no doubt demanded a quality of imagination that was all too often missing in the teacher's haste to fill the blackboard as expeditiously as possible.

Such things, however, were not matters of great consequence, for the vital role of chalk, white or coloured, came in providing certain teachers with non-lethal missiles for flinging without warning at any obviously non-attentive member of a class before them. Irrespective of where the intended target sat, the accuracy of a stick of chalk thrown by a teacher was typically unerring. One or two of the Sir James Smith's teachers could without exaggeration regard themselves as experts in the chalk-slinging art of combat.

In some instances the blackboard duster might also enter the fray as an airborne object of choice, cast outwards with both skill and precision. The duster could well wobble a little as it homed in on its target, but that was at no sacrifice to accuracy. Mr Menadue's skill in duster throwing came as close as any to representing sheer poetry in motion. His blackboard duster, once cast, flew straight and true, its wake marked with a fine line of chalk dust motes which hung and sifted in such rogue beams of sunlight as dared to penetrate the classroom's grimed-glass defences against the same.

Mr Menadue, who had performed distinguished front-line service in the trenches of the Great War, must have used his experiences in battle to hone his expertise as a blackboard duster sharp-shooter. It was therefore probably just as well that hand grenades were not available to him at Sir James Smith's.

In the unwritten rules governing formally thrown classroom missiles, any part of the pupil in the line of fire was understood to be a legitimate target as far as a stick of chalk was concerned; whereas for a blackboard duster, in a near copy of the Marquess of Queensberry rules, only the upper front torso of the pupil could be struck. The head was out of bounds, and the lower body was never a duster issue as it was normally protected by a desk. As a target, when you saw a blackboard duster coming your way, you didn't duck because you knew it was heading for your chest. Raising your desk lid as a shield was an acceptable gambit of the battle plan, however. It was all part of the game.

I saw blackboard dusters thrown by teachers on a number of occasions, at least two of which were intended to seek me out. Once the strike was achieved, the target's duty was to pick up the duster and return it to its rightful place on the blackboard's shelf, in readiness for either cleaning the blackboard or its next outbound mission, or both.

In this gladiatorial arena of learning, a head, or rather the hair that crowned that appendage, was not destined to go fully unscathed as a location to which certain vengeful teachers could apply themselves. However, since slapping, smacking, punching, the use of a cane and even the good old primary school favourite of whacking the flat of a one-foot ruler on the forcibly held-out and turned-up palm of a pupil's hand, or bringing down the edge of the same across the knuckles if the pupil was reluctant to present the palm, were outlawed practices at Sir James Smith's, attention to a head needed by definition to be as surreptitious as it was subtle.

Some teachers elected to rap the top of the skull, under varying degrees of severity, using one or other of their index finger knuckles. Mild hair pulling was also favoured, but for that to be acceptable the hair in question needed to be long enough, clean enough and relatively free of Brylcreem, which considerations served to rule out most of the boys for that sort of treatment. Stabbing the scalp with the point of a pencil was another technique popular with a few teachers, among whom Mr Menadue stood out on his own. A pencil stab was swift, sure and almost entirely un-resented by the selected victim. HB-grade pencils were the weapon of choice, since with H grade and counting the pencil point was apt to penetrate the scalp to a shallow depth and then break off.

Tony Robinson, the son of ace driver Ted and inflicted with "Ted" as his nickname, was adamant that pencil jabbing of the scalp could result in lead poisoning. Nobody else seemed to worry about it much, probably because of uncertainty over exactly what lead poisoning consisted of, but Tony was taken very much at his word.

The school end of the Assembly line-up corridor, as distinct from the Fifth Form end, opened into what, compared with the confines of the corridor, felt to be a grand and airy hallway. The hallway's walls were clad in a brown wooden panelling redolent of academic timelessness. On stepping into that amphitheatre of mute magnificence, the eyes were at once drawn towards the light fighting its way in through thick panes of glass set in the upper reaches of a heavy and somewhat worn portal to the exterior on the far side of the confronting expanse.

Immediately to the left, another corridor, this one not especially well illuminated, turned away almost unobtrusively to pass the entry door to the Chemistry Laboratory and to go on under containment of the outer school wall on its right hand side and a solid partition on its left which on its other side formed the inner wall of the library. The partition gave the library a sense of identity, along with an air of bookish rectitude. The upper half of the library walls were adorned with an impressive sequence of imposingly large honours boards, on which, blocked out in gold-leafed script, it was possible to read a wide range of names set against dates recording their special sporting and academic achievements.

A mighty array of years was covered by the display on the honours boards. Most felt, and some knew for sure, that they were never going to see their names emblazoned in that golden company for future glories, whether they be great or small. The boards spoke their volumes in silence, gazing down upon a library caparisoned with a welter of little-read tomes rich with foxing and the smell of must. The library shelves were replete with a weighty cornucopia of literary and reference works both ancient and less ancient, occasionally enlivened by a title or a publication that could well have been new within the scope of living memory.

In a masterful touch the shelves held a small collection of bound volumes of "Hansard", offering exotic glimpses of ancient debates and point-scoring in the House of Commons which were all of as little significance then as they had been when they actually took place.

I was unable to lay a claim to being a dedicated user of the library facilities, as if I was heeding the advice that I should "neither a borrower nor a lender be", and therefore there we were.

The conventional classics, many in "Everyman" editions, were well represented on the library shelves — or at least I assumed that to be the case, as Miss White, whose demesne included the library and all its works, would not have stood for anything less. I can recall an imposing array of moralistic adventure yarns, many with a historical theme born of Empire, written by the likes of G. A. Henty, R. M. Ballantyne; Gordon Stables and T. C. Bridges. I delved widely into these with some gratitude, not for myself, but because together they made a grand fount of reading material for my father during his extensive times of illness. He gained considerable enjoyment from T. C. Bridges in particular.

There was one book, falling very nicely into the "slim volume" category, that stood out in the popular imagination on the resonant strength of its title, and which was plucked from its place on the library shelves by members of the First Form through to the Fourth with metronomic zeal. It was *Shag, the Story of a Dog* by T. C. Hinkle. A much treasured scenario for many pupils was to be seated in the library with this literary gem in hand while making a great show of pretending to be reading it, and have a teacher, preferably Miss White, come along and ask them what they were reading, because then they could tell her without fear of censure for the use of inappropriate language.

By the same token *Krapp's Last Tape* was borrowed rather more often than might have been expected where a work by Samuel Beckett was concerned. It was always referred to as "Tape's last Krap".

The library then was a fine little unsung treasure house for one and all, and finer yet for those whose pleasure was to read, mark, learn and inwardly digest the inked rivers of words which had poured from the pens of long dead writers to land up on its multiplicity of shelving.

Sometimes, around the two or three long reading tables standing centrally on the library floor, each of which demonstrated on its battered surface the scars of conflicts past and present, sat assembled classes consistent with the requirements of their timetables, keen to be distracted from the pressures of an English Literature lesson by any noises off that the thin partition shared with the external corridor was unable to dispel. Such noises included feet pounding along the corridor, the precipitate opening and hasty slamming of doors, raised voices, the welcome clang of the end of lesson bell, and, for one performance only, the domino crash of a row of desks in the Sixth Form room adjoining the library's inner end.

The Sixth Form room was long and narrow, yet fit for purpose. Like that pitch-dark cell containing Poe's Pit, it could also be felt by those who used it to be shrinking inwards incrementally as the dreaded reality of approaching A Levels swung at them like a razor-edged pendulum in perpetual motion.

It might be said of *habitués* of the Sixth Form room that they were adept at transforming what should have been their house of prayer for constructive salvation into a den of would-be thieves of time. There were no candidates for casting the first stone in the Sixth Form, among Prefects in particular.

The view from the entrance of the Sixth Form room looked directly down the corridor adjacent to the library on the right towards the area of the central hallway. To the immediate left of the Sixth Form room entry, close enough to touch, an inwards-opening door provided access to that large room which doubled as the Third Form classroom and gymnasium.

Boys and girls took gym sessions separately, and for the boys it was normally Mr Jeal or Mr Hooper who led the affray. I don't remember who took the girls for PT — even the thought, let alone the sight, of Miss White or Miss Jones or Miss Holloway leaping about in shorts would have been almost too much to bear. When the young, slender and agile Miss Lyons arrived at Sir James Smith's to begin teaching Biology, the concept of her in charge of girls' PT conjured up a much more pleasing image.

Messrs Jeal and Hooper could only dream about their long departed flush of youth, so that the way it worked with them at PT was that they occupied the centre of the floor, stood inanimate, and barked commands which we followed as best we could.

The PT gear that we wore could be reasonably described as motley, being an assortment of odds and ends cobbled together for the purpose. Perhaps in the welter of our tatty shirts and shorts, (some "more holey than righteous" as my mother was wont to say), lay latent athletic talent worthy of generating a new verse for Gray's "Elegy in a Country Churchyard". The single item of PT apparel that was held in common was a pair of plimsolls. These were blancoed into such thick-crusted uniformity that dry flakes and powder sloughed off at the lightest impact to lie eventually as a slippery deposit upon the floorboards. It was as if the gym were being prepared for a dance

There was no doubt but that PT was a serious business, and everyone took it seriously as a consequence. The main drawback for boys related to their having to change clothes in the cloakroom, as this was a process that could involve various hitherto private parts of the anatomy being exposed to public scrutiny. This caused an embarrassment for some and set up a trial for many. The pursuit of reasonable standards of hygiene and attention to personal appearance were activities that more or less counted for nothing with most boys. Great care had to be taken in order to ensure that nether appendages remained under cover at all times. Changing clothes incorporated the kind of contortions that a circus might have been proud to call its own.

For all that, I had a good feel for PT and was as adept and articulate at the required exercise regime as anyone. I was in any case accustomed to synchronised group calisthenics from my long-term membership of Port Isaac's St Peter's PT Club. What I didn't care for at all were the games of handball laid down by Mr Jeal. Handball moved much too fast for me. When a ball entered the equation I developed instant clumsiness and made haste to stay on the fringes of the action. For his part, Mr Jeal took great pains to demonstrate that he did not believe the meek should inherit the earth.

As well as the entrance (which could also be used as an exit) to the Third Form room alongside the Sixth Form room door, there was another such means of getting in or out of the former that lurked across in the opposite corner. On the far side of that door was the girls' cloakroom and their lavatories, both of which were naturally out of bounds to the boys. Literally a no-man's land, the girls' facilities were neither seen nor desired to be seen by male eyes, although it must be supposed that the feet of Messrs Sammy Coombes and Jim Boundy must have trodden the boards within.

A third door, set rather off centre into the left-hand wall of the Third Form room, was, as previously mentioned, the gateway to the Staff Room. It was hardly ever left open, and rarely even left to stand ajar for any longer than it took for a member of the teaching staff to go in or to come out. Such glimpses of the *décor* and activities taking place within the Staff Room were therefore fleeting at best, and subject to being broadly obscured by a hanging cloud of tobacco smoke. Through that grey haze the outlines of chairs might be spotted disposed here and there, some probably comfortable and some not, around a table or two piled high with exercise books ripe for marking.

At the far inner reaches of the Staff Room, well, who knew what might be hanging around back there? Whatever it was, it was

141

unlikely to spell good news for any pupil. Was the room connected to a lavatory? Even a teacher had to answer nature's call now and then, although the picture that such an eventuality brought to mind was too unedifying to hold onto for long. Where a teacher went to shit was a mystery all right, but it was a mystery best left unsolved.

And so, with the Staff Room leaking its nicotine-impregnated secrets out to the Third Form, this chapter's tour around the school buildings has drawn almost to an end. All that remains to be considered is a venerable, dingy, self-contained unit standing barn-like just outside the girls cloakroom, up at the head of the pathway and steps leading down to the Fourth Form's prefabricated fastness. The floor of the unit was slightly elevated, so that it required a few upward steps to be taken in order to gain entry.

Within lay the art establishment, the province of Miss Holloway. The room dripped with the tools of her trade. There were some benches, a few artist's easels, an ample stock of plasticine, boxes containing sticks of pastel-hued chalk, sets of watercolour paints, tubes of oil paint, pens, nibs, ink, paper and canvas. It all seemed so challenging to those who knew only too well that whatever they did with these invitations to express artistic licence was going to fail to satisfy Miss Holloway's sensibilities.

That good and kind lady shuffled hither and thither around her classes in the manner of a Mother Superior subjecting the unfaithful to the fog of her disapproval. It was just as well for heathen artists that Miss Holloway also did some teaching in the discipline of Religious Instruction, as RI lessons brought with them no hardship at all. In her RI capacity Miss Holloway carried the ball for Mr Hooper, who, in his *alter ego* as a local preacher, was presumably closer to God than anyone else at Sir James Smith's, and who regarded the Holy Bible as something more than a volume of dense print to be read under conditions of coercion.

13

Examinations

It was all to the good that a new First Former was faced with a full shape-of-things-to-come potential of seven years in which to develop a close familiarity with each and every subtlety and nuance of the school's substance and spirit. That time was readily available, even if it wasn't always used wisely. Earth might very well have had many things to show more fair than Sir James Smith's, and yet no encouragement was needed for it to be certain that anyone who could choose to pass by that palace of learning, and subsequently fail to be enraptured by the sight of it, so touching in its majesty, would have to be dull indeed.

Furthermore, it could be reasoned that seven years, if any of us ever made it that far, would surely offer enough time to permit the full impact of curiosities such as what n nuts were all about to be properly taken on board. Forms One through Five each claimed one of the seven years, and the Sixth Form, in both its Lower and Upper identities, added the remaining two. For those of us who made the pilgrimage from the nervous start right through to the bitter end — like MacNamara's band, we were few in number but allegedly the finest in the land — that mystery concerning the value of n nuts would subsequently contain little to thwart our thought processes. That was assuredly consistent with the natural order of grammar school matters.

Throughout the sequence of year-long roads there were many obstacles to conquer, but it was only in the imposition of examinations that fate joined the game to truly test the imperative for progress. The blessed were those of us who could manage to scrape through just enough examinations to be able to move on in the company of the overtly righteous who always passed examinations with ease. Once the end-of-school-year exams were over it was possible to breathe reasonably easily again until the next lot raised their ugly, hydra-like heads a year later. You could pick exams off and figuratively cut them down, but they never failed to resurrect.

For those who didn't succeed in getting through the class exams, the fall-back position was to repeat the year, take it easy, and revel in the role of being a sort of class elder statesman, just as Rossy was in my First Form days. There was no glory in repeating a year, however, and in any case, those who did repeat a year to all intents and purposes represented only an extremely tiny proportion of the total Sir James Smith's pupil complement.

Of much more significance in the matter of attrition of classmates were the pupils who relocated to pastures new with their parents. And yet, by the same token, replacements for them arrived regularly as newcomers who were slotted into classes appropriate to their age and academic ability. As a result, pupil numbers per class from the First Form up to and including the Fifth tended to remain steady at around twenty-five to thirty.

In principle, the majority of the pupils who started out together in the First Form generally held fast as a core group right through to the Fifth. It was then, and only then, that the great shake-out came along in the shape of the National School Certificate Ordinary Level Examinations. The popular title for these Examinations was "School Certificate", but during my time at Sir James Smith's they became more and more referred to as "O Levels".

The O Level question papers were formally set by external education authorities and marked by external examiners. Where Sir James Smith's was concerned, the two external education authorities used were those of the Joint National Matriculation Board (JNMB) and Cambridge University. This marking by external examiners was important since objectivity then ruled on both sides of the papers. Although we were all conditioned to know from hard-fought experience with exams that there were no guarantees that marking either could or would ever be fair, the chances were reasonable that an external exam marker would tackle the job of marking with a lot less prejudice than certain internal ones did.

The Fifth Form introduced its members to their first serious encounter with subject specialisation, following a modest start in the weeding-out of a subject or two during the preceding Fourth Form year. The rule of thumb for the number of subjects to be sat for examination at O Level was eight, although there were exceptions both above and below this. Particularly studious pupils who took it all in their stride often went for nine subjects. The chief difference between those who took eight subjects and those who took nine was that the latter passed them all with ease, whereas the former had to struggle to get there. That was just the way it was.

The minimum number of O Level subjects that could be sat was five. That quota, as well as some sixes and sevens, was fairly commonplace. Specialisation meant that you went for the subjects you liked, and you dropped those that you either couldn't cope with or didn't like. Long-term forward planning as often as not didn't enter the picture. Dropping a subject, irrespective of its relevance to you, could hinge merely on its being taught by a member of staff you didn't get on with.

The O Level examination subjects that I sat for were eight in number, as follows:

Chemistry
English Language
English Literature
French
Geography
History
Latin
Mathematics

Looked at as a group, these eight subjects could best be described as a mixed bag, being neither one thing or the other as far as my adopting a forward route of science or non-science was concerned. I passed them all, however, some better than others.

The most significant decision I had to make over subject specialisation actually came in the Fourth Form when the option presented was to drop either Latin or Physics. I made the choice in happy disregard of third-party pressures, by going in favour of Latin. To some extent Latin fulfilled the role of easy ride, but the real driving force behind the decision to opt for it was the strength of my desire to never again have to attend Physics classes under the tutelage of Mr Jeal. I had no reason to disbelieve that Mr Jeal was not a most competent teacher of Physics, or anything less than an enthusiast for his subject. He looked every inch the part of a Physics teacher, slight and wiry of stature and with a rising wedge of coarse black hair, slightly flecked with grey, that came acceptably close to achieving Brillo pad quality.

Mr Jeal gave the greater part of his attention to pupils whose minds were able to grasp what he was endeavouring to teach, and extended little time to those of us who found Physics, and maybe his approach to teaching it, to be impenetrable. My exodus from Physics and Mr Jeal, and my subsequent entry to Latin and Miss Quick, was marked by an evident failure of Mr Jeal to miss me, or of me to miss him.

The excellent grounding in Latin that I got from Miss Quick provided me with a lifetime benefit relevant to all that was spoken or written or read by me on each and every day that followed. So, when it came to me thinking my farewell to Mr Jeal, "Good-bye Joe, I gotta go, me-o-my-o", I had no regrets in having Latin haul my pirogue down the bayou, there to float away into the future over tranquil waters.

In terms of my successes at O Level, the fact that I managed to achieve a pass in Maths was, no matter that it was borderline, a true miracle to stand beside any one of the New Testament's miraculous manifestations that we were induced to study in RI lessons, and on whose implications we pondered in vain. RI was taught, preached, dogmatised or narrated, depending on your point of view, by Mr Hooper, who must have known what he was waffling on about. I don't know if any of my immediate circle of friends eventually emerged, unlike me, spiritually enlightened, but Mr Hooper did give us a sound grounding in the language and stories of the King James Version of the Bible. Since Mr Hooper was also my Maths teacher, miracles of all kinds would have been very much a feature of his remit.

Having obtained a collection of eight O Level passes, I was deemed to have done enough to qualify for Sixth Form entry and the pursuit of its two years of increasingly hard-pedalling towards an ultimate target of sitting School Certificate exams at Advanced (or A) Level.

My O Level results were delivered unceremoniously. All official communications took place between the external examiners and the school in the august person of Mr Sprayson. I was required to go along to the Port Isaac public telephone box in lower Church Hill, located just across the road from Harry Morman the cobbler's establishment, at a pre-ordained time on a certain day during the summer holidays, there to insert four pennies into the slot provided for the same, to request the operator to connect me with Mr Sprayson by providing her with his telephone number, to press button A when instructed by the operator to do so, and to then get my results directly from the great man's mouth. Port Isaac's only other public telephone box was located up alongside Charlie Lobb's garage at the top of Back Hill. That one was much closer to where I lived than was the box in Church Hill, but it was out of order at the time.

No one that I knew in Port Isaac seemed very interested, let alone excited to hear about my results, and the prevailing lack of enthusiasm rubbed off on me as well. My gaining entry into the Sixth Form was met back at home with a wave of domestic tension that took away any feeling of achievement that might otherwise have won the day. I was then just sixteen, and had for some time been regarded as a ne'er-do-well by my father. The prospect of my continuing to attend school for two more years, and of spending evenings beset by homework and revision, when I should by all rights have been out working and earning money, was anathema to his sensibilities. Throughout that O Level summer of 1955 he kept up a steady and forceful mantra that he could no longer afford to support me and keep me at school, and moreover that it was about "bleddy time" that I went out and got myself a "bleddy job".

This form of bitter contumely, cultivated in wartime service by many Cornishmen who never tired of telling anyone prepared to listen to them that they "dedden fight no bleddy war so's th' likes uv they young buggers kin zit roun' on their backsides all bleddy day", was most likely no stranger to a lot of households all over the country, allowing for variations in accent of course. It must undoubtedly have put paid to the further educational aspirations of many a promising pupil. There is no reason to reckon that North Cornwall was unique in this, albeit that in poor rural communities such pressures placed on children were probably over-stressed.

In my case, remaining at school as opposed to toiling at work helped to heap even more personal guilt onto the great pile of that commodity that I carried around with me as a consequence of also being advised regularly by ex-servicemen of the debt I owed them for all the sacrifices they had made for me. And there I was, reaping the advantages of the great post-war society that those who fought had brought about—"en a bit moo-er gratytood frum a useless bugger like you wooden go 'miss neither".

Had it been left up to me, I might have simply thrown in the towel there and then, but my mother had other ideas and stood like a rock against the tide of work-shy allegations directed at me by my father. She insisted on my continuing at Sir James Smith's in the Sixth Form, and so it came to pass. It didn't dispel my father's sniping, but it did hold it down to a level I could cope with.

My mother was keenly bright and intelligent. Her own potential for educational advancement, which she could have handled with aplomb, had been denied her through the iniquitous stifling of opportunity in rural environments related to the precedence of class. She was clear that as my day was there to be seized, then seize it I should. Faith, hope and charity, the latter in her case being the greatest of these three, marked her in life.

Of my two Sixth Form years, the first expended itself in the Lower Sixth, and the second in the Upper. Although the eventuality of A level exams was never quite absent from the mind's concern, the exams themselves were far enough ahead of us in terms of time that worrying about them felt pointless, and disregarding them was the preferred course of inaction. As the Lower Sixth year neared its end there were some internal exams that needed a bit of attention, as it wasn't enough for anyone wishing to stroll in the Elysian fields of the Upper Sixth to merely scrape through those.

For A Level, most of us studied three subjects. As if the three specialisations were not intensive enough in terms of the time and effort they called for, occasionally a brighter academic light might come along and manage four, provided one of them was a more straightforward option than were the other three. The best A Level pupils might also choose to take certain of their subjects at the academically enhanced grade known as State University Scholarship. I went for one of my three subjects, Geography, at State University Scholarship level, and never stopped wishing that I had just gone along the standard A Level path. State Scholarship Geography probably marked the one overt instance of intellectual pretension that I displayed in all my time at Sir James Smith's, and it sat ill with me.

The truth of the matter was that the phenomenon of a Sixth Form pupil sailing through A Level with top grades in all subjects was a rarity of high proportions. That is not to say that it didn't happen at Sir James Smith's, it was rather that it didn't happen very often. When, though, in a seven-year span of school life such a brilliant talent emerged to illuminate the roll call of academic achievement, then we were all truly blessed by association.

In my years I was doubly touched, as two such stars of super-achievement were there to set the standards for all the rest of us to aim at and fall short of. These prodigies were first of all Derek Pooley, a Port Isaac boy as modest and self-effacing as he was gifted and who was awarded a National Best prize for A Level scientific excellence; and Sheila Oates, known as "Sam", who came from Tintagel and peered at the world through spectacle lenses which were as thick and as ostentatious as she was not.

What the rest of us had to go for, while we stood in the shade of such natural State University Scholarship marvels, was a sufficient accumulation of pass grades in our specialised subjects to win, in order of precedence, either a County University Scholarship or a County University Exhibition. Both of these carried a grant of funds sufficient to cover university fees, modest subsistence costs, basic board and lodging, a certain amount of travel expenses and the purchase of books. Although entertainment costs were not mentioned in the terms and conditions of a grant, the prospective scholar did not identify these to be as vital as they would become once his university feet had been found and the wrong track happily chosen to set them on.

Most pupils who attended Sir James Smith's came from humble backgrounds in isolated village societies where various shades of poverty were endemic. Very few of us could ever have remotely dreamt of obtaining a university place without the benediction of the grant system. It is probably not unfair to allege that even so, university entry then still tended to favour the more elevated layers of society's class strata and was strongly weighted towards elitism — who your parents were and how well-off they were meant far more than did your academic capability. As a result, chinless wonders, egregious toffs and a whole raft of upper-class dolts filled the university ascendancy.

A Level examination pass grades were awarded on a scale of one to ten, where grades one and two signified a distinction; grades three, four and five were passes, grade five being the minimum required for a pass; and grades six onwards acknowledged that you had failed to pass, or, to use the vernacular, that you had "clanged".

The three subjects that I took at A Level were Chemistry, Maths and Geography, for which the respective grades I was awarded were two, five and three. This made a total of ten combined, which was within the limit for the award of a County University Scholarship. Chemistry came easily to me, and Geography was reasonably straightforward, but I was most proud again of scraping through Maths at A Level because passing went so much against my expectation.

14

The First, and Beyond

To recap, in the way that "Twenty Questions" panellists always seemed wont to request, Sir James Smith's catered for pupils ranging in age from eleven to eighteen. These pupils, around one hundred and fifty altogether, were organised into six classes or forms based on ascending order of age. A pupil would anticipate spending one year in each of the forms from the First through to the Fifth, followed by two years in the Sixth. Along this rocky road, O Level exams were taken in the Fifth, and A Level exams in the Upper Sixth.

As far as it went with First Form pupils, it was widely considered by all of the rest, from the Second Form upwards, and no doubt by members of the teaching staff as well, that First Formers not only knew nothing but also merited so little in the way of respect that they weren't going to get any of that from anyone.

The plaintive appearance of First Formers as they joined Sir James Smith's, aided and abetted by brand new school uniforms that were all too evidently intended to be grown into, set such underlings apart from the mainstream. First Formers were like immature puppies, eager to be allowed to please, when or if they could. Almost coincident with the day they began at the school, certain among them were being identified as victims ripe for attention, of both the obvious and the covert kind. Teachers were by no means exempt as willing participants in the cheery process of First Form persecution — cheery, that is, to all but the persecuted.

The rough and tumble of both the Port Isaac County Primary school playground and the St Peter's church vestry had to some extent conditioned me to pay little heed to being the subject of either verbal taunts or threats of physical violence against my person. Although, in fact, actual violence was rare, I usually didn't run away from a fight when one was inevitable, and so perhaps that helped to get me off relatively lightly from too much senior peer attention as a First Former in the Sir James Smith's gladiatorial arena.

On the other hand, Miss White, of English teaching prowess, did her best almost from the word go to compensate for any shortfall in the hard-knock ministrations that I might otherwise have missed. She seemed relentlessly intent on targeting me in her classes with the slings and arrows of scorn and sarcasm, delivered with a keenly whetted edge placed on what I came to think of as a sword of sheer meanness for meanness' sake. Since Miss White's insidious attentions to me continued from the First through to the Fifth Form, I was thereby enabled to carry my fair share of the communal burden of being bullied. Quite why she singled me out I was never able to discover to my own satisfaction. Miss White's satisfaction seemed complete enough for both of us, however, and that had to be fair enough where the satisfaction stakes were concerned. Her attitude probably stemmed from a combination of factors, chief among which was that she had need of a ready foil to deflect attention from her own inadequacies. I expect that in me she saw at least a partial pathway to salvation.

First Form pupils quickly became familiar with the Law of Gravity — shit fell on them, often from great heights. It was a well-known fact that shit always took a downhill route along the line of least resistance, hence from the Sixth it descended on the Fifth where it was recharged, augmented and dropped onto the Fourth, and so on down through the Third and the Second to ultimately spread the bulk of its residual ordure on the First. On the way, some shit stuck fast here and there, and although it never seemed to get too deep, it dropped down in sufficient volume to hold First Formers up to their collective knees in its thrall.

The relative seniority of forms was as well established as was any counterpart organisational chart for a great multinational company or a ponderous governmental institution, although it would need to be said, in the case of the school, that by and large those up at the head of the hierarchical order had a rough idea of what they were doing. Mandates and decrees got passed down from top to bottom, metamorphosing within an intentional fog of misinterpretation as they descended. According to what we sometimes had on offer in gloriously screened black and white at Port Isaac's cinema at the Rivoli, prisoner of war camps appeared to have been organised during the Second World War in a similar way. Of course, at Sir James Smith's we had no active Escape Committee — unless it was held in secret as so many things were, and I just wasn't aware of its existence.

All was not completely lost for the First Form underdogs, however, as, in keeping with each of the school's six forms, the First was as-signed a "Senior British Officer-styled" member of the teaching staff to serve as Form Master or Mistress. The duty of such worthies was to administer advice and counsel to their charges and presumably to make sure that all in the garden was not merely lovely, but also kept fair and above board. Form Masters and Mistresses were experts in seeing what they wanted to see, and formidable in the technique of shelving appropriate action.

The Form Masters and Mistresses that I was required to worship at the feet of were Miss Battle (First); Mr Turner (Second); Miss Quick (Third); Mr Hooper (Fourth); Miss Jones (Fifth) and Miss White (Sixth). My step by step ascent of this ladder of luminaries should have possessed the spirit of clotted cream rising from scalded milk, but a more apt simile would be to liken it to the unwanted froth surfacing during jam-making.

The First Form had so much to learn, and did its best to do so, to the credit of those of its company who took the requirement seriously. They possessed that essential quality of total malleability which, while it lasted, could readily be manipulated into shape. When they became Second Formers and were no longer in the sump of the shit stream, they shook themselves and at once grasped at the new priority of passing some shit downwards in their own right.

Second Formers all too often exhibited a front in which relief gave way to brashness once they had emerged like phoenixes from the ashes of the First. They then considered themselves to be the chosen ones. They had come to know it all. There was nothing, they thought, that a Second Former couldn't tell anyone who was prepared to listen (of whom there were indeed very few) about the school, its personalities, its teaching staff and its secrets and rumours, most of the latter being made up on the spot.

The Second Form lived in a kind of Limbo Land of green pastures, in which responsibility for one's actions mattered far less than the firm feel of springiness in the virtual turf underfoot. The Valley of the Shadow of Death lay comfortably far ahead in O Level country, and in spite of that dread spectre being ever ready to block a new spirit of anything goes, its portents of doom could easily be disregarded. There were a few years of still waters yet to intervene between the now and the then, and for a Second Former a year was an awfully long time.

The slim Atlas of the world issued for use in Geography lessons from the Second Form onwards was, like so many who used it, basic in its format. It contained maps that were either political or physical in design, the difference for beginners being that the latter were coloured in green and brown and blue, whereas the former were fitted with a patchwork rash of many colours, not the least among which was red. What especially caught my fancy in that little Atlas was the physical map of North America, as there, more or less in the centre of the continent portrayed, was a defined area with "Badlands" printed on it.

The Badlands! What an evocative title that was, filling my imagination with the sound of gunfire and the concealment of outlaw hideouts. Games of Cowboys and Indians might well have, as I had so often been told, fallen under the banner of putting away childish things, but, to set that sorrow aside, there stood the Badlands in a Sir James Smith's issued Atlas. It gave me a pleasing feeling that cowboys were still able to saddle and ride.

The name "Badlands" was of much relevance to the Second Form, as if the Second was the genuine Badlands of the school. Second Formers rode well ahead of the posse out to get them, and felt liberated to roam around on the free and open range. One and all, Second Formers lived in a relaxed state of bumptiousness in the sure knowledge that they might still hold a low position on the totem pole, but they weren't down as the lowest of the low any more.

When the Third Form eventually claimed a pupil for its own, that sense of release which had characterised the conduct of the Second Form was subjected to marked dissipation. Their former *joie de vivre* was, at a stroke, compelled to give way to at best a lukewarm sense of foreboding and at worst an utterly cold future reality. Third Formers occupied a *de facto* no-man's land in which, to all intents and purposes, they stood alone, essentially ignored by the battle lines of the school drawn up on both their upper and lower flanks. Theirs was not to reason why.

On entering the Third Form a pupil would find that he or she had moved far beyond the enervating tussle with the First which the Second took as their traditional rite of passage. The Fourth weren't of much help to the Third either — they were themselves more fully occupied in putting their best endeavours into the development of schemes aimed at their own aggrandisement at the expense of the teaching staff in particular, not ignoring a knock-on effect to any innocent bystanders who got in the way. After all, Fourth Form boys were long trouser wearers and well established in the teen stakes, which Third Formers most definitely weren't. In the Third, long trousers stood as eyebrow-raising exceptions to the short trouser norm.

It was as a Third Former at Sir James Smith's, partly in recognition of the shadow land between the senior and junior sections of the school into which I had been cast, that I made my optimum adaptation to school work, abandoning for the time being any search for the means to avoid it. As a consequence, my Third Form year was the only one out of the seven in which I was awarded a class performance prize, presented to me at the subsequent annual Speech Day (which some referred to as Prize Day) by the Distinguished Guest of the day, J. G. Harries Esq., MA; Secretary of Education for the County of Cornwall. The prize was a copy of *The Kon-Tiki Expedition* by Thor Heyerdahl, and, even though I didn't get very far into its pages, I did once make a determined assault on them, which was something I might not have done in the context of any Form other than the Third.

Where class performance prizes were concerned, it was more or less a matter of fact that, form by form, the same names tended to crop up as prize winners year after year. Thus there was effectively a small, established cadre of achievers in the field of academic competence who were expected to win prizes, and so it was that they genuinely strove to be sure they were winners. The great majority of the rest of us whose fate was to occupy the ground around that castle keep of swots were by no means deterred by our comparative failure, since we had come to terms quite early on with the home truth that prizes were not about to come our way. Freed from the burden of expectation therefore, and so immune to disappointment, our middle-of-the-road legion was at liberty to chug its way upwards through school without let or fear — until, that is, we hit the O Level buffers and faced an option of being carried by default into the welcome embrace of North Cornwall's dedicated company of the work-shy and terminally idle.

Apart from the medals awarded for athletic success on Sports Day, which shone like silver but were derived from elements occupying a rather less noble sector of the periodic table, a school prize was invariably a book, chosen by its winner from a Sir James Smith's approved list. Approved books were as long on moralistic content as they were short on providing any stimulation for majority taste.

I would much sooner have received *The Beano Book 1953* than *The Kon-Tiki Expedition*, but was thwarted in that desire owing to the former failing, as always, to make the approved list. No matter what you really wanted, you knew that turgid prose would be what you really got.

My Third Form book prize must have resulted from something of a *bona fide* aberration. The industrious attitude to study that afflicted me at that time was good while it lasted, but only helped to define my year in the Third as being neither-here-nor-there in the mind's eye. The best school memories have to be related to incidences of fun, and fortunately that element of the quality of life resurrected itself when I left the Third and entered the Fourth.

The Forth Form marched with a stiff, take-no-prisoners breeze at its back that was responsible for raising many of the ripples that swept with vigour across what the teaching staff vainly wished to maintain as a smooth-surfaced pond of school life.

In the Fourth we were avid readers of school stories, both from books and out of the pages of the weekly comic papers we were so preferentially fond of. The type of school stories we liked best were always couched on what seemed to us to be comfortable ground, and even if paradoxically it was ground beyond the limits of our experience, the prime characters were normally Fourth Formers, and therein lay a bond.

One notable exception to the rule was the long-running (and perhaps overbearingly serious) saga "Smith of the Lower Third" as presented in the pages of *The Wizard*. Smith remained in the Lower Third for so many years of published exploits that his continuing presence there must have embarrassed him as much as his authors, since eventually he graduated to being "Smith of the Fourth Form". Sadly for most of his fans who took comfort in familiarity, Smith in a Fourth Form guise was never again to realise his Lower Third popularity, and he fell from the pages of *The Wizard* relatively soon.

My own feeling was that Smith was always diminished by the shadow of the most famous of the *Wizard*'s heroes William Wilson, an immortal athletic champion whose trademark feature was the black leotard he invariably wore.

Mostly then, it was the Fourth Form that made the great school stories click. The key players that the action swirled around were anarchistic jokers whose attitude to established authority centred on cutting the said authority down to size through various complicated ruses, while mostly avoiding getting caught in the act. They were perpetrators of cheerful hustles, in which the imposition of detentions and the penalties of receiving either lines or the occasional six-of-the-best piled in both thick and fast but never succeeded in preventing victory being snatched from the jaws of teacher-inspired defeat. Irreverence for authority was the order of the day. Pomposity and pretentiousness were bubbles that were regularly burst — always in a good spirit of fun, and with meanness never being part of the equation. All in all, no one ever got hurt and it all came out right in the end. This was just how we felt it should be in the Fourth Form at Sir James Smith's.

At my favourite fictional school, Red Circle, the stories of which were told in the pages of *The Hotspur*, anything could happen and usually did. Great rivalry existed between the constituent Houses of that school, but it was never taken outside the school gates. To the outside world the school itself was the epitome of focused loyalty by pupils and staff alike, which was just how we wanted Sir James Smith's to be regarded.

We learned and absorbed much from the high calibre of Red Circle's example to apply to our own situation at Sir James Smith's, even though the kind of schools we read about were strangers in so many ways to our day-only attendance and hand-to-mouth existence.

Those make-believe schools were almost all of the exclusive public boarding variety. Much as we might despise them in their real world manifestations, in stories they were all right. Had any stories been written about a Sir James Smith's sort of school, which naturally they weren't, I doubt that we would have wanted to read them. That was another inexplicable paradox. Perhaps by revelling in accounts of adventures and misadventures occurring at schools catering for the offspring of society's upper crust, we were enabled to rise above the circumstances of inferiority that the said upper crust was so fond of laying down on us as being our natural lot in life.

Although I was beset with an advanced level of distaste for chinless wonders, I knew that they had their place in society and we had ours, and well, that was the way it was. It was not until I got into my Fourth Form year that it dawned on me that we were at least as good as they were, and that in all probability we were much better than them when it came to the exercise of tact, humility and charity.

We were brought up to behave with absolute deference to a bewildering array of people identified as our "elders and betters". Having "elders" was naturally enough unavoidable, and so that was something we could live with, but having "betters" to bow the head to at almost every turn served to define us as lesser mortals and pile a sense of feeling on us that we didn't amount to much of anything at all in the scheme of things. In the presence of our elders and betters we were required to speak only when spoken to and otherwise to be seen and not heard. Should there be no way for us to avoid exercising our vocal attributes, it was then incumbent on us to express no opinions which could be construed as contradicting the views of the said elders and betters, as they always knew best. If they said something was, then it was, even when it clearly wasn't. And if you said it wasn't, then what you said was identified as a "mouthful of cheek" and a clip on the ear was your reward.

Such social shackles held me fast until the Fourth Form came along, and then, in the Fourth's willing embrace, the process of chains falling away link by link became no more than a formality. The Fourth Form's cherished objective was to get the better of authority whenever an opportunity presented itself. A multitude of schemes were hatched and executed within the closed ranks of our Fourth Form fellowship, so that, by and large, targeted teachers were all unaware that a steady game of one-upmanship was being played.

Best of all perhaps, when the overall accounts were settled on both sides, honours came out more or less even.

In my capacity as a Fourth Former, I was probably one of those identified by several of our teachers as all too frequently stepping up to test the limits of what they considered to be acceptable behaviour. But then again, those limits were normally only as far as any testing went. You set your foot on them, counted coup, and took a pace back. The old habits of deference refused to lie down entirely.

In one of my end-of-term Fifth Form reports, Miss Jones, the Form Mistress, described me thus: "academically sound, but manner and deportment need improvement". It was, I thought, a most fair assessment, and one that I was rather pleased with. Miss Jones had summed me up precisely — I thought that I could have done a lot worse than have her trenchant observation serve as my epitaph in the Sir James Smith's register of dearly departed to pastures new.

Fifth Formers were, as previously described, thrust up hard against the final bulwark of O Level exams. That fact alone should have helped any member of the Fifth to be taken seriously by all pupils other than those in the Sixth, but all that the imminence of O Levels did was to curtail personal drive and swamp the Fifth's motivation for fun. The Fifth was considered too mature to be still indulging in Fourth Form-type shenanigans, but not mature enough to be associated with any of the authority enjoyed and practised for good or ill by the Sixth.

It may well have been that Fifth Formers carried too much of a burden of having to live up to too many expectations to be left with any hope of meeting those expectations. It was in the Fifth when my being regularly identified as a work-shy idler by my father began to shape up as a self-fulfilling prophecy. My successful breakthrough of the O Level barrier should have stemmed that flow of paternal criticism, but it did so only up to a point.

In a school community consisting of six forms, the onward motion, life and spirit of the school seemed to reside in forms with even numbers, and the great weight of anxiety and hesitancy to be ever-present in those with odd numbers.

With a requisite minimum of O Level passes under a pupil's belt, the Sixth Form was open for his or her legitimate entry, and his or her staying power in having run the grammar school gauntlet to date was finally a reality worth celebrating. The forward path to A Level and the great mysteries that lay in the land beyond was straight and reasonably clear of too many obstacles — it could be walked successfully enough with due exercise of care. The stalwart eleven-plus harvest of pupils, good grain and chaff alike, who had once entered the First Form with fearful hope in their hearts, had been dramatically winnowed down by fate and disillusion by the time the Sixth was ready to open its door to whomsoever remained and had earned the right to enter.

Those who fell by the wayside were always missed, for a while at least. Their absence was noted, although the whys and wherefores of it were not much discussed. The school machine, a behemoth far greater in its functioning than those who fuelled it, was intolerant of regret. It might occasionally miss a beat, but it rolled on regardless. The departure of a classmate caused little more than a momentary shiver as the gap that he or she left quickly closed up tight.

The forward movement of all that was the school and what the school stood for was unstoppable. It held nothing and no one to be indispensable. Its structure was built on a solid foundation of tradition, reputation, history and results, and there was even an element of play-up-and-play-the-game-at-no-matter-at-what-cost involved in the cement of its integrity.

Sir James Smith's in my day was — as Major Oxford, a gentleman from Port Isaac (one of a select few who could make a claim

164

to be such) told me some years later, after the school had "gone comprehensive" and been relocated to far more ample premises to contain a vastly increased complement of pupils — an "old school tie" establishment.

Observations such as the one made by the good Major (retd) had the undoubted benefit both of hindsight and the mollifying effect of time. As the years slipped away and the hard-time sentence of the First Form receded with them, so much about school life in matters both great and small and in habits and practices adopted and absorbed, became essential features of our everyday lives, indelibly writ.

There was a deeply felt debt of gratitude to the teaching staff which time, like an ever-rolling stream, made impossible for some of us to repay. Post-A Level, life looked towards new horizons, and past associations blurred against the onslaught of a storm of new priorities. It was, and is, a matter of keen regret that my opportunities to visit Sir James Smith's as an ex-pupil in order to thank the teachers who strove to instil knowledge and intellect into me against the odds were not so much lost or missed as, by some kind of default, never taken.

All along the way of my charted course through Sir James Smith's, the dues exacted from me or paid to me by members of the teaching staff as a result of my being who and what I was and what I did, were usually more or less what I deserved. Praise came as a rare enough commodity, and my lot before the Sixth Form fell more to gaining a fair share of criticism, censure, penalties and punishment. But then again, with the exception of some of Miss White's excesses, for my part I accepted all of it without a shred of ill-will towards my judges.

As it was, all through the school I had only one reactive confrontation with a teacher to cast a stain on me. It took place when I was in the Lower Sixth, and incidentally holding the position of Head Boy. I hadn't sought to become Head Boy, and nor in my heart did

I really want the appointment — I dropped into it by accident. The Head Boy was normally a member of the Upper Sixth, but as there were no boys available in the Upper Sixth during my Lower Sixth year the Head Boy's appointment had to go to someone and it went to me, perhaps as a result of a popular vote, but more likely by way of rigging the vote at the highest level. I don't think I was the worst Head Boy the school ever had, although not all members of the teaching staff might have accepted that opinion at its face value.

When I was in the Upper Sixth I was appointed Head Boy again, evidently on the principle that the devil that was known was preferable to the devil that was unknown.

15

Badges of Office

That teacher with whom I clashed on a certain day was perhaps a little less than thirty years old, and yet somehow, by virtue (or rather lack of virtue) of his having an unpleasant personality and demeanour he appeared to be considerably older than that. He gave the impression of one who took both himself and his work far too seriously. He pulled rank as if he was adorned with the gilt echelons of superiority. If he had ever had a sense of humour, it must have woken up one day, found its host wanting, grabbed charity by the hand, and fled. He was a relative newcomer to the staff room, and his specialist subject of Biology, which was also fairly new to the school, having been introduced by Miss Lyons scant years previously, was still being integrated into the curriculum from the bottom up. He may well have been a better teacher than the smokescreen of his perceived personality allowed me to see.

What you mought call him, you mought call him not Cap'n, but rather Mr Boothby. I didn't ever hear any Christian name mentioned, but since I didn't choose to enquire about it I have only myself to blame for nor knowing what it was. All the same, he was the kind of man for whom a surname counted most.

My experiences of being with Mr Boothby in the same place at the same time were therefore mostly restricted to the occasions when he was on the duty roster to invigilate in the canteen at dinner time.

Mr Boothby was always smartly dressed in a neat suit, a shirt, with collar attached, that looked as if it might be clean, and a well-pressed tie. He was well built without being stocky, and he glared at the world around him through a type of wire-rimmed spectacles that was known to be favoured by agents of the Gestapo. The impression of there being something undeniably sinister about him was then reinforced by a haircut of some severity which took the classic style known as "short back and sides and some off the top" to its logical limit. That self-same hair was so immobilised by a liberal anointment of commercial dressing that the tracks of the most recent passage of a comb through its glutinous strands were captured inviolate.

If he was not a bully in the strict sense of the word, Mr Boothby at least possessed bullying tendencies — hence he had a need to identify victims that he could pick on and humiliate in front of an audience (a not uncommon trait of the teaching profession) as a means of showing the said audience who was the boss and don't you forget it.

So it was that in the canteen on one fateful day, he chose, for reasons of his own, to go for one of the junior boys sitting down towards the bottom of the dinner table that I then headed, using the boy as a pure sop for his vanity. It was undeniable that the small boy was being noisy, but a certain amount of noise was ever helpful as a welcome distraction from having to contemplate the frequent awfulness of the dinners that came our way. To my surprise, Mr Boothby pulled the boy to his feet and ordered him out of the canteen. Protective of my own, I stood up to bar the way and said to Mr Boothby, "Please, sir, you can't do that!"

Mr Boothby thrust his jaw forward and leaned his face to within a few inches of mine. His eyes narrowed to slits in behind the wired rimmed spectacles. The scene would have fitted perfectly into a black-and-white "B" film involving an interrogation by secret police.

"I can do what I want!" he hissed at me through clenched teeth. "I can throw you out if I want to!" That could well have been his ultimate goal, long in the planning. He knew that I was not one of his admirers. Purely on reactive impulse I replied, with a calm politeness I didn't feel, "Please don't bother, sir. I'm going." Then I walked out of the canteen, and the short confrontation was over, thankfully so as far as I was concerned.

I fully expected to be reported to Mr Sprayson by Mr Boothby for insubordination, and waited in a state of some nervousness to be called to account. I prepared myself to be stripped of my Head Boy and Prefect badges, but strangely enough, nothing at all happened. I found it difficult to believe that Mr Boothby didn't report me. He surely must have done, and all I could assume was that Mr Sprayson, with an insight into Mr Boothby's inner character, must have exercised his discretion and decided to let sleeping dogs lie.

As Miss Jones had previously declared, I had a lot of work to do on improving the quality of my manner and deportment. For all of the truth of that, I was not by nature a conflictive sort, which was why I found the confrontation with Mr Boothby not only disturbing but also personally demeaning to us both.

Following the canteen eviction incident, a rumour rolled around the school, gathering in strength as it went, to the effect that I had raised my fists to Mr Boothby, thereby causing him to back down. It wasn't true, but in the telling and retelling it conferred an increasingly enhanced reputation on me. The thing to do about rumours that acted in your favour was not to deny them, and so let the double negative confer on you a positive cachet.

The little badges of office that were worn and displayed with pride on a blazer's left lapel were probably most prized for the extra status they conferred on everyone to whom they were awarded. The degree of merit relating to the awarding of some Prefect's badges, not omitting to consider the Head Boy's badge as well, could easily be debated, but no one worried about doing so. The Head Girl's badge was something of an exception to the rule, however, since as far as I was able to judge, the girl who held that office always deserved it, although in mitigation of such a positive view, my first-hand experience of the exercising of the Head Girl's responsibilities was not extensive.

Had there been sufficient pupils available in the Upper Sixth to cover the required number of Prefects to be consistent with the establishment, then all Prefects would have been appointed only from that fellowship. The reality was that in the Upper Sixth the numbers were never sufficient, and so members of the Lower Sixth were press-ganged in to contribute.

The appointment of Prefects was allegedly made by consensus of a teachers' conclave — and almost certainly heavily influenced by the Headmaster's likes and dislikes.

A Prefect's badge of office took the form of a small, green enamelled, gilt-edged shield, with the keyword PREFECT picked out on its face in tiny block capitals, also in gilt.

The general duties of a Prefect were directed at monitoring, or otherwise keeping a watching brief on the school precincts, aimed at ensuring that pupil behaviour did not infringe such of the school rules as the Prefect was able to remember. No-one knew them all, and one could be forgiven for thinking that far too many were made up on the spot to counter circumstances of which teachers did not approve. When school rules were seen to be broken and a Prefect was in a position to note the infringement, it was the Prefect's job to nip the action in the bud before it got out of hand. A Prefect was ever ready to break up a fight in the yard in which he wasn't himself a participant.

Prefects also had roles to play as guides and ushers on the special occasions when the public invaded the school grounds, as well as at traditional events defining the school year — these included Speech Day, the Christmas Festival of Nine Lessons and Carols, Sports Day, Open Days and Assemblies. There was a Prefect's rota for reading the Lesson at Assembly, drawn up by Mr Hooper.

Also on a rota basis, Prefects were responsible for running the hand bell around the school to mark the end of each lesson and for invigilating at detentions. Further tasks pertaining to them included sitting as table heads at dinner time; helping to maintain order on the school buses (although the bus drivers never sought such aid and were quite tough enough not to need it); looking out for inappropriate conduct in pupils who went into town during the dinner hour; running internal errands and relaying messages for teachers on request — and so on and so forth.

In short there was an awful lot for a Prefect to do in what was a general exercise of authority to safeguard the integrity of school standards. If all of this appeared to sound too good to be true , it was because it was all of that.

"*Sed quis custodiet ipsos Custodes?*" That telling question, in this instance relating to just who should monitor the monitors, exposed the weakness behind any claims that Prefects were invariably motivated by a sense of duty and the exercise of high ideals. No Prefect was perfect, and some were more imperfect than others. You could take the boy out of the Fourth Form and shove him onwards into the Sixth, but you couldn't take an atavistic Fourth Form spirit entirely out of the Sixth Form boy.

The Head Boy's red-enamel badge was half as large again as a

Prefect's badge and was not to be worn lightly. When I was Head Boy I quickly learned that whatever I tried to do on my own initiative, the institutionalisation of the school system was entrenched enough to render it impossible. The school just went on running itself — I eventually found it best to drift with the prevailing current and do my best to avoid unexpected hazards. In any case, all executive decisions were ultimately taken by the Headmaster, and this included the Head Boy's appointment. What the Lord gave, the Lord could just as easily take away.

In principle, both the Head Boy and Head Girl were supposed to be chosen by a majority vote of the entire school, but in practice the result must have been adjusted appropriately when Mr Sprayson found himself at odds with the popular franchise. As a sop to any vote rigger's conscience, however, the school was also allowed to vote once annually, in something of a popularity contest, for both a boy and a girl who were considered to justify the award of a "Character Prize".

The Head Boy and the Head Girl should have been, it might be surmised, the natural choices for the Character Prize. The fact that this wasn't often the way it worked out could be taken to imply that all was not above board at the highest level. The Head Boy and Head Girl could not serve God and Mammon. They were appointed to serve God, and Mammon didn't like that too much, and tended to show its displeasure when taking the line of least resistance in the vote for the Character Prize award.

16

Those who can, do — those who can't...

Boss

Mr Boothby's gift for generating feelings of negativity — in me at least — found its perfect personal antidote in the person of our illustrious Headmaster, Mr Kenneth A. Sprayson. In his indomitable presence, his warmth of character and his benign vision, Mr Sprayson was for so many of his pupils the One and Only, the undisputed Boss, the heartbeat of the school as a live and functioning entity.

> His life was gentle, and the elements
> So mixed in him that Nature might stand up
> And say to all the world, "This was a Man!"
> (William Shakespeare, *Julius Caesar*, ACT V, SCENE 5)

Mr Sprayson was indeed a Man for all Seasons, "slow to anger, and of great kindness". He seemed impressively imperturbable, and in my association with him was rarely seen to let his air of kindly omniscience deteriorate into anything approaching a genuine loss of temper. It was not, of course, that he was a complete stranger to getting angry. There were more than a few occasions on which I know I gave him sufficient provocation to justify his flying off the handle, but if he ever did head down that road it must have taken place in the privacy of his study, into which sanctum few of us had been, and even fewer wished to step.

The gatekeeper to the Headmaster's study was the school's secretary Mrs Perry, the wife of the Woodwork teacher Mr Perry. The Perrys lived in Boscastle. The diminutive Mrs Perry kept vigil at the study portal with such a bristling degree of energy that it seemed the Holy Grail might lie within. She was, in all senses of the title, a confidential secretary ahead of her time.

Mr Sprayson, a solid stalwart figure of "full round belly", always impeccably clad in suit, tie and lightly chalk-dusted gown of office, glided his majestic way around the school corridors, holding his gown by its lapels, the folds billowing at his back like a train of state. His well-ordered hair fell thickly in careful waves that might have been crafted by a spirit of the sea on either side of a precisely defined central parting. The overall effect was one of trustworthy authority, that being his most distinctive characteristic. He carried it, and it carried him in its turn.

Mr Sprayson held dominion over us, yet he did not flaunt his eminence. It was enough that we his disciples knew that greatness resided in him, and we regarded him with awe, affection and respect. As a consequence, he was not subjected to having his limits constantly tested by us as was the case with most other members of the teaching staff. We all knew a good man when we saw him, and

Mr Sprayson wore a benevolence that fitted him as comfortably as did his suit.

His appearances as duty invigilator in the yard at break time and again in the canteen at dinner time when the common herd of pupils gathered at the trough, were extremely rare events. Such mundane jobs were assigned by roster to his underlings. How Mr Sprayson and his teaching staff related to one another on an informal basis beyond the boundaries of the classrooms was a great unknown. They would certainly have had to come together on a professional level to plan, scheme, cajole and generally organise the life of the school and identify those who either toiled or didn't toil within it, but the general impression was that when it came to matters social, Mr Sprayson kept himself at a distance from the Staff Room's denizens.

His tenure at Sir James Smith's commenced in 1949. He was engaged to replace the implacably long-term incumbent Mr C. E. Leese, whose departure was alleged to have been devoutly desired by the school governors for rather a long time previously, and whose resistance to being retired had become like that of a difficult-to-uproot hardy annual. Mr Sprayson was brought in to act as a new broom, as a reformer of some note authorised to overturn the trappings of hide-bound teaching and school management practice.

His appointment was a watershed moment for Sir James Smith's — Mr Sprayson stood then on a great divide separating a worn-out style of education, some aspects of which would have been familiar to Mr Wackford Squeers, from a modern system of forward-looking and enlightened teaching consistent with the context of post-war aspirations.

It could not have been easy for Mr Sprayson to have inherited a body of teachers inured to the ways of the Leese years and therefore likely to be antipathetic to change. Even in the best-ordered circles of constructive outlook, real change was a commodity quite slow to gain acceptance, and willing adaptation to the process of change was generally manageable only in the longer-term proposition. Mr Sprayson would have known right from the beginning that he would be facing resistance incorporating varying degrees of stubbornness from at least some of his newly inherited subordinates. To him, they were unknown quantities. To them, he was no doubt someone who at best caused them unease, and at worst struck fear into their hearts. Reactions to Mr Sprayson's rule by the rear guard of the former regime were never put on open display, but the tremors of them could be sensed, and were obvious enough even to lowly First Formers.

But then again, most pupils had no more than a perception of any Staff Room undercurrents, and in general the rest was silence. To the majority, the private lives and thoughts of teachers were another country in which things were done differently, if they were done at all. What those things were, or weren't, we not only didn't know but didn't want to find out. It was all best left shrouded in mystery. A teacher's image was like a false front on a western saloon in which a free-for-all melee was an ever-present likelihood — it was kept big on both show and style as a means of concealing any lack of substance behind it.

Mr Sprayson lived in a large detached house set in its own tree-shaded grounds located well up along Victoria Road, about half a mile or so distant from the school at a corner where a secluded lane came in from the right. Victoria Road was the grand name given to the long, slow hill out of Camelford leading towards Davidstow. Mr Sprayson's residence looked rather grand when viewed from the perspective of one who dwelt in a Port Isaac council house.

The house was seen quite regularly by pupils, since on the far side of the hedge set directly across the little lane from its front garden entry gate was to be found nothing less (or perhaps to a reluctant attendee, nothing more) than the school's sports field.

So it was that when we were required to troop up to the sports field on one afternoon each week to participate in what was either, for so many boys, a great escape from lessons or, for others (of whom I was one), trial by football in the autumn and spring terms and by cricket in the summer term, we always got a good view of Mr Sprayson's residence. Girls were naturally enough also required to make the ascent to the sports field, and for them hockey and netball (and sometimes rounders) formed the respective seasonal order of play. It was more than probable that the fine division between eagerness and reluctance to participate applied as much to the girls as to the boys.

That field also gave sterling service when Sir James Smith's sports teams played home matches against one or other of a league of select Cornish grammar schools. Bude, Fowey and Bodmin Grammar Schools and Launceston College, all located within moderate reach of travel from Camelford, were chief among the sports field's regular visitors. We travelled to their home venues for reciprocal away games. Mr Menadue was a driving force in the management of fixtures, and in this respect most certainly, his nerve centre credentials were impeccable.

Launceston College formed a unique element within the general amalgam, as it had to all intents and purposes that essence of a public school which stood rather aloof from craving too much association with the great unwashed of the county's grammar schools. Rugby was played at Launceston College for goodness' sake, and in the Sir James Smith's book of prejudice you couldn't get much more of a public school stamp than that. Although Launceston's visiting teams contained numerous good sportsmen, their credentials were somewhat depreciated by the air of overbearing priggishness that sat

177

on far too many of them. They let it all hang out, metaphorically and literally in the changing facilities. It was not a pretty sight, going far and beyond Sir James Smith's modest norms.

On the other hand, I had no involvement in changing clothes and offending norms at inter-school sporting occasions, since I was obliged to observe the unfolding scene from a position that was fixed somewhere on the outside looking in. I was destined never to be selected to play for a school team, or anything resembling a school team which involved the manipulation of a ball somewhere in its rules.

I was the archetypal boy that no team captain wanted to pick from the usual rag-tag motley lined up for that purpose on sports afternoons at the sports field. I was the epitome of Hobson's choice — the last one left standing as the wind whipped frayed shorts against my knees, and the rain and hail bit my ears and stung my shoulders. Sports afternoons for me were all too often times of irreversibly linked torment and penance.

Matters brought themselves to a head when I became a Prefect, and went on to reach their critical mass on my accession to becoming Head Boy. A holder of such positions was expected to possess at least a hint of footballing or cricketing prowess, on which understanding it had to be conceded that I was a disappointment. To mitigate this deficit I was induced by Mr Sprayson to accept a peripheral association with both the cricket and the football teams and function as score keeper for the former and linesman for the latter. I carried out my allotted duties in these instances entirely to my own satisfaction.

Who could have said that, if I had been more familiar with the rules of either game, I might not have achieved a measure of probably undeserved success? In my capacity as linesman I ran up and down the white line on my appointed half of the pitch with, in my hand, a not altogether clean hankie to flutter and wave in order to offer an impression of accord whenever the Referee blew his whistle. I knew how to award throw-ins and corners, but mostly the objective was to keep moving in an attempt to give an impression of competence.

One of the personal benefits to come out of all this was travel to away matches, especially to Bude, which was always a lively town to visit. It was in Bude on an away day that, unbeknown to the accompanying supervision, Gordon Keat introduced me to draft cider, which further hindered any line running endeavours.

Keeping cricket scores mainly required me to pencil dots in little rectangles on a large printed form, each rectangle representing an over of six balls bowled, one dot per ball. Concurrently I recorded the number of runs scored both per ball and cumulatively; which players were in and which players were out; and then, when they were out, what the cause was of their dismissal. I also had to register such bowling errors as no balls and wides, and note any incidental decisions made by the umpire. Much of the intelligence that came my way was signalled by the umpire by means of gestures that looked as half-hearted as they were incomprehensible. I viewed them from the scorer's seat in whatever rustic edifice served as the designated pavilion for the day,. Distractions came along all too easily and the accuracy of my scoring records was not above suspicion, but by and large it was muddled through.

Mr Sprayson appeared to approve of my putting-a-brave-face-on-it enthusiasm for having a go from the fringes of team sports, especially where cricket, his great love, was concerned. I did my best not to disillusion him, as he deserved no less than to have my good heart rising above the fact that my good heart wasn't really in it.

The sports field was also conscripted as the arena for the school's annual Sports Day, held during the ebb of the summer term. On

Sports Day, opportunity knocked for one and all to come into their own in the pursuit of athletic challenge. There were running events covering a range of distances from one hundred yards up to a mile; throwing a cricket ball (one of the few things connected with cricket that I had no qualms about); cycling in a slow bicycle race (provided you had a bike); jumping long, high and with a hop and a step thrown in for good measure; racing while enveloped by a sack, or tied to a companion to make three legs, or carrying an egg (or a substitute thereof) on a spoon; and — well, the picture was clear enough.

I was acceptably fleet of foot, having honed my technique in the Port Isaac area and hinterland when being chased by, *inter alia*, farmers, fishermen, certain property owners and miserable old buggers in general, all of whom seemed to be forever at odds with the appearance of boys in the vicinity of the fruits of their seasonal labours.

Points were awarded to competitors for performance and placing in each Sports Day competition. He or she who achieved the highest number of such points would be declared Victor of Games and be granted the respective titles of "Victor Ludorum" and "Victrix Ludorum". Both titles merited a small, lozenge-shaped medal that looked as if it should be made of silver but wasn't, and which would be formally awarded at the subsequent Speech Day.

Mr Sprayson did not give the impression of being one who set much store on individual sporting achievements. For him, team effort was what sport was all about — play up and play the game being a declared principle, with humility ruling the winners and graciousness marking defeat. As we were a community of well-established good losers we could comfortably follow his *credo* to the letter.

My principal foray into sport's individualism had nothing at all to do with Sir James Smith's, however. As an established member of the St Peter's Church PT Club in Port Isaac, I boxed regularly over a number of years — boxing exhibitions were a popular feature of public performances given by the club at various North Cornish open air summer fete and carnival events. As PT Club members, we normally boxed between ourselves, but eventually the level of local interest became high enough to ensure that a series of boxing tournaments against similar clubs from other village and town localities came into being. In truth, there were not all that many other clubs, but nevertheless, at each of the tournaments there was standing room only for spectators, so great was the interest in boxing.

Invoking the word "boxing" to characterise the tournaments gave the true character of the bouts involved a formal dignity that they didn't quite deserve. There was a lot of harmless prancing and left-hand jabbing at a distance to begin with, but that all changed for me when I realised that as I wasn't afraid of being hit *en route* to achieving an inside position where I could hit back harder, in most cases I was almost certain to prevail.

Most tournament boxers that I came up against were averse to taking a punch in order to give one back, which always put them at a disadvantage. Once I was in the ring I found that the action seemed to be taking place in slow motion, which gave me ample time to place punches precisely where I wanted them to go. For one whose eye to ball co-ordination was so far wide of the mark, my ability to slip a glove through an opponent's defence came as a personal revelation. I thought of how advantageous it would be for me if the practice of cricket could be slow-motion rendered in the same way, even if cricket was already soporific enough in its own right.

On one occasion my ability to do better than my opponent in a contest was reported in the pages of the *Cornish Guardian* weekly newspaper. The article chanced to be read by Mr Sprayson, who thereafter summoned me to come and see him in the sanctity of his study. As I waited on the threshold of entering that room of many mysteries, he appeared before me, holding up a copy of the relevant edition of the ubiquitous broadsheet. He stood in the sort of un-nerving pose which he habitually adopted when elevating into public view a discarded wrapping from a piece of consumed confectionery that he had just spotted and picked up from the ground — within or without the precincts of the school, it made no difference to him; that sort of heinous criminality knew no boundaries.

And so, when Mr Sprayson stood majestically before me (unless it was I who stood trembling before him), brandishing the *Cornish Guardian* as if it was the giant king of all toffee papers while he turned his full attention on me, I believed myself to be in line for a carpeting. However, it turned out that he had come to praise rather than to bury me. He made it plain that an individual sporting achievement, on the unlikely assumption that close-encounter boxing as practised by me could be considered a sport, was not a foreign word in his lexicon. Indeed, he went so far as to inform me in a confession that I had no reason to either disbelieve or believe, that he himself had been associated with boxing throughout his life. He hinted, rather strongly and very directly, that it would please him if, at any future tournaments in which I participated, I could be identified with Sir James Smith's as well as — but with a subtext that "rather than" would be his preference — the St Peter's PT Club. In his eyes it shaped up that any form of positive publicity for the school, well-earned or not, was better than no publicity at all. He made an uncharacteristic attempt to suborn me, and that wasn't quite cricket. I couldn't agree, and didn't want to disagree, so took the middle road, and was non-committal without closing the door. With all due respect, however, I would sooner have been what in the

Fourth Form was referred to as "in the shit" than ever switch my Port Isaac allegiance.

With regard to that Fourth Form expression there wasn't much open use of what was euphemistically known as "bad language", in any part of the school by boys who, to borrow a line from Cole Porter, came from societies that once knew better words but now only used four-letter words. Swearing was of course not unknown, but it was rarely heard. Although as a general rule anything went in the yard, bad language wasn't included. The invocation of "shit", that universal medium, was about as far as anyone dared take it, although in the eyes of our elders and betters, shit was substantially exceeded in gravity by any means of taking the Lord's name in vain. The usage of the good old all-purpose words "bugger" and "bleddy", either separately or in cheerful combination, was so inured in the vernacular that those words had long since lost any cachet of profanity.

We were naturally only too well aware that it would be to dice with disaster if we should utter even these everyday epithets within the audible reach of a teacher. It was a truth universally acknowledged, to our cost, that the range of a teacher's hearing far exceeded the human norm.

Maurice Brown, that Port Isaac boy of some note from whose cast-off wardrobe I had obtained essential items of my school uniform, once recounted to me a tale concerning an utterance of allegedly inappropriate language in the Sixth Form room. It so chanced that he and a few other members of the Sixth were lolling about and idling their time away when the room's door was thrown open rather suddenly to reveal Miss White in its frame. She stepped in and looked around. "Ah, Brown!" she said, "I see you are all having a nice little fug in here!" The collective jaws of all present under Miss White's gaze dropped open as one, and remained open until well after she had departed, or alternatively until she had fugged off, as precipitately as she had arrived.

Had they heard Miss White's words correctly? Although they were astounded, they relished the forthright brevity of her visit. Clarification was sought, and was obtained, but it only brought disappointment in its confirmation of her legitimate use of language. However, for a while afterwards the Sixth Form room was thought of as "Fug Hall" and that was all right.

That Mr Sprayson included in his portfolio of teaching attributes the ability to make the rudiments of algebra and its bag of n nuts reasonably comprehensible to the hitherto uncomprehending was made plain to me during my very early days at Sir James Smith's. In modulated tones he read to his algebra classes from a textbook, as if he was a senior politician patronising a rabble. He was anxious to secure our votes, yet not quite able to disguise the edge of condescension to his eagerness for divulging a message that he wanted to be accepted, but in which he himself didn't quite believe.

The subject he taught at which he was the unquestioned master, however, was Chemistry. In this sphere he was eminently qualified, having, at some date in a past which was dim to all his pupils yet very much alive to him, graduated from the Faculty of the discipline of the same name at the University of Birmingham.

Mr Sprayson carried the banner for Chemistry in the manner of an elder statesman as he strode between and around the benches in the school's quite well-appointed chemistry laboratory, still gripping at the lapels of his gown with accustomed grace and dignity. He instructed in matters mundane and intricate, a veritable colossus in the elucidation of chemical equations, providing advice on the art of lighting Bunsen burners safely, and performing a wide range of experiments to illustrate in practical terms what happened when you mixed various compounds and corrosive liquids together and sometimes heated them up, thereby transmuting into reality the symbols of an equation written up on the blackboard.

Many of the chemical reactions which we witnessed were so lacking in spectacle that they required a leap of faith on the part of the beholder to accept that anything had really occurred at all. Sometimes there was an instant change of colour or a surge of heat in a test tube or flask as the selected ingredients met and reacted with one another. At other times there came the startling manifestation of a voluminous precipitate to elicit gasps of restrained awe from the assembled class.

Mr Sprayson's guarantee for holding our attention and interest, however, was that every once in a while he made something exciting take place, such as when he allowed access to a Kipps apparatus from which hydrogen sulphide gas could be generated. The chemistry laboratory had but one Kipps, maintained in a recess over on the left-hand wall as you entered. The recess was fronted by a glass isolation panel to contain the diffusion of any rogue emissions, although the panel wasn't equipped with any locking device, and the absence of such security let the Kipps apparatus be considered fair game by fart-minded individuals.

An ever-popular lab experiment was the oxidation of aniline by concentrated nitric acid — Mr Sprayson poured a small quantity of the latter onto a similar quantity of the former in a glass dish to create a volcanic eruption in miniature. However, the most popular demonstration of all that he performed was the so-called "green tea experiment". This consisted of placing a portion of orange coloured sodium trichlorate crystals in a broad-diameter test tube, clamping the test tube to a vertical stand at an acute angle, and applying the flame of a Bunsen burner to the base of the test tube for as long as it took to trigger the reaction, which wasn't usually all that long. The result was a dramatic spectacle as the crystals transformed into a powerful gush of copious green chromium sesquioxide flakes. It was all extremely satisfying, and it didn't take long for some of us to realise that if the test tube containing the orange crystals were to be tightly fitted with a rubber bung prior to the application of heat, that mighty surge of green tea would guarantee the forcible propulsion of the bung out of the test tube. Such rubbery missiles were able, we discovered, to travel from one end of the laboratory to the other, and, then on impact with the far wall, to bounce a goodly part of the way back again.

The floor of the laboratory was fitted with four massive work benches, thickly capped with hardwood of a type which time, wear and tear and the frequent spillage of chemical compounds, of corrosive elements and of solutions representing the whole gamut of the ph range, had rendered anonymous. Each bench was fitted with a pair of sinks with running water (cold only) plus manifold outlets to a gas supply intended for the use of Bunsen burners. The benches stood at right angles to the long axis of the lab, with separating aisles in between and along the line of the walls on either side.

Down at the far end of the lab behind the blackboard, two not inappropriately, but rather optimistically, named "fume isolation" rooms were located. The rooms were the sort of vulnerable holy of holies with which the Wizard of Oz would have been familiar. As there was no fun in keeping fumes in isolation, fumes were released to run free by pupil preference, although not with Mr Sprayson's approval. A favourite trick we had was to go in and open a bottle of concentrated hydrochloric acid alongside an equally opened bottle of full strength ammonia, and then stand back to watch the clouds form.

As previously noted, the Kipps apparatus was displayed in its glassed-in alcove, and there were other similarly recessed sanctuaries further down towards the fume isolation area in the same wall, these intended for holding concentrated acids and various inflammable organic volatiles.

The right-hand wall of the laboratory was characterised by an abundance of shelving on which an army of closed bottles and jars, displaying a full spectrum of colours and contents, were lined up in a proud array. There were solids, crystals, powders, nodules, pellets and so on and so forth. To an uninitiated beginner emerging from the scientific desert of North Cornwall, these were wonders indeed, presenting the substance not only of the periodic table, a descriptive chart of which was affixed with drawing pins for our delectation on the end wall, but also of all things known to man.

Among the more exciting contents of those open-access ranks and phials of glassware were sticks of phosphorus and pellets of sodium and potassium, all submerged in clear oil as if they were sardines; acids of the big three persuasion, both dilute and concentrated; chloroform; and one jar of sodium cyanide pellets. If locks and keys to any of this cornucopia had ever existed, they were long gone.

The pale green, lead-based paint with which the walls were covered was significantly shrouded in grey-black shadows drawn by the ghostly fingers of acid fumes past and present. Ah, but the laboratory was a garden of delights, with Mr Sprayson as its horticultural kingpin.

I went on to sit Chemistry at A Level under his attentive guidance, and obtained a distinction for it — my one and only A Level distinction in fact, be that as it may. I was not a natural scholar, merely one whom Mr Sprayson had inspired with his enthusiasm for the subject. Organic, rather than inorganic, chemistry fitted me like a glove. Organic chemistry was sheer poetry and I saw it with crystal clarity. Actual poetry, according to Miss White, was something I knew nothing about, but where the beehive lyricism of organic chemistry was concerned I greeted my element.

It was therefore something of a pity that similar scales did not fall from my eyes where an understanding of Maths was concerned. I was always reluctant to give an impression of one who genuinely worried about that, even though I did.

Battle

The school's total complement of pupils waxed and waned only marginally, holding at roughly one hundred and fifty, and consisting of an approximately equal mix of boys and girls. This pupil balance of male and female applied with a like weighting to the teaching staff.

One of the female teachers held the title of Headmistress, appointed not so much as a counter to the supremacy of Mr Sprayson, but rather to add a formal touch to the staff pecking order, and to help, perhaps, in stifling unrest among the members of the teaching regime. The title of Headmistress was to all intents and purposes honorary, but its authority was no less real for all that. Any inherent grandeur that went with it never quite seemed to rise up and declare itself, though, as if it knew in its heart that subservience to the Headmaster was paramount.

To secure his own position following his arrival at the school, it could be surmised that Mr Sprayson no doubt found the need to wage some form of counter to the pretenders to his throne whose allegiance to the defunct Leese regime died hard. Not least among the dissenters at the time when I came to the First Form was the Headmistress of the day, the appropriately named Miss Battle. Whatever took place in the struggle for power was played out behind the seemingly united Staff front presented to pupils, but it was not unlikely that eventual resolution involved blood spilled on the floor of the Headmaster's study.

Miss Battle, who appeared to have no nickname for the very good reason that her surname spoke volumes, was a fixture at the school through most of my First Form year. It was towards the end of that year that she disappeared forever. Her departure was sudden, and came not with a bang but with a whimper. Expressions of regret thereafter were not widespread and were mostly expressed in muted tones.

On the official photograph of the school's pupils and teaching staff taken in the summer term of 1951, Miss Battle was not to be seen, implying that she was definitively gone by then. Central to the photograph, seated as erect as a ramrod in the Headmistress' chair at the right hand of Mr Sprayson, whence she might come to judge both the quick and the dead, was none other than Miss White, looking as though she had just smelled something noxious and was keen to create an impression that she was not its originator.

Most pupils would not have felt motivated to give Miss Battle much thought after the event of her leaving the school community, once the sense of relief had worn off, that is. She was not particularly popular — not at all popular in fact. She ruled the classes she taught with an iron hand. I don't know the extent to which she inspired fear in others, but she surely inspired fear in me.

Miss Battle took the First Form for both Latin and Musical Appreciation — the latter being an oxymoron in the prevailing pearls-cast-before-swine context. Her tastes in music were strictly Third Programme. A majority of pupils listened to the Third not at all, unless it was tuned into by accident and then tuned out of too slowly. So many of them, not least myself, were raised musically on a radio diet of "Two-Way Family Favourites", "Henry Hall's

189

Guest Night", "The Billy Cotton Band Show" and "Variety Bandbox" among others of similar ilk, none of which appeared to resonate with any pleasure in the flinty heart of Miss Battle.

Musical Appreciation *à la* Miss Battle required that the class should sit and listen while she played a succession of obscure classical numbers on gramophone records using a wind-up gramophone set to run at a rate of seventy-eight revolutions per minute. The sense of numb disbelief which all this engendered in us had to be well hidden behind a front of feigned interest. I don't believe that we carried out much appreciation or analysis of the works we were obliged to listen to. Miss Battle should, however, be given the benefit of the doubt, as her objective of providing us with some cultural enlightenment was undoubtedly sincere. Unfortunately, although she could lead Philistines to water, she couldn't make them drink of its bounty.

It was probably at a fairly early stage of my short association with Miss Battle and Musical Appreciation that she decided I was a lost cause. On the rare occasions that she spoke to me she was apt to snap, and her tone was harsh. On the other hand that wasn't too far removed from her normal manner, which helped to make me just one among the crowd of recipients of her disdain.

Her image was hard to reconcile — she was clearly struggling to regain any element of an opportunity to feel and even look as if she were forty again. She looked something like a blowsy version of Phyllis Calvert, being well dressed, matronly of figure, severely regal in her *coiffure* and rather heavily made up. An odour of face powder overlain with tobacco surrounded her in a palpable aura.

Since it was evident that Miss Battle and I did not share similar tastes in music, my presence in her Musical Appreciation class was probably as distasteful to her as it was purgatory to me. One day she demanded that I tell her exactly what, if anything, my musical tastes were. Fear of the consequences made me reluctant to answer, and so I kept my silence. The tongue lashing that I received from her for what she defined as a display of dumb insolence was preferable to the mockery that would have been my lot if I had told her I liked Big Bands. There were no renditions by any Big Bands in her stack of seventy-eights.

Then, as Miss Battle flounced into the classroom at the commencement of a Musical Appreciation session on a certain day, trailing both her gown and her characteristic aroma, she instructed Mike Ferrett, with my assistance, to make a selection from the stack of records for the challenge to come. Mike and I shuffled through the records, examining labels both front and back with false enthusiasm. For all that what was on them meant to me at least, the labels might as well have been written in Latin.

We eventually came up with a selection as random as were our thoughts, and handed the chosen discs of pressed Delafila over to Miss Battle, not without trepidation. Following a rapid once-over scrutiny, she looked up at us with a rare vestige of a smile, enough to register a mild gleam of pleasure while stopping somewhere short of being make-up cracking, and declared to the class that her lost faith in human nature had just been restored.

I drew two lessons from that successful endeavour. The first of these was that the hard to please Miss Battle appeared to have a chink or two in her armour. The second lesson was that when the chips were down and all else had failed, then using bullshit to baffle brains was always worth trying.

The air of bustling command which Miss Battle threw into Musical Appreciation took something of a back seat when it came to her teaching of Latin. Her technique regarding the latter embodied the certainty that Latin was not only a dead language, but likely to remain so if she had any say in the matter. When she entered the classroom at the start of a Latin lesson she seemed to insinuate her presence into its every corner, nook and cranny in a manner calculated to chill the hearts of all who stood before her waiting anxiously to be instructed to sit.

She bade us open our Latin textbooks to a page of her own choosing and then ordered us to copy down in our exercise books the very words which already stood in print on that and subsequent pages. We picked up the basics of our Latin vocabulary through repetitive copying. We learned by rote and repetition, although we weren't exactly taught anything particularly insightful. Miss Battle was well able to transform the uninteresting into something far more stultifying to the mind. Perhaps that marked the strait way of her valediction.

As we sat and toiled over densely printed pages of Latin narrative allegedly describing events related to Caesar's Gallic wars (unless they were Punic), a lack of understanding of what it was all about hung over the class like a cloud. Miss Battle sat in regal isolation behind the teacher's desk up at the front of the room, having shifted her chair back a little so that she could lean into it, relax and put her feet up on the desk, casually, as if no one else was present in the room.

She then opened a newspaper, disappeared behind its wide spread, and gave every indication of being in the process of reading all that lay within. The silence was broken only by the occasional rattle of pages of newsprint being turned by her, and by sporadic coughing from an otherwise mute class.

Now and then the sight of a thin, grey-white plume of smoke rising from behind the screening newspaper signified not only that Miss Battle was still awake, but also that she numbered smoking among what was felt by us to be an impressive list of personal vices.

The one relief that Miss Battle's desk-bound tableau offered to help make the ordeal by Latin tolerable was an occasional glimpse of her voluminous bloomers as she adjusted the position of her legs atop the desk.

And then she passed into history. In losing that Battle, Mr Sprayson had won a victory, as had the teaching of Latin at Sir James Smith's.

Miss Battle's successor as Latin mistress was a much younger lady named Miss Quick, rapidly coming to be nicknamed "Quickie". Unlike Miss Battle, Miss Quick fortunately did not live up to her name. She had a quiet and engaging personality which radiated both kindness and a pleasing air of innocence. In her own slow and unassuming way she put life into Latin, letting fresh air and new ideas waft through the mausoleum of Miss Battle's creation.

Miss Quick was instrumental in my motivation to choose, when the call came in the Fourth Form, to continue with Latin in her saintly company and to drop Physics, without even a hint of taking the softer ride creeping in. The choice of Miss Quick over Mr Jeal was easy to make. Who might have been selected had Miss Battle versus Mr Jeal formed the scope for choice was a dilemma I was glad I didn't have to solve.

With Miss Battle's unceremonious exit, the position of Headmistress became vacant and needed to be filled by someone who would be unlikely to pose any challenge to Mr Sprayson's hard-won dominion over all. The list of in-house candidates from the existing post-Battle line-up of teaching staff was not extensive, namely consisting of Miss Jones, Miss Holloway and Miss White. Respectively they made a virtual faith, hope and absence of charity trio – but the greatest of these was the latter.

Polly

My experiences of being taught by Miss White were not all especially happy ones. It did not take long for me to decide that she was mean-spirited, and she never gave me good cause to consider that I had misjudged her. My opinion of Miss White, it should be pointed out in all fairness, was not necessarily shared by others. However Miss White's accession to being Headmistress only served to emphasise my perception of her focused unkindness.

She wore her hair in a severe knot, high up on the head. It gave her a rather Regency-inspired look. She was in any case not the type of person to let her hair down, either literally or figuratively. The starkness of her hair style extended downwards into a prim cast to her mouth which slipped all too easily into a curl of contempt, with which I became all too familiar. Her eyes were narrowed and accusatory, filled with the implication that those on whom she focused her flinty gaze needed to watch out, or face the consequences.

The best that might be said of the quality of Miss White's professional wardrobe was that it was wholly complementary to her character. Her attire was as sombre as it was drab. She fortified her role as Headmistress with a talent for trailing anxiety in her shadow. She strode the corridors unsmilingly, and when our paths crossed, I shrank against the wall as she bustled by.

One of Miss White's more obvious physical attributes was a garish red tint at the peak of her cheekbones. It was always there to see, a badge perhaps of barely pent-up anger, ever-ready to seep, diffuse and flood her cheeks without warning once she found a victim, or better yet, once a victim inadvertently found her. The more intense the flush, the more was the trouble that was about

194

to devolve on the unfortunate person who had opened its gate. A kinder view would perhaps have considered that Miss White was an easy blusher, although blushing from embarrassment or guiltiness of conscience were not evident features of her character. Mark Twain may have had someone not unlike Miss White in mind when he wrote, "Man is the only animal that blushes — or needs to".

Her ultimate ascent into high tones of facial colour, reaching up to purple and even beyond, occurred when I was in the Third Form. I hasten to add that I was not the cause of it.

On a certain evening (or night) when the school was closed and empty, a person (or persons) unknown obtained access to the Third Form classroom (cum gymnasium) by dint of forced entry, and proceeded to make some changes to the *décor* by painting slogans on the walls referring to Miss White in a somewhat derogatory manner. To emphasise some of the points made by the slogans, using the kind of artistic licence that Miss Holloway would not have awarded very good marks for, a few stick-like caricatures were added, allegedly representative of Miss White and Mr Sprayson in compromising positions.

Sadly enough, what the inscriptions actually stated, and what the stick renditions were all about, was never made known to the scholastic body of the school. Immediately following the discovery of the nocturnal artist's work, the Third Form classroom was declared off limits to all but the members of the teaching staff. It had to be sufficient unto the day for most pupils to understand that a few simple and presumably well-chosen words were able not only to cast a range of shades of apoplexy across Miss White's face, but also to place broad grins on the visages of very many of her pupils.

An intensive investigation, closely resembling a manhunt, was carried out under the direction of Mr Sprayson. In line with Miss White's natural ability for causing grief to far too many of her pupils, the in-school suspects were legion, but since so also were their alibis, the trail soon ran cold.

Putting the satisfied grins aside, most of us found the incident of the writing on the Third Form wall to be more than a little shocking in its uniqueness. Sensibilities were shaken quite as much by it as they had been at Belshazzar's feast where *"Mene, mene, tekel, upharsin"* on the wall had been the written order of the day. It was too much to hope that Miss White's kingdom was numbered, even finished, but we could well accept that she had been weighed in the balances and found wanting. We had no Daniel to interpret for us, but on the other hand we didn't need him as we were able to make up our own minds.

Where it went with me, I knew full well that my aptitude for both of the subjects taught by Miss White — English Language and English Literature — was not bad. I had an intuitive feel for spelling, word usage and grammatical construction that ought to have put me in good stead with her. In spite of this, however, any promise I might have shown and any nurturing encouragement I might have been given were overcome by Miss White's evident desire to depreciate me. There was clearly something about me that didn't sit well with her, not that I could blame her for that of course, as it was her entitlement. Unfortunately, when dislike got coupled with meanness it turned into a form of harassment, even bullying, on which account Miss White and I had no meeting point. In retrospect I was surprised at how little I let her attitude bother me — perhaps my knowing that I was better than she made me out to be was what kept me going.

I read avidly, but not to put too fine a point on my cultural leanings, much of my primary reading source was drawn from the pages of the great D. C. Thomson stable of weekly story papers. That was all good, solid stuff with a limitless cast of characters, many of whom felt like long-standing friends, taking part in exploits combining imaginative locations and situations, an abundance of action, laugh-out-loud humour and high adventure all in equal measure.

I once used the name of the celebrated "Adventure" detective, Dixon Hawke, in an answer to a question in one of Miss White's exams which asked for the name of a well-known fictional detective to be specified. The story that I associated with Hawke in that context was "The Case of the Black Cat". Miss White was expecting Sherlock Holmes to put in an appearance, and my answer, though perfectly correct, was summarily dismissed by her.

I didn't mind, as this was merely symptomatic of our unfortunate relationship. Giving me low marks, irrespective of whether I had been right or wrong, was Miss White's *modus operandi*. She seemed especially fond of holding the way I spoke up to taunts and ridicule (she had no discernible regional accent herself), and because this mockery appeared to give her pleasure I broadened my Port Isaac accent whenever I was called on to speak or read aloud in any of her classes — which was naturally enough fairly often. Thus did I aid her scope for criticism, and for a good while my accent kept the game afoot, as her detective, who was not Dixon Hawke, might have said.

Since all good things eventually had to come to an end, this process of challenge and counter-challenge became a burden when I entered the Third Form. I then lapsed into silence in Miss White's classes, not so much to throw in the towel as to take the line that if she was intent on making me appear stupid I could just as easily do that for myself by not reacting to her any more.

So, when she threw questions at me, I set a dull haze of incomprehension on my face, even when I knew the correct answers to give. I whispered them out of the corner of my mouth to Pat Sleeman who sat in the desk alongside me. Miss White gradually gave up on singling me out, not that it ever prevented her accusing me of being obdurate, or stopped her continuing to give me low marks in English exams.

A *dénouement* of sorts came along to plant its seeds on the day of the O Level English exam, as for that one I was no longer incarcerated by Miss White's marking standards. I achieved a distinction in English Language at O Level, and did creditably enough in the English Lit exam as well. These results, when they became known, only seemed to make Miss White more angry with me. She acted as if I had worked for O Level in a way that I never had with her. She was not glad for me — quite the contrary in fact. What I owed to her teaching was much, but what was less clear was whether or not I succeeded because of her or in spite of her.

I was in any case then moving to the Sixth Form, and even though Miss White was the form mistress for the Sixth, I was no longer being taught by her. As a consequence, her ability to deter me was greatly weakened. However, she didn't entirely sheathe her sword, and there was one last hurrah that came to pass between us at a moment during the spring term of my Upper Sixth year.

The trail leading to the incident began with the school's annual Christmas Concert at the conclusion of the preceding autumn term. The Concerts, ever popular, programmed performances by pupils ready to highlight their personal talents or lack of the same, together with Form presentations inserted like stepping stones along the way. A Christmas Concert took up an entire school day, and, with a little help from a few members of the teaching staff behind the scenes, the show was compiled and produced by the pupils themselves. For continuity purposes it was compered by the Head Boy and the Head Girl, the bulk of this duty falling on the Head Boy.

His job was to introduce acts and once in a while throw in a joke to amuse the audience, which consisted of staff and pupils. The jokes were not subjected to staff scrutiny or censorship in any way, but it was generally understood that extracts from Mr Max Miller's Blue Book were not acceptable as a source of gag material. When the compere's task fell to me as Head Boy, the radio work of Messrs Bob Monkhouse and Denis Goodwin, lifted for the occasion by Pat Sleeman and myself, formed the fount of continuity humour.

My Christmas Concert playwriting credentials were reasonably firmly established by the time the fateful Upper Sixth year was reached, as I had had two plays to my name, even if not to my credit, performed in previous years. The earlier play relied heavily on the format of Mr Wilfred Pickles' immensely popular BBC radio programme, *Have a Go*; and the second was a parody of Shakespeare's *A Midsummer Night's Dream*, entitled "A Midsummer Night's Nightmare". The latter was served up with impressive topicality as a company of school players under Miss White's direction had recently given a highly successful performance of that very play, much as Shakespeare might have intended it to be performed.

Enlivened by the fact that my two plays were accepted by a non-paying captive audience with the sort of enthusiasm that rose above apathy but fell somewhere short of rapture, I proceeded to write a further piece for the Upper Sixth to present as the closing highlight at the final Concert of my Sir James Smith's career. It was a play about nothing of consequence, which bore a loose relationship to *Under Milk Wood*. The best that could be said about its reception was that a growing rumble of discontent from the audience, led by those sitting in the teaching staff seats in the front row, did a good job of suppressing the sound of Dylan Thomas turning in his grave.

The play was indeed an unmitigated turkey. Few if any of the cast had learned their lines — I tried to cover it up with improvisation, but the limit of damage control was reached all too soon. The play attempted to set sail, only to lose its means of propulsion and slowly founder in a narrow strait that bore a remarkable resemblance to Shit Creek.

When Eugene Field commented with respect to a performance by a celebrated Shakespearean actor that "he played the King as though under momentary apprehension that someone else was about to play the ace", he could well have been suggesting an epitaph for my Upper Sixth play. It was not so much that the school wasn't ready for the play, more that the play wasn't ready for the school.

From my position as one of the *dramatis personae* on stage I could not help watching as, from his seat at the centre of the front row of the audience, Mr Sprayson whispered a lengthy instruction to Mr Turner, whereupon Mr Turner rose to his feet with uncharacteristic haste and made his way around to stage right wing. There, in full view of a large proportion of the audience, as if a part had been specially written into the play for him, he launched into a sequence of gestures designed to leave no doubt in the minds of any of the hapless performers that the ever-burgeoning debacle should end forthwith. The sense of relief as we folded was at its most pronounced among the cast.

The song had ended, but the malady lingered on. Pupils from Forms throughout the school kept coming to ask me, well into the spring term it seemed, just what on earth the play had been about. I fell back on an answer I had heard to a similar question about the meaning of modern poetry in a television play entitled *Drink Doggy, Drink*, namely that a detailed explanation would take too long to give, whereas the short answer was that if they didn't know, I couldn't tell them.

I took all the sarcasm, criticism and condemnation without rancour, and decided to see the incident of my play's failure as one of those memories which enriched the heart and added colour to the tapestry of school life. The calm waters of my acceptance of this fact, however, were ruffled by random cats' paws pushed along by the sneering wind of a certain boy in the Lower Sixth whose motive, in this instance certainly, was the intent to wound. He was a Camelford boy, and although his origins couldn't be used to justify his attitude, they could well have made at least a contribution to the same. His Christian name was Edwin, but everyone called him Stan. He was shorter than me, and quite slight — not that being slight or even thin amounted to anything as most of us had the kind of figures that made bone identification on exposures easy.

A handful of us Sixth Formers were in the Sixth Form room during a rare free period one spring term afternoon when Stan chose to raise the matter of my failed play. He made a number of jibes which seemed to get increasingly personal in tone, harping into a fairly pointed diatribe that didn't appear to contain any element of knowing where to draw the line. I suggested to Stan that he might give his mouth a rest, but he made it plain that he wasn't up for that, and continued to regale the company present with further caustic observations. He was bespectacled, and that feature, since a tenet of pupil etiquette was that a fellow-pupil wearing glasses should not be subjected to rough treatment, was a useful instrument for his security. Nevertheless, as it went on and on, enough eventually became more than enough, and my temper got the better of me. I snapped, stood up and punched Stan in the nose.

This sudden burst of classroom violence took place at the back of the Sixth Form room. On receipt of my blow, Stan, to the accompaniment of loud gasps with shriek-like overtones from one or two of the girls present, staggered backwards and collided with the end desk in a spaced column of six. He and the desk went over in unison, both falling against the desk that stood next up in line, which in turn toppled against the next one, and so on. The whole column of desks went down like a set of dominoes, albeit making considerably more of a racket than dominoes were capable of. The reverberations of the crashing seemed to linger in the air well beyond the point at which the front desk of the column of six hit the floor.

It was at this point that Miss White entered the fray, as it so happened that she was conducting a First Form reading class in the library adjoining the Sixth Form room. The crash of tumbling desks was wasted on neither the First Form nor Miss White in terms of the excitement it engendered. All that transpired thereafter was devoted to rapid sequence action and reaction. Without a by-your-leave, the door to the Sixth Form room was wrenched open, although flung open might have been a better description of the precipitate nature of its movement. Miss White stood again at the portal. She surveyed the room, and gave a loud shriek to complement the look of horror and purple outrage on her face. There before her was a frozen tableau of fallen desks, with me standing at the back, Stan sitting on the floor, and the incidental members of the Sixth Form hanging around on the fringes in a state of nervous anticipation.

Having made her observation, Miss White did not attempt to seek an explanation, but took off post haste down the corridor in the direction of the central hall, screeching incomprehensible words, which could well have been obscenities but probably weren't. The gist of it seemed to be that in all her years as a member of the teaching profession she had never witnessed such monstrous behaviour or come into contact with such appalling violence. And as far as it went with me as the perpetrator, a punishment of some severity must be the least order of the day.

I had committed unseemly conduct of egregious proportions. That much was clear to Miss White, and I knew it only too well. It would have been importune enough had I been a member of any other Form let alone the Upper Sixth, but the additional fact that I was Head Boy transcended any option for mitigation or leniency to come my way. I felt that the slender thread from which my personal status always hung as far as Miss White regarded it, had, at a stroke (or maybe a punch), been frayed to breaking point both irretrievably and deservedly. She must have been secretly delighted by it.

From my blazer I removed my badges — both HEAD BOY and PREFECT — followed along in Miss White's turbulent wake down the corridor, and handed them in to Mrs Perry as a pre-emptive measure. Mr Sprayson was not available to take charge of the badges himself as he was then in conference in his inner sanctum, no doubt receiving Miss White's report and spit-flecked advice.

The school afternoon was by then over, and as I went down the hill to get the bus back to Port Isaac, Miss White's vituperation hung over me like a vindictive cloud. I was deeply sorry, not for the loss of the badges, as being Head Boy had never really sat easily with me, but rather for my action against Stan. He ought to have been handled diplomatically, although a little more circumspection on his part would not have gone amiss. All the same, the overwhelming bulk of the blame devolved on me. The odd thing was that I had no small sense of wellbeing in knowing that I had provoked such a choleric reaction in Miss White.

On my arrival at school on the following morning, and just prior to Assembly, I was summoned to see Mr Sprayson. Much to my surprise he handed me back my badges and instructed me to pin them back on my blazer. With that done he launched into a short but keenly sharp lecture, admonishing me for having lost my temper with Stan. He was fair and right to the point, as always. I suspected that his younger daughter Moira, a fellow Sixth Former and present in the room at the time of my dust-up with Stan, might have told him at home on the previous evening that I had been subjected to a certain amount of provocation, and on that basis I got a conditional reprieve, the condition being that I shouldn't do it again.

Whether or not Miss White was consulted about the outcome, even though I never actually lost anything to be reinstated back to, was not made clear.

Poor Miss White. She is remembered by me with pleasure and no lack of gratitude for all that she taught me. Her choice of me as a victim was, paradoxically, a force for ultimate good, as it gave me the motivation to do what I could to rise above it.

Mena

With both a Headmaster and a *de facto* Headmistress in place, Sir James Smith's one hundred and fifty pupils could be reckoned as well catered for in the field of Authority Figures begging for their homage, even if the grip on authority placed in the hands of the Headmistress was more illusory than real. However, to enhance what could have been a veritable triumvirate of governance had Miss White been just that little bit more masculine, there was yet a third incumbent sitting at the centre of the school's circle of power.

The Third Man was the acknowledged Deputy Headmaster, Mr Menadue, popularly and affectionately known as "Mena". His prime teaching subject was History.

Mr Menadue was a former Leese acolyte, solidly cast in that "old school" tradition. It was said that, as heir apparent to Mr Leese, he had expected accession to the Headmastership to be his following Mr Leese's alleged shove into retirement. That honour, however, was destined not to be, as the influence of the old guard had foundered in the immediate squall of Mr Leese's passage. Given the nature of his antecedents, Mr Menadue's destiny at Sir James Smith's was to hold fast and remain frozen forever as the ship's first mate.

Mr Menadue, suited, gowned and bustling, was cut from archetypal material. It was tempting to compare him to Red Circle's Mr Smugg, but he could have stepped straight out of any of the pages of a host of school stories featuring battles of wits between Fourth Formers and their custodians. His face was rounded, yet curiously sharp-featured beneath well slicked-down hair, that for all its garnish could not avoid demonstrating a tendency to thin out. On his nose, which defied attempts to be described as anything other than aquiline, sat a pair of thin-rimmed spectacles redolent of much more severity than he was capable of summoning up.

As well as History, Mr Menadue took classes in basic Arithmetic and presided with magisterial aplomb up at the sports field on Wednesday afternoons, as if he were born to the manner of boot, bat and appropriately sized balls. His History campaign was fought largely on two fronts. First of all came the saga of the British Empire, ranging from its eighteenth century excesses through to the early twentieth century when the first signs began to appear that, sooner or later, the days were numbered for the whole unfortunate project. The Indian episode, featuring high-stakes rogues like Clive and Warren Hastings, was given substantial attention by Mr Menadue, as was the nineteenth century's Grab for Africa. The events that he taught us took place in lands of which good North Cornish children knew little and for which they probably cared less, but in spite of ourselves we absorbed by reluctant osmosis all that Mr Menadue had to offer us.

His second, and clearly preferred, historical teaching theme dealt with the origins of the First World War, wrought all about in intricacies, complications, the playing fields of Eton, and a cloying spider's web of petty jealousies and intrigues that were common in most of the crowned heads of Europe. The sorry mess that he outlined to us offered a convincing indictment of the perils vested in the maintenance of hereditary monarchies as well as in the bloody-minded stupidity of its aristocracy, its sycophants and its military officer class. A full cast of blue-blooded dimwits stood revealed in Mr Menadue's spotlight. Strangely enough though, even as late as we were in the mid-twentieth century, we still continued perversely to pay great deference to such people whom we were instructed to regard as our betters.

Mr Menadue's First World War credentials were impeccable. He was a man of the trenches who had seen far too much front-line action and had come home shell-shocked. The vestiges of this condition presented themselves not only in his relentlessly analytical pursuit of the causes of the First World War, but also in an impressive range of nervous tics and twitches which now and then flickered alarmingly across his face, or jerked his shoulder, or trembled his hand.

Perhaps it was as a result of his battlefield experiences, coupled with what was no more than a thinly veiled sense of frustration at being condemned never to serve as school Head, that Mr Menadue sought to take no prisoners in the course of his History lessons. He was well accomplished in the barking out of orders, and was all too evidently desirous of having any orders obeyed without delay and without question at all times. To seize the attention of daydreamers or slackers his methods were impressively direct. From his command centre alongside the blackboard he was able to hurl its wooden-backed eraser at any pupil suffering from attention deficit and to hit his selected target every time. Duster throwing was a trademark action for him, and he was famous for it. Complaints there were, but resentment for this Great Game there was not.

Now and then, Mr Menadue elected to stroll unannounced into the no-man's land of the nether regions of the classroom and awaken anyone he observed to be obliviously dozing by virtue of jabbing the point of a freshly sharpened pencil into the somnolent head and repeating the process if it was deemed necessary. It was not unknown for the pencil's lead point, especially if it was of H grade, to break off in a punctured scalp. Mr Menadue sometimes varied that technique by grabbing a lock of pupil hair between his thumb and forefinger and then simultaneously tugging it up and down while beating a rhythmic rat-a-tat-tat tattoo on the head in question with his forefinger knuckle.

He had his foibles, all of which were savoured by his pupils as being the stuff of legend. Key among Mr Menadue's specialities, or so it was alleged, was the technique he used for marking History exam papers set by himself. On good authority it was held that you didn't need to know anything much about the subject matter in order to pass a Mr Menadue exam. All you had to be able to do in the time available was to cover as many sheets of paper as possible with writing — the more the better. You could of course write straight to the point, but you could also write drivel — the quality didn't matter. All that was important was quantity.

It was said that Mr Menadue never read the handed-in exam papers. He simply counted the number of pages and used that figure, together with a merit or demerit weighting related to term-time performance, behaviour and whether he liked you or not, to estimate and award a final mark. I didn't have the nerve to test the page-count waters myself, but there were two or three boys I knew of who said that they had done it, and that the volume concept had worked perfectly for them. It was history graded by the ream, if not by the quire.

On those Wednesday afternoons dedicated to slow torture by

football or cricket, Mr Menadue tucked his trouser turn-ups into his socks, put on footwear appropriate to the season, and stepped seamlessly into the role of coach/referee/trainer in a single pass. He gave his full attention to all who were sports-adept and left those of us who weren't to shiver in the outfield or along the side lines. He assigned team captains (usually the same ones on each occasion) and delegated the captains to select their teams of the day in turn from the huddled mass of assembled candidates, both the hopeful and the hopeless.

The team selections were made in descending order of prowess, running the full measure down from eagerness through indifference and so on to the barrel-bottom scrapings that neither captain wanted, and in which I stood, focused only on my desire to hear Mr Menadue blow the final whistle.

Those sports afternoons were all too often felt by me to be grey, wet, windy and forbidding, all at the same time. They weren't entirely like that of course, and owed their negative perception — an admitted disservice in many ways — to my antipathy for activities that I had little or no aptitude for.

The one time that Mr Menadue paid me a full measure of attention at the sports field was related not to football, but to cricket, at which I also didn't manage to excel. His attention followed the previously described "Willie Wallop" accident, featuring Mike Ferrett as the innocent bystander and myself as the sincerely contrite, although inadvertent, perpetrator.

My usual role in the cricket season was two-pronged. To begin with, in fielding team mode, I was banished to the long grass in the vicinity of the boundary, where I had to stand and hope that a ball would never be struck in my direction. Secondly, I was always one of a group called on to help push the heavy roller when its use was necessary. I didn't so much mind pushing (and pulling) the roller, which consisted of a huge cylinder of granite fitted with an axle and a yoke-like cart handled frame. We usually pushed it down the twenty-two yards long pitch in one direction and pulled it back in the other. It was not an unsatisfying activity.

One day the edge of the roller went over someone's toes. It was an avoidable accident according to Mr Menadue. He delivered a long and loud verbal remonstration to the roller team of the day. Fortunately the ground had been soft enough to yield, and so the toes the roller passed over had a certain amount of natural cushion to sink into and no lasting harm was done.

Mr Menadue met his sporting match on a certain memorable winter's day. I was then in the Second Form, and at the time knew him perhaps not well, but well enough. On that day the snow fell heavily and lay round about, deep and crisp and even, offering an open invitation to all to partake of its blessing and to grant it appropriate benediction. The school buses had struggled to get us to Sir James Smith's through the early accumulation of snow, and the question as to whether or not they would be able to get us home again at the end of the school day was there to be worried about when the time to go home came around. The thought of cancelling school never occurred to anyone, as always. Prior to Assembly line-up we enjoyed a rather cheery period out in the yard of milling and shuffling around in the snow, which was by then a good six inches deep. Only a few snowballs were thrown, no more.

We trooped into Assembly with our minds set on making the most of what the snow might offer at mid-morning break time. The hymn, lesson and prayers ran their usual course. Then came the day's announcements, into which Mr Sprayson inserted a bombshell to the effect that the throwing of snowballs anywhere — repeat, anywhere — on the school premises was banned. Anyone caught throwing a snowball would be subject to a penalty yet to be defined, but which, by implication, would be undoubtedly harsh. An immediate consequence of the banning order was to cast a cloud of gloom over the boys. What good was it to have snow, we thought, if you couldn't pick it up and form it into balls for throwing at objects both animate and inanimate.

It was therefore a disarrayed and doleful mob which filed out into the snow-decked yard at break time. The daily ration of milk was imbibed by the habitually compliant, and secretly disposed of by the rest. As it was, snow proved to be a handy medium into which to pour unwanted milk.

It was of course entirely inevitable that someone was going to grab a handful of snow, make a ball, and lob it at someone else. It could not have been otherwise. Before long, Mr Sprayson's prohibition edict lay in tatters.

Mr Menadue was on monitoring duty in the boys' yard at the break time under consideration. He took his duties seriously, and came came storming out among the increasing numbers of snowball-tossing miscreants to demand, in forcible tones, an immediate halt to the practice. He was most eager, almost frenzied, to take down names as his eyes darted hither and thither to identify the guilty. There in the yard, with his black gown of office sharply etched against the grey-white scene, Mr Menadue stood out as a target *sans pareil*. Seizing the moment, a single snowball sailed in his direction, met him with a good deal of accuracy and triggered a spontaneous onslaught. A flurry of snowballs followed. They found their mark and a general barrage then ensued.

As the blitz targeting him intensified, Mr Menadue was driven to seek cover. With snowballs bursting on him and all around him he made a tactical yet ignominious retreat out of harm's way into the Assembly line-up corridor. Battle honours had gone to the school's snowballing battalion. It was a victory to savour, even though it was known full well that the war was already lost.

Names were gathered. A few of the guilty and a lot of the innocent were hunted down. All were brought together to have the school's version of the Riot Act read to them by Mr Sprayson. A summary sentence was handed down for immediate execution. My name found its way onto the list of rule violators, although since I was guilty as charged, I couldn't complain about it.

We were all condemned to miss a succession of mid-morning breaks in order to sit in detention in the First Form room, where, for our punishment, we were required to copy out what seemed to be an endless array of chemical equations chalked up on the blackboard for us by a Prefect. The equations were utterly mystifying to juniors like me with yet an extremely limited experience of chemical formulae.

When I first saw the blackboard covered with the equations, I sank into a deep well of despair. I thought that I was required to solve them as I was just learning to do in Algebra, and I feared for the consequences of failing. However, it emerged that the name of this particular game was that the equations should be copied out neatly, and if not neatly then at least legibly.

This detention task resembled the "lines" that were always getting handed out at Red Circle. It would have been all to the good if any feature of the reactive interplay involving acids, bases, elements and compounds both organic and inorganic specified in the formulae had rubbed off during copying, and strange to relate, a lot of it did.

It would have been equally good had there been a collective sense of remorse over the breaking of the snowball banning order and the pelting of Mr Menadue, but regret for throwing snowballs could never be on the cards, and that was that.

Jonesie

Although the Headmaster had an appointed male Deputy in the mercurial person of Mr Menadue, Miss White appeared to have been granted no such formal support figure whose deputising presence she could count on. Had there been a Deputy Headmistress position though, it must, in terms of both seniority and suitability for the job, have gone to Miss Violet Jones, known to us as "Jonesie".

Her age was best left undefined, and although she was not as ancient as was sometimes unkindly alleged, Miss Jones was separated from any former flush of youth by a substantial spitting distance. Advancing middle age bobbed up all about her, yet she bore an impressively erect posture as she strode around and taught with a brisk determination suggestive of a spark that would not be easily extinguished.

Miss Jones was very much a maiden lady. She resided with her father, not far away from the school. Mr Jones' credentials for elderliness were very well established, as was his sense of good humour. He had enough of the latter to benefit both himself and his daughter, which was just as well, as Miss Jones' sense of humour normally surfaced slowly and with some reluctance. Her hair was grey, and sometimes when it caught the light it seemed almost white. Her mouth was wide, a slash-like feature accentuated by very thin lips. She had a disconcerting habit of pausing in mid-sentence to swallow deeply while speaking, as if she was anxious to gain a moment of thinking time.

We of North Cornwall's great unwashed tribe might have been forgiven for attributing a lah-di-dah quality to Miss Jones' way of speaking. Flowers to her were always "flahze".

She was the appointed Fifth Form mistress, holding serious court on that class in its splendid isolation up at the top end of the

Assembly corridor. Miss Jones' specialist teaching subjects were Geography and Euclidian Geometry, the former taken right through from the First Form to A Level and the latter probably pursued to O Level, but with more emphasis on the junior school. She taught Geometry with the aid of a thin textbook containing the basis of numerous theorems, each of which was associated with a statement addressing its immutable geometric truth, and the means of proof that the statement was not only absolute, but also worthy of being believed. Each theorem was neatly arranged on a single page of the textbook and graced with the suffix "Quod Erat Demonstrandum", shortened to QED.

Miss Jones read and discussed each theorem in turn with us from the start to the finish of the textbook. We followed her, learning the theorems by heart. We were thereby enabled to provide the proof of very many theorems without quite knowing why. Miss Jones was always convincing, apart from when she wasn't, both to us and for herself it was suspected.

The ultimate pinnacle in Miss Jones' mountainous range of proved theorems was reached by crossing over what she referred to as the *Pons Asinorum* (the "Bridge of Idiots" being an approximate translation of this grand title). She bade us cross this bridge via proving and appreciating a theorem drawn up by a gentleman named Pythagoras, or "Pythag" as we called him.

In the realm of Geography, Miss Jones led her classes along a path of enlightenment that was much more amenable to set foot on, Danny Kaye notwithstanding, than were the creaking struts of the *Pons Asinorum*. Under her informed tutelage most pupils managed to end up with a reasonable understanding of what was where in the world; who traded with whom; who liked whom; who didn't like whom; what varieties of physical geographical characteristics and climate were to be encountered where; and what peoples, cultures, flora and fauna either graced or defiled their lands of origin. She knew it all and willingly passed it on.

And as for what we ought to have been making of it, well, much of the World Political Map on the good old Mercator projection was coloured red, so it didn't much matter what anyone thought outside of that crimson reality. We all picked up the general idea that quite a lot of world existed beyond the boundaries of North Cornwall, although relating to that greater expanse was another matter altogether, not that many of us put too much effort into it. The tone of debate with respect to the situation pertaining to overseas localities was still to some extent vested in a dictum of Mr Cecil Rhodes, in that having been born into England (or rather into Cornwall) we had already won first prize in the lottery of life.

The alleged last words of Rhodes might incidentally have served to sum up the state of revision on the eve of every examination that we took in our school lives, including Geography and Geometry —"So little done, so much to do".

In teaching Geography to the more senior classes, Miss Jones hosted presentations cum discourses by individual "volunteers" on relevant topics of her choice. The delivery of the presentations was, in effect, sometimes somewhat halting, rarely very enlightening, and only marginally reliant on research. In fairness, however, a few of the Geography presentations given by fellow sufferers in my Sixth Form days were quite good and well delivered, although they were perhaps not striking enough for their entire substance to remain for too long in the mind afterwards.

My own efforts in the presentation field were probably neither good nor well delivered, as I wasn't much cop at research, and I tended to adapt my imposed topics to Port Isaac themes. What I didn't know, I made up. What I lacked in the way of facts I more than compensated for with imagination. It was as well that I didn't seek Miss Jones' approbation, as it was rarely forthcoming. I think I managed to rise above my shortcomings in a cloud of genuine guilelessness, using soft answers to turn away wrath. These, together with some self-effacing asides, served to give me a not undeserved reputation as a modest buffoon with Miss Jones.

The Geography presentation sessions were occasionally supplemented by what could be described as "field trips", if not "educational excursions", to sites of local importance, chiefly of an industrial nature. There were in addition special external guest lecturers who had probably agreed to come along and talk to us at moments when they were vulnerable to suggestion. To support such guests, the entire school complement was as like as not to be readily dragged along to the lectures, since a well-feigned interest was a small price to pay for an extended break from lessons.

On one memorable day a gentleman who hailed from the Gold Coast of West Africa, shortly to become the independent nation of Ghana, came along to give us a talk on West Africa's natural resources. Gold from the Gold Coast received honourable and frequent mention, but ivory from the neighbouring Ivory Coast somehow failed to get a look in. The fascination of the lecture was not so much in what was said but in who was saying it. Few pupils at the school had ever seen an African man in the flesh before. We were all thoroughly impressed by his magnificence, his accent, his charm and his articulation. He was indeed what education was all about.

Field trips out of school, with Miss Jones as party leader, took in celebrated localities such as the great Delabole slate quarry; Tintagel's Rocky Valley; Slaughter Bridge and its surrounds; and a new cheese factory up at Davidstow, already famous for the excellence of product and volume of production of what hitherto had been a strictly rationed commodity.

The most ambitious field trip, undertaken in my Lower Sixth year, was to Birmingham and the surrounding Midlands, where for a few days those of us who went sensed that we were genuinely venturing to the outer limits of civilisation. The visit, organised in association with Bude Grammar School, was intended to give the participants, from both centres of learning, some exposure to both heavy and light industrial establishments of national importance. The primary attraction was not unnaturally a tour of Cadbury's chocolate factory at Bourneville.

There were twenty-four of us altogether on the Midlands trip — twelve from Sir James Smith's and twelve from Bude — all being boys drawn from the Fourth, Fifth and Sixth Forms. The supervision consisted only of two teachers from Bude Grammar School, so the omission, whether intentional or inadvertent, of any of the Sir James Smith's teaching staff permitted the Sir James Smith's contingent to assume that the trip was as good as unsupervised. Hence, at best, our general conduct was less decorous than it ought to have been, yet we failed to consider that the supervising teachers would be very unlikely not to report back on our manner and deportment to Mr Sprayson. But, it was ever thus.

I was instructed to write a short article on the Birmingham trip for publication in *The Camel*, the annual Sir James Smith's end-ofsummer-term school magazine, and proceeded to do so. I concluded with the flowery homily, "it was much more than a tour of Midlands industrial centres, it was a lesson in life". My article was not only derided but also highly censored. Its final version became so watered down that I couldn't imagine I had written a word of it.

In my Upper Sixth year I attempted to get my own back by inserting a piece in *The Camel* which bypassed the censor. As I was then on the magazine's editorial committee, that kind of undercover activity was not all that difficult to effect. No more than a few copies got run off, however, before my material was seized, confiscated, and probably destroyed by the person with ultimate editorial control for *The Camel*, namely Miss White. Some things just weren't meant to be.

I only once saw Miss Jones in a state of being nonplussed, when even the thinking time resident in her gulping swallow failed to provide its customary salvation. That moment of truth shone out in a Geography lesson when, possibly carried away by a sense of occasion related to the imminent prospect of a visiting lecturer, she began to recount to the class her memories of a visit to the school by a team of Hawaiian dancers whose appearance combined an exotic cultural experience with welcome entertainment. She described the traditional dress worn by the dancers. Commenting on grass skirts came easily enough to her, but then, as she swallowed profusely while her hands insinuated voluptuous curves at chest level, she was singularly unable to find the word that specified the type of garment relevant to the dancers' upper torsos. Her hands moved ever more rapidly as the silence extended. She swallowed again. "Vests", she said.

Joe

Mr E. J. Jeal, teacher of Physics, was nicknamed "Joe". Whether or not Joe was the name that his second initial signified was felt to be a matter of no great importance. As well as Physics, Mr Jeal not in-frequently took PT lessons. Attendance at PT was compulsory, and he made it self-evident that he was more than determined to hold fast to PT always remaining compulsory as long as he had anything to do with it.

As far as physique went, Mr Jeal's version of that was not

particularly prepossessing. He was thin, slightly built, and rather hunched up about the shoulders. Taken at face value, he could have been said to be "weedy". He exhibited a kind of trembling nervous energy that suggested he might be expecting a stick to fall hard across his back at any moment.

The reality was that Mr Jeal was a bundle of toughness to his very core, and therefore constituted an unpredictable force to be reckoned with. His most distinctive feature was a great wedge-like shock of black hair (admittedly shot through with a few fine threads of grey), which leaned forward to almost, but not quite, obscure his eyes. There was no gainsaying that his looks made him the very model of a scientist; a backroom boy broken free from the restrictions of his cocoon and ready to spread wide his wings and take on the world.

Mr Jeal resided in an isolated bungalow surrounded by wind-blasted fir trees standing at a road junction known as White Cross, where the road up from Port Quin and Lundy Bay crossed the Polzeath road coming down from St Endellion via Plain Street. The location meant that Mr Jeal lived a lot closer to Port Isaac than I for one found comfortable, given that my having no great affinity with the science of Physics had created a mutual antipathy between him and me that felt as unnecessary as it did real. In fairness to me, however, Mr Jeal never seemed quite able to shine a spectrum of tolerance in my direction. Our shared lack of common purpose gave me all the motivation I needed to drop Physics like a hot potato in favour of Latin when I entered the Fourth Form, and to appreciate with relief thereafter a lift to my spirits.

Mr Jeal was distinguished from his fellow members of the teaching staff by having had a single verse song written and dedicated to him at an inspired moment in the past by an anonymous lyricist. It was to be hoped that Mr Jeal was unaware of the unique honour done him, as the piece could have been construed as being a little unflattering. Sung to the tune of "John Peel" I heard it performed in the boys' yard on a few occasions, usually in vocal undertones. The lyrics suggested that certain of the subject's private appendages were made from metal alloys of a durable and commercial nature.

It was an interesting song.

As far as I was aware, Mr Jeal was not a horseman, which was probably just as well if the attributes assigned to him in his song had been valid. He commuted between White Cross and Sir James Smith's in a car of substantial vintage — it, like him, kept going in spite of itself. The car seemed to do what was asked of it without inspiring much confidence that it would keep on doing so for very much longer.

Mr Jeal's age, at a guess, might have been somewhere on the far side of forty. His extra-curricular life was additionally a great unknown, although that sort of mystery, which few if any pupils ever attempted to solve, could have been applied equally to all his fellow teachers. Mr Jeal left a trail of watts, volts, ohms, energy, friction, velocity, joules and what have you in the dust of his passage, all girt about in rafts of symbols and formulae larded with letters that were literally all Greek to his pupils.

As an ancillary responsibility, Mr Jeal had charge of the school's stationery cupboard, which he opened at a fixed time in the week for the issue of new exercise books. To get a new one you had to hand over the old one to him, which he would then inspect minutely to check that each and every page was properly filled with the fruits of either in-school exercises or homework. If the old exercise book wasn't full up with writing on every one of its pages, you wouldn't get a replacement. Mr Jeal's technique of refusal was rarely cordial. Indeed, he treated the stationery cupboard and its contents as his own personal fiefdom, and regarded any stationery-usage irregularity as a personal insult.

What roused his wrath to its greatest heights, however, was not so much the discovery of blank pages as the improper treatment of exercise books. He was in his most unhappy frame of mind when he identified an exercise book handed in for replacement as having had pages extracted from it. He evidently assumed that such a major infraction as page theft could only have been committed for personal gain. Mr Jeal knew, by feel alone, precisely how many pages an exercise book was light by, and denounced the perpetrator of the extraction outrage in stinging tones.

Transcribing jokes heard on the radio into a school rough book, as Pat Sleeman and I did, also went very much against Mr Jeal's grain, promoting the inevitably angry reaction. A rough book was intended to be used to work school tasks out in pencil (on any subject) prior to copying the results in ink into a subject-specific exercise book. Of course, it didn't take much for Mr Jeal to give a bawling out on those grounds, whether or not it was deserved. Being the subject of his inclement attention didn't bother me too much, even if now and then I had to forgo the provision of a new rough book until an assigned period of penance had been worked through.

I was sure that by his own lights Mr Jeal was a decent man with a good heart, it being only a pity that he didn't wear that good heart on his sleeve.

Bert

Mr Jeal's wire-brush stiffness, brittle demeanour and abrasive tongue were neatly counterbalanced by the character of Mr B. S. Turner (known as "Bert") who was himself the epitome of suave gentility, a man as warmly avuncular and jovial as he was dedicated to his culturally rich teaching regime of both French and Music. The hair that he didn't quite have on his head was made up for by his trademark moustache. His average height and solid build leaned towards providing him with a jowly rotundity. He and Mr Jeal might have been Watson and Holmes respectively.

Mr Turner taught his pair of subjects as if the one was an extension of the other, with both being definitively interchangeable. To the extent that each of them was foreign to so many pupils and couched in language and symbols they didn't pretend to understand, Mr Turner played it all just right. He made Music especially enjoyable as they sang along to his piano accompaniment. If the way forward wasn't exactly adventurous, it was at least walked with enthusiasm and managed to avoid highbrow overtones.

The musical repertoire that Mr Turner exposed us to was tightly constrained, however. No element of it was knowingly permitted to stray into the realm of popular songs of the day. Our choral renditions were typified by numbers of the classic calibre of "Drink To Me Only With Thine Eyes"; "All Through the Night"; "Sweet Lass of Richmond Hill"; and "Gaudeamus Igitur", to name but a few. At one time his arrangement of "Nymphs and Shepherds" rose to the top of our musical bowl as did cream from scalded milk, as he endeavoured to reprise a surprisingly successful recording of the same by the Luton Girls' Choir, which for many of us had hitherto helped to mar the reasonably smooth flow of Sunday afternoon's "Two-way Family Favourites".

The Sir James Smith's pool of vocal talent was not especially rich in soloists, which was no major handicap, as we relied on singing in groups to iron out any individual discordancy. The plaudits which we won were perhaps awarded less for what we sang than for the fact that we had finished singing it.

With all that set aside, community singing brought a class to-gether, since whether or not you could carry a tune you were always welcome to stand in a choir. I was living proof of that reality — Mr Turner declared me to be tone deaf, although I didn't think I was, yet he allowed me to be a member of the class choir without hindrance or let. He positioned me at the back of the group with instructions to move my lips, but not to exercise my vocal cords. This was a handsome compromise, typical of Mr Turner's good will and chari-table nature.

For all his self-evident skill in merging the least with the best and allowing everyone to contribute in their own way though, Mr Turner liked things to be just so. He was fussy about details, and in particular where French was concerned his spirit of teaching was no less than meticulous. Mr Turner liked the disciplined rigour of enumerated lists and idealised the use of economy of space. He lined up verbs, phrases, genders and grammatical niceties with a precision that excluded all frills. The tried and true assumed pride of place in his directory of priorities.

Nothing defined Mr Turner's methodological mind better than did his approach to list enumeration. Numbers encased in brackets, whether square or round, single or double, were pet hates to him. In his view, an itemising number in any list could only be followed by a full stop — no more, no less and sufficient unto the day. There was a simple elegance to this, and almost as with the Lilies of the Field, even Solomon in all his glory was not arrayed like one of those.

Mr Turner smoked, as the popular expression went, like a train. A noticeably strong presence of many expended packets of twenty surrounded him. He would undoubtedly have made a significant contribution to that blue-hazed cloud which roiled its way out of the Staff Room into the Third Form room whenever the common linking door was opened.

Mr Turner's teaching of French was gently but thoroughly done. He suffered all fools gladly, and as a consequence even the most impervious among us absorbed something of the language in spite of themselves. I had a moderate flair for French, and I managed to do fairly well in Mr Turner's set exams, all through from the First Form to the Fifth Form and O Level. My facility with French went some small way towards making up for my shortfall in the field of Music.

I was therefore expected to do well in French at O Level, and it was much to everyone's surprise, including mine, that I barely escaped failing the exam. It may have been that in his regular marking of my work, Mr Turner had accredited me with rather more than I deserved — in the very antithesis of Miss White's marking technique. On the other hand, I might simply have had a bad O Level day, as I knew full well that I should have done much better than I did.

The grounding in French that I got from Mr Turner was sound enough to reside within me and provide a firm foundation for building on in later years, as was his enumeration system of numbers succeeded by full stops. He was indeed a gifted teacher, but even if he hadn't been, he was a man that it was impossible not to like and admire.

His musical talent provided the accompaniment for all of the school's traditional functions throughout the academic year. Be it piano or organ, Mr Turner was a master at the keyboard of either.

And so it came to pass that at the Christmas Festival of Nine Lessons and Carols in the year following my departure from Sir James Smith's, held as always at the chapel in the heart of Camelford, Mr Turner, while seated at the organ, suffered a sudden seizure and left this world on a literal high note. The sadness and the shock of his passing stunned all who had been his pupils, far and wide. And yet, on reflection, there was something poetic about his final exit, made in the service of Sir James Smith's, doing what he loved, doing what he did best, and leaving a legacy of being remembered with pleasure and affection.

Alfie

Compliments of a similar kind to those due to Mr Turner could be equally heaped on Mr A. J. Hooper, who taught Mathematics (Pure and Applied) and Religious Instruction, and additionally put in what was probably more than an adequate devotion to sports duties. For some members of the teaching staff, the supervision of sport and games was an assigned chore which the evidence suggested had not been eagerly sought. However, where Mr Hooper was concerned, taking charge of sports seemed to agree with him.

Known as "Alfie", Mr Hooper was a man blessed with the comfort of middle age. His redoubtable personality and warmth of character overcame the fact that he could not be described as handsome, no matter how far the imagination might be stretched. His hair was receding like an ebb tide on either side of his forehead, leaving such greying remains as lurked in the middle to form an accentuated quiff that only a scalp hunter could have coveted. His face, heavy featured, weathered and clearly lived in, expressed a vaguely simian quality. On him, it all conveyed an air of pleasing gravitas, which, since he was an itinerant local preacher of the Methodist persuasion, did him no harm at all.

Once in a while, Mr Hooper came along to preach at one or other of the two Methodist chapels in Port Isaac — I didn't ever attend his services though, as I was of the Church persuasion and hence required to be unsympathetic to all Chapel activities that smacked directly of Bible punching. This weighty obligation was open to adjustment, however, when it was time for the Chapel Sunday School Christmas party. In addition, activities at the Chapel Youth Club, held under the warm-hearted direction of Mr Harold Provis, another local preacher of note and a man I took pleasure in calling my friend, were by no means off limits. Thus was the spirit of religious tolerance maintained when good cheer was afoot.

Because of, if not in spite of, his prowess as a local preacher, Mr Hooper made a perfect fit to teach Religious Instruction (RI). He set a steady course, letting ecumenism reign as the great charade played itself out. Most of us who regularly attended Sunday services of worship, whether of Church or Chapel affiliation, did so under the duress of elders and betters who in so many instances had not set foot in any religious establishment for many a good year. Religious backsliding was not something any one of them would ever have been prepared to admit to, however, since that implied hell as their not unlikely eventual destiny.

I only knew of one pupil at Sir James Smith's who was excused attendance at Mr Hooper's RI lessons, and was told that it was owing to her being of the Roman Catholic faith. A Roman Catholic was a rare breed indeed in North Cornwall. Not much was known about them, and they were regarded with the kind of air of nervous acceptance that was normally used to mask fear of the unknown.

An examination of the Bible that I used in Mr Hooper's RI classes confirms that our greatest intensity of focus was directed at the Gospel according to St Matthew. The relevant opening pages of the New Testament are tattered and dog-eared at the edges, and bear various annotations singling out inspiring parables and unconvincing tales of miracles. The Bible was one of my St Peter's church Sunday School attendance prizes. Since Sir James Smith's didn't provide its pupils with copies of the Good Book, we all had to provide our own. RI lessons were conducted at an easy pace, in general calling for no great effort to be made beyond the need to memorise and quote various passages of scripture. We tended to see RI lessons as green pastures in which to lie down until the end of lesson bell was rung.

One day in a Fourth Form RI lesson, Mr Hooper introduced us to the author C. S. Lewis through the medium of one of that author's books, a slim volume entitled *The Screwtape Letters*. We were invited to read passages from the book, which was in all likelihood very well written, informative and thought-provoking. All one might say about it is that in the maw of the Fourth Form, the one thing which was learned from the book was that its title was more interesting than its contents.

Mr Hooper was also a wholly proficient Maths teacher, and it must stand as a true measure of just how good he was that he managed to condition me to be able to grasp the basics of a range of aspects of pure maths, with algebra, calculus, integration, trigonometry and co-ordinate geometry looming large, and concepts like the googol and the googol plex thrown in for good measure. Applied maths, however — statics and dynamics — were totally beyond my ability to comprehend, and nothing Mr Hooper or anyone else could do succeeded in raising any genuine glimmer of understanding in me as to what they were all about. I found applied maths to be a dense and impenetrable jungle that blunted the steel of my resolve to cut through it.

Yet, in spite of that constraint, I obtained a marginal pass in A Level maths, which I owed both to Mr Hooper's tuition and to my learning by heart the templates of all the applied maths textbook examples and using them where they seemed to fit the A Level exam questions. There was little or no academic merit in it, but a pass was a pass, and where applied maths was concerned, that was near enough for me.

Mr Hooper was the appointed Fourth Form master, and so naturally it was during my year in the Fourth that I saw the most of him, down in the Fourth Form room adjacent to the canteen. As a result of the Fourth's comparative isolation, members of the teaching staff were not easily able to sneak up to us in order to put in a sudden appearance and catch us off guard. They could almost always be seen descending from the main school level above, and forewarned was forearmed after all. Boisterousness and various patterns of horseplay all too often took on an excess of their own in the Fourth Form room, in a way that would not have been feasible up in the more intensively patrolled reaches of the school.

It was a well-known fact that a desk lid had to be slammed shut rather than being gently lowered for that purpose. Slamming was a satisfying act, done normally on an *ad hoc* basis. One morning after Assembly, a kind of mass class hysteria seemed to generate itself, in which the entire body of the Fourth engaged in a frenzy of desk-lid slamming. The action created a thunderous clatter and was supremely satisfying for as long as it lasted. As it was, we all became so involved in slamming desk lids up and down that Mr Hooper's approach and arrival took place for once without warning. He came in haste, drawn by the imminence of the first lesson of the day, and driven by an urgent imperative to quell a volume of noise that might well have been audible down on the River Camel bridge.

The mass crashing of desk lids triggered latent heat in Mr Hooper that had little in common with local preacher norms. He trembled not with the flames of the Holy Spirit as much as with the fires of

Satan's Pit — Satan's other pit that is, not the one at Delabole. He entered red of face, yelling wild entreaties at us to stop that went unheeded for a long few moments, until the resounding clatter of desk lids slowly faded and died, as if a final encore had reluctantly run its course. As far too many of us were implicated as desk-lid slammers for individual examples to be made, Mr Hooper put the entire Fourth Form on report to Mr Sprayson for what he could only describe as an outrageous infraction of the mystical school rules as well as for the wanton abuse of school property.

An incident like that didn't happen again, which was a pity really, as it had all been so enjoyable in its execution.

The Fourth Form desks were set up in four columns, each column consisting nominally of six desks. Each desk was skid-mounted with a fitted bench-like seat, so that, when you were seated, it took very little footwork to move your desk forwards or backwards in order to bring it into respective contact with the desk in front of or behind you in your column. Through teamwork, and operating in minutely surreptitious increments, we discovered that in the course of a lesson we could not only shunt a column of desks a few feet forward, but also withdraw the column to its original position while leaving the desk at the head of the column to fend for itself out at the front in splendid isolation. The front desk in my column of six was occupied by Pat Sleeman, who, with little in the way of meat on his bones, was easy to push forward, although much less easy to placate afterwards.

I don't think that Mr Hooper, or for that matter any of the others among our teachers, ever quite cottoned on to the snail-pace to-and-fro shuffle of Fourth Form desks, but if they did then perhaps they reckoned it to be not without some secret appeal to their sorely tried senses of humour.

Mr Perry

Mr Perry, who had no discernible nickname, dwelled in Boscastle, taught Woodwork, only Woodwork and nothing but Woodwork, and as a consequence of his exclusive Woodwork credentials he didn't seem to be quite as real in professional teaching terms as were other members of the teaching staff. Woodwork, a practical subject, was taught only to boys. The equivalent subject of specialisation on the girls' side of the school was Domestic Science, taken by the Art mistress, Miss Holloway.

Mr Perry was a Woodwork master in all senses of the term. He clearly had an affinity with the smell of sawdust, the rustle of wood shavings and the performance of interesting acts using bits of cut wood. He demonstrated much expertise in assembling and precisely integrating the said pieces of wood into artefacts pleasing to the eye, with never a nail, a screw or an element of brute force in sight.

The positive qualities of Woodwork lay for me in the clean smell of the timber, its beauteous grain, its timelessness, its variety, and the manner in which it all fell together so ideally in the hands of a gifted craftsman. Wood combined the aesthetic with the historic. What I knew about it as a working medium was not much, although I was proficient in a depth of knowledge of the identity and the natural history of every species of tree that grew in the valleys around Port Isaac, together with the wild flowers they sheltered, the wild animals they nurtured, and the birds that nested in them.

The darker side of the Woodwork coin was that when it came to handling seasoned wood to construct acceptable household items, utilities or even pure *objets d'art*, I was as ham-handed as they came. Precision in measurement, drawing lines with a thick carpenter's pencil, removing a bit of wood here and a bit more there with a saw, a plane or a sometimes lethal chisel, left my mortises rattling in their tenons and my dovetails moulting, hanging together by much less than a wing and a feathery prayer. A line from a song—"To be a farmer's boy"—that we gave great voice to in Mr Turner's choral sessions more or less summed me up: "For those who 'wood' work, 'tis hard to want and wander for employ-hoy-hoy-hoy-hoy-hoy".

Mr Perry was fair of skin, with a face rife with freckles. He had sparse reddish hair which fell in light waves on a head he held down and thrust a little forward. It gave him the quizzical appearance of a man on a quest who had not been fully briefed on what he was supposed to be looking for. He gave the impression of one well used to being disappointed by pupils who demonstrated scant aptitude for his subject.

Once in a while, however, as always, a rare talent would emerge to grace one or other of his classes, and that would provide the motivation for Mr Perry to end his woodworking day feeling justified. On the other hand, he generally made a good showing in terms of amiability and calmness of presence—when and if he was present, that is, since in class his comings and goings had much in common with the wind.

Mr Perry was a fully fledged member of Sir James Smith's staff of dedicated smokers, and for him, nipping out of his Woodwork theatre of operations to partake of a cigarette or two was a gift horse never to be looked in the mouth when opportunity knocked. Hence in his classes we were frequently left to follow our own devices for periods consistent with the life span of a Woodbine smoked from end to end.

The high point of my association with Mr Perry, which ended in the Fourth Form when the onset of more academic priorities rendered desirable my discontinuing with Woodwork lessons, came with my making a mirror frame in stained pine. Its dimensions were about a foot and a half long by a foot wide. Its rigidity was a tribute to the holding power of the evil-smelling and horribly glutinous wood glue that we were induced to apply to shaky joints. The final product, with fitted mirror, did singular duty for a long time in our bathroom at home in Hartland Road. It was a poor thing, but mine own, a modest triumph destined never to be repeated. Sometimes I wondered if there might ever be a limit to the list of school subjects that I wasn't any good at.

Mr Perry's wife, as noted previously, was the School Secretary. She was in every sense of the word the Headmaster's gatekeeper and guarded access to the great man with the utmost zeal. Mrs Perry always seemed to be full of energetic efficiency, and in all likelihood came to assume far more powers that could have appeared in her job description, if she ever had one. She was most likely not too popular with the rank and file of the teaching staff, whose ability to approach Mr Sprayson directly was severely blunted when she was around. On the other hand, that might have been all to the good. Mrs Perry was always nice to me, and that allowed me to place her on a bit of a pedestal.

Holloway

The most easy-going of all the teaching staff was Miss Holloway, the Art mistress. She moved slowly, as if she was wading through treacle, and she bore such a personally distinctive air of dissociation from what was going on around her that it gave her character an almost saintly quality.

Miss Holloway was generally referred to by her surname when we spoke of her. That was tantamount to having a nickname, being in its way an affectionately honorific device. Her youth lay in tatters a long way behind her. Her advancing age was emphasised by that slow and dreamy manner which hesitated not far short of the border of doddering country. Miss Holloway was either unwilling to tell anyone off properly or blissfully incapable of doing so. Her Art lessons, not simply for pupils of artistic temperament but also for those who like myself were in various phases of being devoid of the same, were pleasantly constructive oases within the ephemeral desert of serious school business. No one had to work at putting one over on Miss Holloway, as there was no need for that sort of thing where she was concerned.

In *School Friend,* a popular comic of the day intended to be read by girls yet perused with equal avidity by many boys, a regular page was devoted to the exploits of "Dilly Dreem, the lovable duffer", an encapsulated title that could have been made to measure for Miss Holloway. She was wholly charitable, and unto her pupils, most of whom had yet to learn that charity never failed, Miss Holloway suffered long, and was kind. She rejoiced not in iniquity, rejoicing only in the truth.

I don't remember a great deal about being taught by her, although I must have dealt with her classes well enough, even if Art and I once again had little in common. I stopped doing Art as a subject before O Level, most likely when I dwelt in that early graveyard of Physics, the Fourth Form.

The Art room was located in the stone-built out-house annex at the back of the school. It was furnished with long work benches, the surfaces of which were festooned with pencils, paints, inks, slabs of plasticine, modelling clay and sheets of blank paper. Miss Holloway, in her characteristically dusty dishevelment, presided over both the majesty and the crudeness of output generated by the tasks she set, casting her pearls willingly before swine.

She invigilated regularly in the canteen at dinner time, leading the assembled hopefuls in Grace before letting them loose to do their worst with what the menu had to offer. The standard Grace for recitation at dinner time was "For what we are about to receive, may the Lord make us truly thankful" (not that there was much chance of that happening), but one day Miss Holloway surprised us all by pronouncing "*Benedictus, benedicat*" as the Grace. It was such a break from tradition that it came as quite a shock and made a great talking point thereafter, not least for those of us who wanted to find out what it actually meant.

Quickie

Miss Holloway's graceful excursion into Latin may have risen to the fore through her great friendship with, and mentoring of, Miss Quick, who came to Sir James Smith's to teach Latin following the sudden retirement from the field of Miss Battle. I was fortunate to be taught by Miss Quick, or "Quickie" as she soon became known.

Miss Quick was as demure as she was mild of manner and staid in appearance. She dressed and looked as if she had just stepped out of the mid-nineteen-forties, even though she was young enough to have gone in for something of a more cutting-edge style of attire now that the rapidly burgeoning fashions of the nineteen-fifties were with us.

It appeared that Miss Quick probably shared accommodation with Miss Holloway, as they both seemed to come and go from the school in one another's company. Together they must have formed a garland of tranquillity in the otherwise smoke-decked wastes of the Staff Room.

The Latin brought to me via Miss Quick provided a link to those far off days when speakers of that tongue ruled the world. Latin had subsequently come to form the time-honoured basis for drafting and defining the substance of state, legal and religious documentation, current even to our very day. Miss Quick's gentleness of character was to a large extent wasted on the stony ground trodden by more than a few of her pupils, but, on one like me whose manner and deportment needed improving, I liked to think that she planted fertile seeds of conduct that blossomed up into a fair and constant harvest with the years.

As with almost all my Sir James Smith's teachers, some of whom went on to that great Staff Room in the sky, and others who no doubt relocated to the fiery, smoke-filled corridors down below, I don't know how Miss Quick fared with her career in the years after my leaving Sir James Smith's in 1957. She became unwell during the time when I was her pupil, which meant she had to take various absences from school, and these, in what is a sad commentary, generally went unremarked. Whatever her destiny or fate, her presence in the world made it a better place for me.

Pam

At about the time when I entered the Fourth Form, the school introduced the subject of Biology to its science curriculum. The teaching of Biology began in the lower forms and built up from there as the guinea pig juniors progressed to reach the senior levels. I had no connection with Biology of course, but was able to observe, at arms-length as it were, the nature and foibles of the teaching staff brought in to service the innovation.

The first of these, the founder teacher, was Miss Pamela Lyons, who became known as "Pam" or "Pammy". In her essence, Miss Lyons was everything that her Staff Room colleagues, both male and female, were not and never could be. She was young, vivacious, fashionable, glamorous, immaculate and devil-may-care, an immediate focus for the attention of all boys from the Fourth Form upwards. With such credentials we thought, this lady's tenure at Sir James Smith's was not likely to be long lived.

It was interesting to speculate on how well, or alternatively how not so well, Miss Lyons' flamboyance resonated with her rather less colourful fellow-members of staff, or alternatively with the ponderous gravitas of the school's board of governors, led by that noble aristocrat from the Molesworth St Aubyn lineage, Sir John (Bart), Sir John's presence at any of the school's annual functions, most especially on Speech Day, provided a total assurance that fluent cliche cloaked in sentimental platitudes would be visited on all.

On one monumental day, Miss Lyons, having changed into sports supervisory gear somewhere or other in the school precincts (a moot question as to locality since the available facilities tended not to be conducive to that sort of thing for teachers), accidentally (allegedly) dropped an item of her intimate apparel when she was on her way back to the Staff Room. The garment was discovered where it fell by a Second Form pupil named Duncan Andrew, who appeared not to realise that what he held in his hands was pure gold. He thereafter became an instant celebrity and the envy of his peers, not least those of his peers who sat concurrently in the Sixth Form. Unfortunately, the item of clothing was not made available to them to be passed around, as Duncan took it at once to the Staff Room, knocked on the door, and entered holding it aloft in a triumphal endeavour to be showered with plaudits for finding it. He didn't quite get the praise he sought, at least not right away, but he was rewarded by a silvery laugh from Miss Lyons as she accepted the flimsy piece from Duncan's hand.

Mr John Williams, who had at that time recently arrived to strengthen the teaching of English, and who had thereby brought a touch of much needed milk of kindness to infuse Miss White's bitter tea, wrote a piece of blank verse in Shakespearian metre for *The Camel* of that year in commemoration of the sporting occasion for which Miss Lyons had seen fit to change her clothes, and included in it a reference to "how Andrew bore away the Lion's belt". Miss White neither could nor would have been able to write with such tongue-in-cheek vitality — or if she had, she might then never have recovered from the experience.

Miss Lyons, invigilating in the canteen one dinner time, found me with a mountainous pile of rice pudding on my plate. This surfeit of rice came about as the result of the common practice in which bigger boys dumped food they didn't like or want upon the plates of smaller boys. The rule was that your plate had to go back to the kitchen with no left-overs on it to mar its surface — otherwise you were in trouble. So if you couldn't eat what you got and there was a victim handy, onto his plate it went. Fortune always favoured the strong, as the ancillary rule was that the weak must neither complain nor tell tales.

Looking at the great heap of rice on my plate, Miss Lyons bet me sixpence that I wouldn't be able to eat it all. I had no alternative but to accept the bet, even though I had no sixpence to my name nor was ever likely to have if the truth be told. I tackled the consumption in a spirit of false bravado, knowing that the capacity of my belly was not nearly as great as my desire to win the bet.

The situation was resolved with recourse to the time-honoured resort of subterfuge that was so often employed in pupil versus teacher contests of will. It had so happened that on a certain day a long while previously a forceful struggle had taken place between two boys sitting across from me at the foot of my canteen table. The boys, both a year senior to me, were Bob Pethick and David (known as "Joe") Callaway. The latter had endeavoured, as was his standard practice, to relieve Bob's plate of an item that he fancied for himself. Joe was adept at doing such things. He was much bigger than Bob (and me), and well accustomed to using his native St Teath cunning in pursuit of personal satisfaction. Since plenty was so often in short supply, the strong were rarely backwards in coming forward to grab what they wanted.

Joe had a firm hold of one of Bob's hands, which Bob was trying in vain to pull free. As if relenting, Joe released his grip, whereupon Bob's arm, suddenly released, whipped back at an uncontrolled speed, causing Bob's extended elbow to impact with considerable force on the thin fibreboard coating the canteen wall. Fortunately there was a hollow behind the fibreboard, and all Bob's elbow did was to break through and push a flap of the fibreboard into the hollow. Fate decreed that the incident was not observed by the invigilator of the day, a short frisson of horror at the foot of the table being the only consequence of note.

It was quickly decided that reporting the damage to the wall was likely to do the miscreants more harm than good, as the flap could be easily pulled back into position with judicious use of a little finger, so that the break was only evident to someone who was intent on looking for it. Should it be discovered, all knowledge of how it got to be where it was could be readily denied. And so it was that the existence of the indented flap in the wall was known only to a few.

That this was a blessing in disguise quickly dawned on those of us who were in the picture, as all it needed to permit a spoon to be inserted into the interior cavity of the wall was a light push on the flap. Thus were we provided with a facility for the disposal of unwanted dinner, associated with the surety of always being able to send an empty plate back to the canteen. And it was into that cavity that a fair proportion of my plate's great charge of rice pudding went to join the substantial fruits of the kitchen that had gone before.

Miss Lyons was shown an empty plate, and much to my discredit I was rewarded with her sixpence. She was a good sport of the best kind, and I on that occasion surely wasn't. However, as far as I can recall, that episode represented the sum total of my cheating activities at Sir James Smith's. Nevertheless, regret for what was done remains with me to this day.

Miss Lyons taught at the school for no more than a couple of years,. She was sincerely missed when she left, but hopefully went on to achieve grand things.

Boothby

Miss Lyons' role in the great task of enshrining the subject of Biology into the school curriculum was taken up, following her departure, by a young man named Mr Boothby. He was tall, square of build, clean-shaven, bespectacled, and always turned out immaculately in suit and tie. His hair was fairly close-cropped and held in place by what must have been an adequate, although not excessive, application of something like Brylcreem.

What it all added up to was that Mr Boothby's appearance was stereotypically that of a ranking member of the Gestapo. All that was lacking to complete the picture was to have him don a long black overcoat made from leather. Perhaps he kept such a garment at home for wearing on special occasions.

As far as it went, the perceived image suited the man. He took no prisoners in carrying out his teaching duties, and snapped instructions as if they were military commands. Mr Boothby was, I thought, a genuinely unpleasant and intolerant piece of work. Behind the rimless lenses of his spectacles his eyes peered out through hard slits. As a dinner-time invigilator his patrolling was merciless — his book of alleged infractions seemed limitless and he held the record for canteen evictions by many a country mile. He threw people out for no better reason than that he could.

As previously described, I was one of his higher-profile victims given that I was Head Boy at the time. That incident, which gained much in the telling and re-telling around the school, won me a surge of popular support from the junior boys in particular, as they were only too well aware of Mr Boothby's uncharitable foibles. Their votes were probably instrumental in winning me the Character Prize for that year.

If further moves in the reactive battle of wills with Mr Boothby were not sweet, then they were at least not without a certain fragrance. Whenever fate and the school timetable came together and set Mr Boothby to conduct a Biology class in the Chemistry Lab immediately after one or other of the day's two breaks, it seemed that during the break in question a person, or persons, unknown must have entered the Lab for the sole purpose of opening the release tap on the Kipps apparatus for a few moments. The action allowed a substantial waft of hydrogen sulphide (H_2S) gas to pass into the contained atmosphere of the lab. A little H_2S went a long way, but in order to obtain the assurance that it would travel, the perpetrator, or perpetrators, chose to bleed more rather than less of the gas from the Kipps' storage chamber.

The flaw in the practice was its repetition. Had it occurred only once, or even twice, the smell greeting Mr Boothby at the start of his lesson could have been put down to pure chance, but after it had happened three times the impression that a plot was afoot must have dawned on him. The options open to whoever was responsible were to either stop or face the consequences. It was evidently decided to stop. An odour of rotting eggs might have been a fitting judgement on Mr Boothby, but he had a class with him as well, and they deserved better.

I was in no way gratified by my lack of regard for Mr Boothby, even though I knew that he took considerable satisfaction in demonstrating that power to do good or ill (well, perhaps not good) resided in his hands. In a school environment the big and the strong almost always prevailed, some rightfully so, but there were others, like Mr Boothby, who used their might as a means of living with their own demons.

John

As I knew it, the complement of teaching staff at Sir James Smith's was by and large a quality establishment. In that scheme of things, personal differences that I may have had with some of them were of no long-term significance. There was bound to be a joker or two (or more) in every pack, but they were far eclipsed by the aces, among whom Mr John Williams was not the least.

He joined the school to teach English under Miss White when I was in the Lower Sixth. He was a breath of fresh air and more. Like the US cavalry in a host of memorable "B" films that we saw on Fridays at Port Isaac's Rivoli Cinema, Mr Williams brought along salvation for the many, yet he sadly arrived too late to save those who had fallen to Miss White's slings and arrows in the last stand beneath the shadow of O Level.

Mr Williams didn't have a nickname as such, but nor did he need one to be worthy of affection. He exuded a mighty intellect in all he did, and from his cut, manner, total lack of side and sheer adequacy, a first guess at which institution of learning had brought him to be a master of his craft would not have bothered to look beyond either Oxford or Cambridge, the latter being preferred. For Mr Williams was "donnish" in just the way we imagined a don ought to look — ready, willing and able to take his place in a "Brains Trust" at the drop of a venerable mortar-board.

He was tall, and thin down to the barely decent edge of being emaciated. His hair was longish and slick, quite consistent with the incidence of long hair being a hallmark for intellectualism. A single lock hung on his forehead as if by design. One of the things that impressed me most about him was that, as he told us, he counted the celebrated actor Michael Gough among his close friends.

Truly did Mr Williams have many admirable traits, although what distinguished him most from Miss White was that he was as interested in the pupils he taught as he was in what he taught them. He was tolerant of the slow to learn, encouraged one and all without fear or favour, met triumph and disaster head on, and treated those two impostors just the same.

Mr Williams exuded bland competence. We could all feel it and benefit from it, and yet it came so naturally to him, seemingly without effort, that he must have been unaware of how positive a figure for good he really was in a hitherto Miss White dominated field of fire.

It was when I was in the Upper Sixth that I had the good fortune to take a course of lessons under Mr Williams in the general appreciation of English literature. These lessons were in effect discussion forums on topics related to the works of Shakespeare and certain of the greater and lesser known Victorian and War poets. Some teachers weren't much interested in pupils' opinions, but Mr Williams was not of that ilk. To begin with, we as pupils probably came over to him as ducks' backs in the face of the flowing river of national treasures that he opened to us, but we were to rise eventually like lions to the sonorous grandeur of works such as *Under Milk Wood*. Dylan Thomas's resonance shook me to the core of my being.

That masterpiece of word play appealed to me so much that it went on to inspire the catastrophic play that I wrote in its image. Dylan Thomas would never have guessed at the calibre of events that he set in motion when he took up his pen to commence writing *Under Milk Wood,* and when his words went forth to Sir James Smith's carried by his disciple Mr Williams.

17

Assembly

If the world of Sir James Smith's was a stage, then we who moved through it were merely the players, anticipating both our exits and our usually unremarkable entrances, although without being especially attentive to the script.

Act One, Scene One saw us entering from stage left to join the company of the First Form, whining pupils all, with new satchels of creaking leather, and our morning faces set with varying degrees of grubbiness as we crept like unwilling snails towards Assembly.

The passage of time leading to its inevitable abuse notwithstanding, a good leather satchel was expected to serve its owner for the full seven-year stretch of a grammar school career. A satchel's strap was stout, its buckles stiffly secure and glinting on the carapace, and its capacity as well able to contain the limited needs of the First Former as to strain dangerously under the homework burden of the Sixth Former.

The universal priority attending to a satchel was that it should be observed by members of the general public to be clearly laden to its limits, irrespective of whether or not the contained load, or any part of the same, bore any relevance to either homework or study.

The undeclared objective was to create an image of much work in progress, with whether or not that work would ever be completed being unrelated to the observer's business.

With satchels slung in various styles of carelessness on shoulders ready, with reluctance, to be set to the wheel of the day, and the pushing and shoving contest which marked the school bus disembarkation once again behind us, we wended the slow and desultory way up College Road towards the school, much in the style of a poorly led lynch mob milling around in the vicinity of a sheriff's office and town jail. Although any sense of haste seemed absent, the morning's school Assembly at nine was a pressing deadline antipathetic to too much dragging of feet.

Once we arrived at the school we dropped the satchels off in our designated classrooms. Anyone who possessed an overcoat or a raincoat then hung up that item of apparel in the casual repose of the cloak room, along with any occasionally carried paraphernalia such as PT bags. And then, as the Assembly bell intoned its initial clang, we were galvanised into rapid action as we scrambled to take up processional order-of-seniority line-up places in the designated corridor — boys to the left, girls to the right, with Prefects being ignored in between as they went in vain through the motions of order-keeping patrol.

The bell signalling Assembly, which was incidentally also rung to mark the end of each lesson during the day, was made from fine bell metal and equipped with a wooden handle. It was portable and of an appropriate size to allow it to be swung manually by the appointed ringer of the day, who was required to parade the bell throughout the school buildings so that there was no danger of its metronomic notes being missed by anyone. The bell monitor regarded his or her bell-ringing duty as a genuine privilege, not least for the opportunity it guaranteed them to leave class without let or hindrance at as early a moment as could be got away with in the waning stages of a lesson. Censure descended on the head of the monitor if the bell got rung too early or too late, and so the swinging had to commence spot on time. And so it came to pass, for the most part. There was also undeclared competition between bell monitors as to who among them could ring the bell the loudest. Ultimate clanging volume was vested in rhythmic technique and an arc of swing exceeding one hundred and eighty degrees.

In the manner of a flock of starlings bunching in patterns of effortless unity over a late autumn landscape, the assembly lines moved as one to the Second Form classroom. Slim, green-jacketed hymnbooks could be picked up on the way in. The room filled forwards from the rear, boys on one side and girls on the other, with a column of Prefects occupying the aisle in between.

The teaching staff entered last, marching in to take up their accustomed places in a row of chairs set against the front wall. The Headmaster and Headmistress held the centre ground in the row, immediately behind a tall wooden lectern supporting an intimidatingly massive black leather-bound King James version Bible on its upper slope.

Then, as if at a given moment, Mr Sprayson rose to his feet. He stepped forward to the lectern. The sound made by a falling pin hitting the floor could have been easily audible as his eyes took in the assembled ranks with a searching glance that every individual felt to be directed specifically at him or her. In tones as clear as they were resonant, Mr Sprayson announced the number of the opening hymn to be sung. A great rustle of pages took place, only marginally masked by the introductory bars struck up by Mr Turner.

With the preliminaries out of the way the Assembly had no alternative other than to give vent to song, at which juncture it was at once evident that if harmony was not a strong-point forte, then neither was timing. Everyone started off more or less together, but as in any race to a final Amen, the end was reached with the field rather strung-out. I was very familiar with *Hymns Ancient and Modern* from my St Peter's church background, and knew by heart so many of the hymns in that masterful collection, but the school's little hymnbook drew much of its content from sources other than *A and M*, and as a consequence I never came to develop a great affinity for it.

One hymn sung quite frequently at Assembly, which wasn't from *Hymns A and M* but which I grew to really like, was John Bunyan's "To Be a Pilgrim". As a rule, I felt that school hymns had something of a Chapel core to them, not surprisingly perhaps as it was that arch-Methodist and local preacher Mr Hooper who stood behind the religious fibre of Assembly.

Indeed it was Mr Hooper who selected the passage from the Bible to be read as the lesson that followed hard on the heels of the hymn. Lessons were read by Prefects on a strict roster prepared and posted by Mr Hooper. The order of the roster was not open for debate. When a Prefect's turn came up, he or she stepped up to the lectern, opened the Bible at the correct place (previously marked with a slip of paper) and read the selected passage aloud at a measured pace.

Lessons tended to involve the more well-known Biblical passages, thereby avoiding any of the linguistic pitfalls of the unfamiliar and outright obscure. Special pains were taken to ensure that no passage contained any element of either innuendo or *risqué double-entendre* for senior pupils to snigger at.

There were only two occasions in my experience when lesson reading went a little awry, both instances being attributed to Mr Hooper's roster being either ignored or forgotten. Those respective moments subsequent to the tailing away of the hymn when no one broke ranks to move in the direction of the lectern were fraught with tension. Sir James Smith's thrived on the comfort of familiar routine, and deviations from the same were disturbing. To ease one of the painful breaks in continuity a quick-thinking Prefect threw caution to the wind, ran to the lectern, opened the Bible, and read a passage from the first page his eyes fell upon, which chanced to be somewhere buried deep in the impenetrable meanderings of the Old Testament prophets. So selflessly was this deed done that apart from Mr Hooper and the situation-rescuing reader, few who were present at that Assembly seemed to take note of the irregularity of hearing a lesson which made no sense — probably because as usual most of them weren't listening.

At the second instance of lesson reading failure, Prefect action was very much lacking. Following a pause of intensely pregnant proportions it then fell to Mr Sprayson to heave the Bible open and do the honourable thing. This occurred during my tenure as Head Boy, and led to some heavy criticism being thrown my way by Mr Jeal, who made no secret of his feelings that I had shirked both duty and responsibility in not taking hold of the situation. That was fair enough comment I thought, even if it was voiced by a man who was not always so objective in his dealings with me.

At the conclusion of each lesson reading, in order to dispel any doubt in anyone's mind that the reading was indeed over, the lesson reader was expected to pause for a couple of heartbeats before coming up with the traditional advice to listeners and non-listeners alike that "Here endeth the lesson". It was then required that the Bible should be closed in a manner that was both decorous and respectful, slamming being off-limits, prior to the reader going back to his or her place.

On one occasion when I was lesson reader I deviated from the script by declaring "That is the end of the lesson". These few words made Mr Sprayson very unhappy. It seemed that you messed with the lesson-ending tradition at your own risk.

A significant hurdle for me in lesson reading was contained in the passage One Corinthians, Chapter Thirteen. This was always read at the final Assembly on the last day of each term by the Head Boy, and so it came to be that when I was Head Boy that particular task fell to me. The chapter served as a *de facto* herald of the prospect of holidays to come. I lapped the passage up and savoured the truth of its words, but never seemed quite able to get away from mangling the sixth verse with its "rejoiceth not in iniquity, but rejoiceth in the truth". These words were a genuine tongue twister for me, and try as I might, I couldn't get my tongue to press against the back of my front teeth in the right sequence.

Almost before the echoes of here-endeth-the-lesson had ceased to resound in the dusty eaves above the lectern, Mr Sprayson launched into a recitation of the day's notices and announcements. The little snippets of information that he divulged to the Assembly were supposed to be informative, and sometimes were, but more usually they leaned towards being too mundane to merit much in the way of close attention.

In the notices and announcements, things that had already happened, and which we all therefore knew about, were confirmed; suggestions were made as to things that might be likely to happen (and we only needed to worry about them if and when they did); positive declarations were made as to what would definitely happen in terms of immediately scheduled events on the school's calendar; advice was given on sporting fixtures and lists of team members, on award ceremonies, on pupil achievements and honours and on arrivals and departures of members of the teaching staff (such departures occurred only infrequently in any case, and all too rarely seemed to feature unpopular members of staff).

Once in a while the announcements got to be enlivened by an

admonitory harangue from Mr Sprayson, usually with an emphasis on reported infringements of the moveable feast that was the School Rules. Hardy annuals among the litany of abhorrent and unseemly acts perpetrated were the dropping of litter and incidences of surreptitious smoking within the already less than fragrant confines of the boys' lavatory block.

The imminence of the bell to mark the start of the day's initial class placed a definite curb on the time available for announcements. Mr Sprayson wound the proceedings up with the delivery of a prayer or two for the health and wellbeing of the school community, and led the Assembly in a communal recitation of the Lord's Prayer. Since the school seemed to thrive well enough those prayers must have worked.

At that, there ended (or here endeth) the day's Assembly. We filed back out under the sternly critical scrutiny of the row of teaching staff at the front to go to our specific classrooms. It was all over; a story, a hymn and a prayer, not unlike "Five to Ten" on the Home Service.

Staff smiles were rationed at Assembly, and only likely to be seen if Mr Sprayson evoked a witticism, or cracked a characteristic joke worthy of making even the most hardened devotee of *Workers' Playtime* cringe inwardly. It was likely that anyone who had to deal with the likes of Sir James Smith's pupils on a daily basis would have had little to smile about anyway.

In rare instances, an extraordinary touch of drama would come to the Assembly proceedings, as for example when a pupil fainted and needed to be carried out of the room amid much commotion, some of which was sincere and some of which wasn't. A few Sixth Formers once pulled a contrived faint as a ruse to get out of Assembly early. The alacrity and eagerness with which they sprang into action to remove the victim contrasted so much with their normal torpor that suspicions were raised in the minds of a few staff members that all might not be exactly as it seemed. That it worked in their favour was a credit to all concerned with the plan and its execution.

A St Teath girl, two forms senior to me, could always be relied on to produce a genuine epileptic fit somewhere or other in the school precincts on a once or twice a term basis. Sometimes such a fit would come upon her in Assembly. Her classmates were familiar with her medical condition and knew how to handle her in a matter of fact way without any fuss. They placed a pencil between her teeth for her to bite down on. Many a good pencil must have met its splintery end in that way, but where disrupting Assembly was an incidental factor, the pencil went down in a good cause.

18

Sufficient Unto the Day

The little tune of a regular school day, as they said in *Much-Binding-in-the-Marsh*, ran something like this:

08.45	School buses arrive in College Road
09.00	Assembly
09.10 — 10.00	First Lesson (and calling of class registers)
10.00 — 11.00	Second Lesson
11.00 — 11.15	First Break (Milk issue)
11.15 — 12.15	Third Lesson
12.15 — 13.45	DINNER TIME!
12.30 — 13.00	*First Sitting*
13.00 — 13.30	*Second Sitting*
13.45 — 14.45	Fourth Lesson
14.45 — 15.00	Second Break
15.00 — 16.00	Fifth Lesson
16.15	Departure of school buses from College Road

Sometimes the First and Second Lessons might be set back to back, integrated into a Double Lesson on a single subject. Double Lessons were always a daunting prospect to confront, as much in the anticipation of them as in actually having to sit through them. They

251

mostly seemed to involve English Literature or Geography, neither of which was a subject conducive to easing the burden.

The inter-lesson bell brought no relief when a Double Lesson was in play. Most probably the doubling-up was an artifice used to fill a gap in the school's lesson timetable that could otherwise not have been closed, much like force-fitting a wrong-shaped piece into a space in a jigsaw puzzle, once the failure to find the correct piece had gone on long enough to become too much of a frustration to be borne.

However, there was always the First Break of the day to look forward to, although even that wasn't all sweetness and light, as we were each required within its short compass to imbibe that distasteful half a pint of milk. Not everyone was a milk drinker by choice, although it had to be admitted that milk played a vital role as an additive to tea (milk in the cup first and tea afterwards and definitely not the other way around), and was equally beneficial in a watered-down and heated-up role when poured over small squares of sugar-sprinkled cut-up bread for breakfast.

All in all, the milk distribution process cut far too big a hole in the precious fifteen minutes of First Break time. The peripatetic bell rang all too soon at a quarter past eleven to summon the faithful as well as the reluctant back to their classrooms to put in the hour leading to Dinner Time.

Dinner Time was a fulcrum of peace on which the struggle for survival against the odds which constituted the bulk of the school day on either side was balanced finely. The thought of dinner should have ensured that no matter how bad the morning had been, there was always something to look forward to at the end of it, but unfortunately, school dinners at Sir James Smith's were all too often mere headstones in a churchyard of blighted hope.

School dinners had also been available at Port Isaac County

Primary School, but there were only a few who lived in the near and relatively near vicinity of the school who availed themselves of the facility. The majority of recipients of this culinary largesse hailed from outlying areas too far removed from the Primary School in terms of distance to allow them the time to walk home when dinner was due.

In Port Isaac, I lived just across the road from school in Canadian Terrace, so was always able to go home for dinner and took great comfort in the opportunity. Irrespective of how meagre our fare at home might be, it was always welcome, and moreover I knew that my mother or my Gran would have cooked it to my taste. Indeed, it was pretty universal that no serious thought was given to eating any-where other than at home. To have done otherwise would have been tantamount to practising blasphemy. There was a sanctity in eating dinner at home that was not to be taken lightly by non-believers.

Thus it was only when I began at Sir James Smith's that I was confronted for the first time in my life with a requirement to partake of school dinners. Yet when there was no chance to go home, and no possibility of avoiding the inevitable, you just had to bow your head, swallow your unease, and get on with it.

Not the least hurdle facing the would-be diner in the Sir James Smith's canteen, irrespective of his or her unwillingness to consume what was on offer, was that the meals came at a price, payable in advance. Dinner money for the week ahead had to be brought to school and handed over to the teacher when your name was called out from the class register before the first lesson on Mondays. The cost was not exceptional at no more than a few pence per day, but for all that, there were families that struggled to come up with the few bob each week. On several occasions I was one of those who had nothing in hand to put on the teacher's desk when I was summoned by the register.

It was always obvious that the teacher knew full well why dinner money was not forthcoming from certain individuals, and yet an explanation for the shortfall was always demanded, as if the dues of humiliation were being sought in lieu of cash. No pupil ever confessed poverty openly, as to do so would have damaged such vestiges of pride as the pupil possessed.

I took the same tack as others by declaring that I had brought the dinner money with me from home, but must have lost it through a hole in the lining of the pocket I had put the money in. Holes in pockets were common, and pockets could easily be turned inside out to provide the supporting evidence. Some pocket linings were graced by holes big enough to push your hand through, but you didn't want to exhibit those for fear of having embarrassing conclusions being drawn as to the purpose of the holes.

Among other well-worn excuses regarding the non-payment of dinner money were that the money had been forgotten at home and would (hopefully) be brought in tomorrow, or that you had put it down somewhere, had forgotten to pick it up again, and now couldn't remember where that somewhere was. No-one who was registered for school dinners was ever refused canteen entry for non-payment, however, so in the end it didn't really matter, just as long as the dinner money turned up sometime, as it generally did.

Dinner Time took place in two sittings, each with a duration of half an hour, the first for the girls and the second for the boys. This formula of segregation had nothing of discrimination about it, and simply worked for the best in the context of its time. We were all used to eating in a hurry at home, so that the time allocation did not pose any constraint. Apart from the need for decorous behaviour in all its many guises to be observed in the canteen, the governing rule was that there were to be no leftovers. The most fortunate were those who possessed the art and skill of rapid swallowing without tasting.

Any inequity of share-out caused much resentment in the hearts of those who bore the brunt of it, and blatant unfairness was likely to set classmate against classmate. We were all ultra-sensitive to the fair apportionment of food.

As to the meals themselves, to put the best gloss on what turned up on our plates, it could be described as plain fare with the emphasis on plain. Words like tasty, appetising or wholesome did not immediately spring to mind on a daily basis, although occasionally something good might come along to hit the mark. The rareness of such events made them all the more welcome, but as a rule, expectations were never elevated.

During the Dinner Time period, irrespective of whether or not you were on the first or second sitting, there was a chance to take a walk outside the school premises for half an hour or so. By turning left up College Road at the entry to the school you could follow the road to where it transformed into the sylvan path leading down to and along the left bank of the River Camel. If you turned right, you descended College Road and could then turn left at the bottom to walk along to and over the bridge across the river, and then proceed to greet either the well-concealed delights of Camelford's town centre, or visit the park that flanked an upstream section of the right bank of the river.

As one who was conditioned to what Port Isaac had to offer, I thought that the town of Camelford was, frankly, not up to much. In Camelford's favour, it was vastly preferable to Delabole, although the achievement of that kind of superiority didn't call for anything especially exacting.

The rules for going into the town were few and simple, seemingly designed to curb the enthusiasm of any pupil whose manner and deportment needed improving. They were, namely, that school uniform (inclusive of the much-hated cap) must be worn at all times; that the observation of absolute decorum was mandatory; and that the dropping of litter was forbidden, and would, if spotted, cause the perpetrator to be regarded by Mr Sprayson as the author of a crime against humanity.

The shops of Camelford were off-limits to Sir James Smith's pupils only to the extent that entry purely for browsing purposes was not looked on fondly by the shopkeepers. If you were not intent on buying something you were forthrightly exhorted to stay away. Therefore the impecunious kept the displeasure of shopkeepers at bay by peering through their windows at the stock within.

One dinner time, I went down into Camelford to buy for my father, a keen if perennially unsuccessful flutterer on horse races, and Mr Donald Kent, his equally less than adept partner in racing form, a copy of the weekly racing journal, *The Sporting Life Guide*, at the shop of Mr Batten, the newsagent. Both my father and Donald shared an additional bond of having been wartime submariners who had consequentially contracted serious tuberculosis. The *Sporting Life Guide* was not stocked by Mrs Rowe, the newsagent in Port Isaac, and nor, evidently, could it be ordered from her. I found out why when Mr Batten became at once aghast at my request and instructed me to leave his shop forthwith. He further admonished me by declaring that he was considering reporting me to the Headmaster for involvement in gambling. It took all sorts of qualities to make a society, and it seemed the Chapel outlook was not the least of these. Through town I wandered, not quite as lonely as a cloud, yet still floating through wind and chill, and not forgetting the sun, if and when it shone.

Mid-afternoon brought the Second Break of the day, in this

instance devoid of any rigid structural formality of the type represented by the First Break's milk distribution. If we were lucky, a fight might get going in Second Break time, and be joined by an instant ring of spectators several deep, whose job was to hinder the access of Prefects or members of the teaching staff who might be anxious to stop the action.

Those who fought with one another entertained alleged grievances for the *causus belli* that were thought to hold at least enough substance for ritual translation into aggressive showmanship. Few if any of the blows struck during confrontations would have threatened the integrity of a rice pudding skin — flailing, pushing and impressive gesticulation formed the order of battle, all choreographed on the full understanding that some form of authority would be along to halt the display well before it could get out of hand.

Needless to say, no such contests ever took place during the four-o'clock exodus down College Road to the buses waiting to take us home. That particular moment of transit was wholly antipathetic to time wasting, prevarication and procrastination. The straight, narrow and smooth path home was held to be inviolate.

19

Hardy Annuals

For the most part, the school day ran its allotted course under the umbrella of a familiar routine. It rolled along as if by rote, much like chanting the twelve times table. Doing things in the right way was what counted. Routine was the core ingredient in the recipe holding the school intact, so as to ensure that it always moved forward in strength and as a whole. If you thought too much about it, then the momentum might be lost. The routine was bland as if by definition, but was always open to be spiced up by an addition of the unexpected.

On the other hand, not all of the Sir James Smith's extraordinary events were unexpected in themselves, since they in their turn were integral parts of the well-established routine, even if they weren't always blessed by plain sailing. Pivotal to the life of the school in this context was a supposedly well-ordered sequence of annual functions and traditions. These undoubtedly lifted many spirits as their time drew nigh and preparations for them gathered pace. It was probably only for a few that expectations fell short of reality. Such functions were naturally at their most agreeable in the late autumn term, when the all-consuming anticipation of Christmas embraced them as its own. The great delights then were the Christmas Festival of Nine Lessons and Carols; the school's Christmas Concert; and the individual forms' Christmas parties, all of which were devoutly looked forward to.

The winter cum spring term delivered up Speech Day, which centred on the awards of prizes for academic, sporting and personal achievements made in the previous school year. The summer term was graced by Sports Day; the publication of *The Camel*; and the official photograph of the entire school establishment, at once uniting the pupils and the teaching staff in a single frame defining "The School".

And as if to guarantee that this cornucopia of delights could never be accused of insubstantiality (an allegation sometimes made but seldom proven), the bill of fare was leavened with occasional dramatic productions, these being intended for the consumption of the public at large. Produced and directed by members of the teaching staff, Miss White being not least among that company of some being more equal than others, the cast was drawn entirely from the ranks of pupils. They invariably performed to great critical acclaim, and if the plaudits were now and then overdone and once in a while spread too thinly, wholesomeness always won the day.

The Festival of Nine Lessons and Carols

The Spirit of Christmas at Sir James Smith's was as tangible as it was joyous. If peace on earth as a guiding principle had a tendency to fall by the wayside, goodwill to all mankind met the jollity challenge head on, bursting to the fore and lightening the darkness.

Christmas was nothing without tradition, and no one at Sir

James Smith's wished for it to be otherwise. The magic lay not in Christmas Day itself, which for me was always something of an anti-climax, and absolutely not in the dog days which followed. No, the thrill of Christmas was related to its Advent, filled with anticipation, preparation, and the heartfelt feeling that life was for a little while likely to be less negative than usual. We were brought up to recognise the birth of Jesus as the Christmas catalyst, but with all due respect we intuitively didn't want to sacrifice too much of our goodwill on the altar of religious considerations.

A Christmas season imperative was the singing of popular carols. We all possessed a broad repertoire of carols, learned by heart through years of repetition. A carol sung in a summer month might sound and feel quite dysfunctional, but in the build-up to Christmas it was able to take on its true colours and come alive. The resonance of Christmas carols was never heard to be more profound or up-lifting than it was at the school's Festival of Nine Lessons and Carols, held shortly before the autumn term ended and the Christmas holidays began. Compared to the Sir James Smith's Festival we thought, the broadcast version from King's College, Cambridge, on Christmas Eve displayed all the hallmarks of inferiority.

This carolling and lesson-reading *tour de force* took place on a designated afternoon in mid-December, when the tide of term was very much at the ebb. The venue was the sanctified (a Church person might say sanctimonious) hallows of Camelford's large and venerable Methodist chapel. This redoubtable edifice stood on the left-hand side of the road heading into the town, at a modest distance beyond the far side of the River Camel bridge. Attendance was compulsory, as was the wearing of full school uniform and the maintenance of piously good behaviour. Decorum of a high order was particularly demanded of any pupil selected to read one of the Nine Lessons, which in the string of their entirety provided not only a piecemeal narrative of the Christmas saga in accordance with the King James Version of the Bible, but also a tuneless counterpoint to the carols sung between the readings.

At an allotted moment on the big day, dinner time being over for good or ill, an Assembly was called, and, in ascending order of form seniority we were marched off to the chapel as to war, in a great column of pairs, uniformed, capped, and in some instances even motivated — although we went with a teacher rather than the cross of Jesus going on before. Out of the school we filed, down College Road, along a stretch of the main road, over the bridge and so on to the chapel. Prefects harangued the stragglers, and by and large the column held its integrity. Had the route been longer, a different form of order might well have occurred before we reached our destination.

On entering the chapel we filled the pews sequentially from front to back. Apart from Lesson readers who sat on the aisle, both for ease of access to the lectern and to avoid any unseemly struggle in fighting their way clear of the ranks of the masses, there were no pre-assigned seating places. Parents and other guests in attendance were expected to occupy the pews at the very back of the chapel. The more senior pupils revelled in the lack of exposure to be enjoyed beneath the overhang of the chapel's balcony. It was invariably a full house.

As the congregation assembled, Mr Turner at the organ ran through a set of voluntary improvisations on well-known carol theme tunes. The organ was that self-same fateful instrument at which he was destined to end his honoured days. The sound of the organ was barely audible above the cumulative background noise of backsides shifting on seats, feet shuffling, order of service papers rustling, hymn books being riffled, and a surf-like murmur of conversation. Talking in chapel was banned by an order from the very top, but it had clearly fallen on deaf ears. What could not be banned, given that the service was set in the winter of the year, was a moist ripple of multiple throat clearing to the accompaniment of a discreet fusillade of coughs, without which no congregation seated in a place of worship anywhere would have been complete.

And then behold, suddenly, as if a switch was thrown, or a tap had been wrenched shut, silence reigned with a sibilance-laden depth. A long moment of tension seemed to hang in the air, only to be lifted when the unaccompanied voice of a boy soprano launched into a rendition of the first verse of "Once in Royal David's City" and the show was on its way in the dawn of all its glory. For a few years, until his teenaged vocal cords gave up their high-notes ghost, the school's boy soprano of choice was a St Kew lad appropriately named David, whose surname was Keast. He was a gifted singer and his voice fit whatever happened once in the royal city of his Christian name like a glove.

As David's last card intonation of "Jesus Christ, her little Child" faded and expired, the school's first-choice choir showed its hand by taking up the second verse with "He came down to earth from heaven", only to have the congregation win the bet with "Who is God and Lord of all". Interestingly, this wasn't a question, even if it ought to have been.

The interplay of Lessons and Carols generated an increasingly festive atmosphere, in spite of being temporarily let down by an interlude for prayers and a homily appropriate to the occasion. In the seasonal spirit of peace and goodwill, this was a small price to pay, however. The keynote Lesson in the order of reading was the ninth, traditionally taken from the Gospel according to St John, chapter one, verses one to fourteen. It was read by Mr Sprayson. He stood before the congregation in the fullness of his majesty and in his very own mellifluous manner delivered the piece as if it was gospel, which come to think of it, it was.

The final Carol was traditionally "O come, all ye Faithful", a rousing number to lift up our hearts for the retreat back to school prior to the formal end of school hours. And a good time was probably had by all.

Inclusive of the regimented commute from school to chapel and back again, plus all preambles and postscripts, it came as a surprise that the Sir James Smith's Festival of Nine Lessons and Carols took up in the order of only two hours of time.

The Christmas Concert

In benevolent contrast, the school's Christmas Concert, held in the almost great hall in which woodwork classes were also known to be given, lasted for the best part of a full school day. That particular investment in time met with universal approval. Transformed for the occasion, the hall could boast of a stage complete with facing curtains and modest, yet serviceable, back-stage facilities for the performers and stage hands. A number of random paper chains were draped around the walls of the hall for decorative purposes, and, where benches, sawdust, wood shavings and an occasional bloodstain had once occupied the floor, an impressive number of rows of chairs were set up for the audience on either side of a narrow central aisle.

The Christmas Concert was nothing if not a major undertaking. In principle, the responsibility for the show was in the hands of the pupils. Guidance from the teaching staff was available on request, although it was sought only infrequently. The leading lights — not necessarily by choice — for compiling the programme for the day and in ensuring an efficient line of continuity between acts by virtue of on-stage patter, were the Head Boy and the Head Girl, the former being the concert's official Master of Ceremonies.

The "all day" spread meant that the curtain rose (or rather was drawn open) at ten o'clock, with the final curtain falling (or being drawn closed) just ahead of four o'clock. Dinner Time performed the function of an extended intermission.

It was more or less decreed that each form must contribute a performance of its own to the Concert's bill, casting as many of its form members in the performance as was feasible All players were allegedly conscripted on a purely voluntary basis, but, when there was a shortage of volunteers, a more coercive approach, involving the persuasive skills and arm twisting techniques of Prefects chosen for the task, was used to swell the cast's ranks.

The forms' contributions were the salient moments of the Concert, leading off with the First Form's sometimes noble effort, and running — all the while padded out with continuity gags and leavened with performances by solo talent, in ascending sequence through the rest of the forms' shows — all the way up to the Sixth Form's masterwork. The latter was the top-of-the-bill presentation, which was hopefully intended to close the Concert on a high note, although, as my pastiche of *Under Milk Wood* had demonstrated, there were gravely muted exceptions to ending the show with thunderous applause.

And, since the concert had to last all day, no time constraints were placed on any of the acts. All the same, the blood, sweat and tears that it took to stage a group effort were all too real to everyone present, and therefore, in the sure understanding that the Sir James Smith's audience's tolerance for crap should not be tested too much, an approximate duration of five minutes for any item on the bill was a good target to aim at.

In spite of there being a seemingly inordinate amount of time available to fill, even allowing for the help of extended entrances, exits and pregnant pauses, in general it was a very rare thing that

264

time ever dragged. Anyone possessing a vestige of musical talent was certain to be conscripted to support the guarantee that the show must go on. Any pupil who was able to carry a note (let alone notes) in song was prized, as were those who could string a few recognisable chords together in the correct order on a musical instrument, or remember enough of a classic poem to be able to get up and recite it. Dancing, conjuring tricks, patter and banter were also featured to keep things going. Some of the talent was marginal, but it was talent nevertheless, and a welcome resource to call on.

Some pupils tried to keep their talents secret for fear of being discovered, yet invariably at some point during their climb through the school the truth would out and they would be compelled to turn their performing arts specialities into a variety act. Once an act was "discovered", opportunity then knocked for them annually for so long as they remained at the school. In this respect, the likelihood of talent existing in members of the First Form came under extremely exacting scrutiny.

Prominent among the solo artistes I knew and admired was Hugh Menadue, Mr Menadue's son, already a Sixth Former when I started at the school. Hugh was an accordion virtuoso, willing and able to pick up his instrument and slip into any slot at any time. His repertoire was immense. He could lead a singsong or accompany any singer and enhance the singer's performance. In 1964, when I was working as an exploration geologist in deep bush in the remote Lundazi District of the far east of an African country then known as Northern Rhodesia, I met up by chance with a small party of officers of the country's Agricultural Department. One of these was Hugh Menadue. It was a huge surprise and a happy reunion, although a story for another time.

The order of programme for the Christmas Concert was drafted and committed to paper. As a matter of principle all acts, from soloists up to Form groups, were responsible for providing their own stage props. So much hidden drama lurked behind the scenes during the build-up phase that the finalised programme might well have been written in blood. However, in the best show business tradition it was fairly assumed that it would be "all right on the night" (or rather fair enough on the day with a break for dinner time), and it seemed to work out that way, if for no better reason than that it had to.

The Head Boy's role as MC consisted not only of introducing various acts and performances while struggling to find something nice to say about each and every one of them, but also of maintaining the continuity flow between acts with a line of cheery chat sprinkled with jokes. The jokes needed to appeal to the tastes of an audience with an age range from eleven up to sixty (and perhaps beyond), and therefore were forced to take the line of lowest common denominator.

My two years of service as Head Boy meant that I was MC at two Christmas Concerts. I possessed quite good comedic credentials in restricted company, but they didn't translate quite that well when set before a large audience. My performance as MC may not have been nearly as bad as I thought it was, but only the kindest of souls would have said that I rose too far above mediocrity. I quickly learned that there were no hard and fast guidelines to follow in order to guarantee a good reception from the audience. The tenor of the jokes which I told, much as they had been with my predecessors, owed a lot to the back covers of matchboxes, and carried the sort of air of pending desperation that marked opening comedians on *Workers' Playtime*.

As previously noted, any material with blue overtones or innuendo or which could be in any way be considered even modestly *risqué* was subject to a banning order instituted at Headmaster level. "Honi

266

soit qui mal y pense" cut little ice at a Christmas Concert. If the least hint of Max Miller type suggestiveness crept in, Mr Sprayson would be out of his seat and backstage to dress the MC down well before the recently introduced act had begun to display its flaws.

The Concert's strait-laced constraints additionally governed what was and what was not possible for an act to present on stage. A musical rendition of a popular number, as for example something drawn from the Top Twenty as broadcast each Sunday on two-oh-eight, was tacitly understood to be *non grata*. Most musical offerings were therefore redolent of a musical soiree in a Victorian drawing room.

It was only in the field of sound effects that music of the moment, invariably extracted from gramophone records, could enter the equation — in my "A Midsummer Night's Nightmare" I used the opening bars of "Cherry Pink and Apple Blossom White" (Eddie Calvert — the "Man with the Golden Trumpet"); "The Man From Laramie" (Mr Jimmy Young, who else?); and "Heartbreak Hotel" (Elvis Presley, a promising newcomer).

The opening scene of "A Midsummer Night's Nightmare" provided a short exchange which inadvertently placed an undetected foot across the line guarded by the censor. It had Duke Sleazius, played by myself, remarking to Hiphoorayta, his bride to be, "Now, fair Hiphoorayta, our nuptial hour draws on apace! Ah me, I cannot wait for four more days to pass!" To which Hiphoorayta replied, "Four days shall quickly steep themselves in night!", and Sleazius rejoined, "Or the next four nights!" It was mild enough as things suggestive went, but could well have marked a small victory against the system.

I also took the role of Bottom in the same play. I wasn't allowed to get away with changing his name to Backside, or worse, so Bottom it had to be. Playing two parts required a few ultra-rapid costume changes, one or two of which did not go very smoothly, much to the appreciation of the audience.

Taking it all into consideration, there was no gainsaying that a few well-chosen jokes were the quintessential accessories for light relief. Many of the gags in the "Bumper Fun Book", compiled by Pat Sleeman and me, were lifted from various BBC radio comedy and variety series, with, of course, that great emphasis placed on the quick-fire routines of Messrs Bob Monkhouse and Denis Goodwin. Other contributions were harvested from the fertile fields of all-time greats such as Ted Ray, Arthur Askey, Jimmy Jewell and Ben Warris, Robert Moreton, Tony Hancock, Jimmy Wheeler and Arthur English. Together they provided a glorious vein of blessed comedic genius.

It would have been so good had Pat and I been able to draw on the repertoire of the greatest of them all, the aforementioned Max Miller, the Cheeky Chappie. However, copying gags from his act was dangerous when there was uncertainty as to whether Max was using his White Book or Blue Book, and we were too nervous to take a chance on it.

It was only in the individual Form performances that there was granted a little licence to test the limits of propriety by alluding, indirectly and not unkindly, to faults, foibles and unique characteristics of some members of the teaching staff. As a rule it was all taken in good spirit by the teachers being lampooned. They knew who they were, and appeared to regard on-stage references to them as accolades. The Form performances were rarely serious in content — they typically leaned towards satirising aspects of school life and the personalities who drove it (although the concept of satire as such would, at the time, have eluded the understanding of almost all of us at the school); parodying classical works of literature (as with my Lower Sixth attempt at wringing a few laughs from "A Midsummer

Night's Nightmare"); and reprising certain radio programmes of the light entertainment genre, among which *Educating Archie, Hancock's Half Hour, Top of the Form* and *Have a Go* were all graced with the cachet of Christmas Concert success.

The deep bottom of the barrel that I plumbed with my Upper Sixth adaptation of *Under Milk Wood* was also, fortunately perhaps, my Concert swansong. The play was a botched-up affair with an under-enthusiastic cast, not one of whom managed to learn their lines. It was a disaster from the curtain-up to the plug-pulling disarray of its premature death scene, Mr Sprayson having dispatched Mr Turner to the wings to convey the strength of his displeasure by virtue of a feat of gesturing that made it obvious that the turkey must be put out of its misery. Mr Turner was almost as impressive as John Wayne in a funeral scene in *The Searchers* when he demanded of Ward Bond, as the presiding minister that he should "put an Amen to it!"

The audience's one regret must have been that a long hook was not available with which to yank me and the rest of the sorry cast from the stage. Such an action might at least have finally elicited a laugh. There was no business like show business, although even Mickey Rooney and Judy Garland might have had qualms about putting on an over-ambitious show like that one.

Christmas Parties

Apart from the mixed blessings of the Christmas Concert, the end of the autumn term still had a little more to do in order to ensure that our great expectations of personal gratification in the Advent might be justified. One manifestation of festivity was laid down in Form-dedicated Christmas parties, held on five separate afternoons in respect of Forms One through Five, and during a designated evening for the Sixth, Upper and Lower.

The afternoon parties were held in the respective classrooms of each Form involved, the rooms being cleared of desks for the occasion and made to look modestly festive with hanging streamers and home-made paper chains. The form teacher presided over all the fun-whether-you-like-it-or-not with the aid of one or two colleagues, who in fairness did their best to demonstrate that even if fun was not a strong point with them, they did possess some recognisable human characteristics.

The presence of gaiety at the parties was not particularly un-restrained, as the emphasis on festive abandon tended to be played out in a low key. The chairs lined up around the classroom walls became a sort of haven where cronies gathered in groups in apparent attempts to get as far away as they could from the yawning no-man's land of the classroom floor.

Although there was ample discourse at these parties, there was little to be had in the way of full-blown social intercourse. The party highlights were perhaps not that prolific, but everyone had learned to be grateful for any mercy, however small, and an afternoon free of lessons fell very well into that category. There was usually some fizzy pop or strong tea to drink; a thin slice of fruit cake to appreciate; a variety of small sandwiches to appeal to anyone whose taste ran to meat paste or fish paste or finely sliced cucumber; and a whole plethora of party games.

The disbursement of the comestibles was closely supervised and was carried out in a fair-handed manner which precluded the kind of free-for-all that unrestricted access might have engendered.

Among the games, a perennial favourite was Musical Chairs, which rarely failed to offer welcome opportunities for boisterous pushing and shoving. Blind Man's Buff provided an additional diversion, as did Postman's Knock, although not all teachers were

270

supportive of the latter's inclusion in the party's schedule. With no effort having been spared in assembling multiple wrappings interleaved with written jokes, quiz questions and forfeits to test everyone's patience and dignity, Pass the Parcel appealed also to the popular consciousness.

As bus departure time drew nigh, the party traditionally ended with its attendees undertaking a spirited "Okie-kokie" session. With perhaps an over-emphasis on modesty, only those parts of the anatomy that decency would permit were put in, put out, in–out, in–out and then shaken all about. We did the Okie-kokie and we turned around, and that was what it was all about — Oy!

The musical accompaniment to the festivities relied strongly on gramophone records fit for a King, which is to say either Edward VII or George V. Post-war musical trends were not a consideration. Mr Turner, an excellent pianist, was in any case always available to be brought in to run his practised hands over the ivories to lead a sing-song of old favourites, the stress being on "old" rather than on "favourites".

Music, with acknowledgement to the gramophone record repertoire of Mr Victor Sylvester, was a dominant feature of the Sixth Form party. Had music been all that there was, it wouldn't have been so bad, but unfortunately Victor's music meant that Sixth Formers were all expected to get up and dance to it, boys with girls. It wasn't cricket, even if for some of us cricket wasn't exactly cricket either.

To try and establish an awareness for the Sixth Form boys of which foot was which and where it ought to go in the context of dancing, a much reviled course of lessons in ballroom technique was forced on the said boys during the month preceding the Sixth Form party. To ensure the boys' attendance, the dancing lessons took place unexpectedly during school hours whenever an opportunity presented itself.

The principal characteristics of the dancing practice sessions were an air of deep embarrassment and movement of feet that had scant co-ordination with Mr Sylvester's strict tempo criteria. Given that the objective of the exercise was to spread oil on the troubled waters of Sixth Form party-goers, the thickness of the lubricant seldom managed to exceed that of the minuscule depth of iridescent bilge-pumped sheen gilding the sea around many of the fishing boats at their moorings in Port Isaac harbour.

Nevertheless, the Sixth Form party was as often as not a noble effort — a good shot at an evening of informality and with fare as festive as it could be at a time of rationing exigencies. My sole recall of the party that I attended when I was in the Lower Sixth was that it was no better, although certainly no worse, than I had expected it to be.

When I was in the Upper Sixth, the Friday evening of the Christmas party coincided with my returning to Cornwall by train from London. I had been up in the Big Smoke for two days to attend an interview for an undergraduate place at the Royal School of Mines, a constituent college of London University's Imperial College in South Kensington. The journey was a major undertaking for me. It was my first time ever to go to that fabled city, the gilded reputation of which made my other urban forays to Plymouth, Bristol and Birmingham seem like also-rans by comparison.

I travelled up to London on the Southern Railway, boarding the train at Port Isaac Road Station and disembarking at London's Waterloo Station. Naturally enough, I returned home by the same route, and since I was then travelling on an evening train, I considered that I had been granted a tailor-made excuse to miss the Sixth Form party thanks to the great benefit of my not only being late but also probably having eventually to walk the three miles or so back to Port Isaac from Port Isaac Road Station.

Unfortunately for me, when the train made a scheduled stop at Exeter St David's Station, perfidious fate brought a boarding passenger, who was none other than Mr Sprayson's elder daughter Jennifer, into the compartment in which I was sitting. Jennifer eventually disembarked at Camelford Station, where she was met, with transport to Camelford in hand, by Mr Sprayson himself. I heard Jennifer say to him from without, "You'll never guess who I travelled down with!" Whereupon the great man emerged from the steaming billows at the door of the compartment, crashed the door open and dragged me unceremoniously out just as the Stationmaster was blowing whistle for the train's departure. I only barely had the presence of mind to seize my luggage and have it accompany me on the precipitate exit.

Mr Sprayson exuded affability, and was at his most effusive in declaring how fortunate it was that I arrived when I did, since I could now accompany him to the Sixth Form party. I would miss very little of it, he said, as it would be only just getting into its opening throes.

To go to the party was not quite what I had any desire to do, but then again I was the Head Boy and had to believe that duty, cruel as it might be, was calling me. In other words, if you couldn't fight them, you joined them, especially when you had been shanghaied. Besides which I was, in the words of a popular song of the time, "too pooped to pop".

When we were in his car on the way to the party, Mr Sprayson quizzed me on the nature of my London interview as well as on my feelings for a positive result. I could only answer in monosyllables, as I had no idea of how well the interview had gone. It had seemed to be all right, but I was just too glad that it was over to devote any time to worrying about the outcome just yet.

My biggest concern about the Sixth Form party was that I would

273

be judged to be inappropriately dressed. My mother had bought a suit for me to wear to the interview, modestly grey in colour, and the first of such a distinctive item of garb that I had ever owned or worn. The suit was not made to measure, but it fitted me adequately enough. The jacket was long and double breasted, well cut and good in terms of value for an "off the peg" item. I had had no previous experience of wearing anything quite so formal, but supposed that a switch to being more casual would only require me to take the suit jacket off. That was reasonable, as no one of my acquaintance ever wore a jacket or a coat within the confines of a room. The fact that some members of television's "Grove Family", had an enduring habit of wearing their coats when indoors was always a matter of some amusement to us. *The Grove Family* was very much a must-watch programme.

The deep concern that I had about my suit was that the trousers were cut narrow in the legs — narrow enough to come very close to qualifying as "drainpipes". The drainpipe style of trousers, in conjunction with a long-draped, velvet-collared jacket with an Edwardian look, was then being much favoured by city youths popularly referred to as "Teddy Boys" or "Teds". The Teds formed both a fashion and a cultural movement of some notoriety, seeking to break away from the restraints of post-war austerity by virtue of practising outlandish behaviour, committing *ad hoc* acts of violence, and demonstrating contempt for authority. They liked to hang around in intimidating-looking groups on street corners, and when that activity (or lack of the same) palled, to frequent the coffee bars which were then springing up like wildfire all over the place in the urban environment.

Not a single Ted had so far made an appearance in North Cornwall, although the movement's notoriety, as reported in the newspapers, had surely prepared the way for its arrival. In my narrow-legged suit trousers I was genuinely worried that I might get linked with the Teds through guilt by association.

Thus, and with great trepidation, did I attend the Sixth Form Christmas party. The festivities inched their way so slowly towards the last waltz that they seemed to be threatening never to get there. All the same, time won in the end, as it always did.

At the close, Mr Sprayson called upon me in my Head Boy capacity to say a few words to the assembled party-goers, and I did my best, but was too tired to be very articulate. My performance was sub-standard and I knew it, which was why I wasn't really surprised when, on the following Monday at school, Mr Sprayson invited me to come and see him. In his study he launched into a lengthy critique of my lacklustre party monologue. He accused me of giving way to almost obsessional shrugging, which he claimed had awakened in him a desire to grab me and shake me. This, from one who had dragged me from a train against my will, I felt to be not a little ironic.

Had he grabbed me, I thought, it would have made for a much better party finale. The shrugs that I had larded my closing remarks with were supposed to be consistent with comedic timing, but they were clearly yet another lost attempt to set a trace of *avant-garde* humour before an unfeeling public.

When Saul of Tarsus on the road to Damascus was subjected to a light from heaven shining round about him, he fell to the ground, and a voice, purporting to be that of none other than Jesus himself, advised him (Acts, chapter nine, verse five): "it is hard for thee to kick against the pricks". That advice was no less true on the road to Damascus than it was on my road to Christmas in the Upper Sixth. Since discretion was forever the better part of valour, I chose not to kick so that the pricks could simply keep their own counsel.

Speech Day

Although my shrug-laden end-of-party turn had failed to ignite the imagination of all who heard it, it had not been entirely out of keeping with the Sir James Smith's tradition of calling on reluctant individuals to address the masses. A bean feast of imposed tedium could always be anticipated to soar to its ultimate zenith on the occasion of the school's annual Speech and Prize-Giving Day.

Depending on your point of view, as well as on your name's presence on or absence from the list of prize winners, Speech Day was an event to be celebrated, or tolerated, or endured. It occurred prior to the Easter holidays and took as its focal point the presentation of prizes awarded for individual academic, social and sporting achievement in the preceding school year. The prizes were handed out by an invited guest of some distinction, who was additionally required to make an extended speech to the captive horde, using words both rich in moral rectitude and dripping with sanctimony.

The three or four pupils who were at the academic top of their respective classes from the First through to the Fifth Forms were all awarded prizes. In addition, members of the Fifth Form who did especially well at O Level could expect to be included in the hand-out. Sixth Form academic prizes were a little more nebulous, relating almost entirely to an individual's A Level results. A Level prize winners were of course no longer at the school, and therefore might or might not be able to return to collect what was due to them.

With the best will in the world, it always seemed to happen that once you had left the school, a return under any pretext was something that tended not to be very appealing during the immediate years thereafter. It was only as the few years gradually moved towards becoming many that the attraction of making a reappearance seemed to grow on you. Hence it was mostly the brave and the bold who showed up to collect their A Level prizes and plaudits at the Speech Day subsequent to their departure.

My A Level results were sent to me in a formal letter through the post. I was under instructions to telephone Mr Sprayson when they had arrived, which I did, once more from the Church Hill public call box in Port Isaac. During our conversation, Mr Sprayson's emotions were far more highly charged than mine, to the extent that his enthusiasm on my behalf seemed to know no bounds. He kept exclaiming that the value vested in the County University Scholarship which my grades had won me would amount to one thousand pounds over its three years of currency. Sixpence was a lot more money than I usually had access to — Miss Lyons' generosity aside — and the concept of forty thousand such tanners being allocated to me in a grant was too much to be easily understood.

In practice, class prizes didn't visit themselves upon members of the Lower Sixth as they faced no promotion trial by examination beyond that of demonstrating that they had done enough in the Lower Sixth year to justify Upper Sixth entry. Not all Lower Sixth Formers succeeded in surmounting that hurdle — the road to the Upper Sixth was paved with faint hope and thwarted ambition.

There were, however, two traditional prizes which kept the Lower Sixth in the game with a chance, one of them being the Leese Sixth Form Prize for academic achievement, named of course in honour of Mr C. E. Leese, who not only established the prize, but whose shadow still hung indelibly around the corridors and corners of the school. The second opportunity was the Character Prize, awarded by democratic vote of the school establishment, one "Character" elected by the boys and one by the girls.

Apart from the award of silver-like medals for the boy and girl who had been the best all-rounders on the prior Sports Day — the "Victor Ludorum" and "Victrix Ludorum" — all prizes were books, each having an appropriately inscribed plate, emblazoned with the school crest, stuck on the inside cover to display the recipient's name and what the prize was for in beautifully handwritten script. Also included on the plate were the date of the prize's presentation; and the identity of the distinguished guest who had been brought in to make the presentation. The books were chosen by their recipients from an approved list controlled under strict budgetary guidelines of fifteen shillings per title, seventeen and six at a pinch, and maybe a quid under extreme circumstances.

As far as the books went, nothing frivolous was permitted. The guideline for content was that it should have an improving or moral quality imbued with recognisable educational value. As a consequence, and speaking for myself without wishing to do any other prize winner a disservice, it was probable that most of the volumes handed over on as prizes by the distinguished guest of the day went unread.

I didn't pick up very much in the way of school prizes, but, for the record, here is what they were and when they were awarded:

- ✦ 2 February 1954 — Third Form prize — *The Kon-Tiki Expedition* by Thor Heyerdahl.
- ✦ 21 March 1956 — Character prize — *Science and its Background* by H. D. Anthony
- ✦ 21 March 1956 — Victor Ludorum medal
- ✦ 31 March 1958 — County University Scholarship prize — *The Petrology of the Igneous Rocks* by F. H. Hatch, A. K. Wells, and M. K. Wells
- ✦ 31 March 1958 — Leese Sixth Form prize — *The Petrology of the Sedimentary Rocks* by F. H. Hatch, B. K. Rastall, and M. K. Black
- ✦ 31 March 1958 — GCE Advanced Level prize — *Rutley's Elements of Mineralogy* by H. H. Read

My Big Year on this modest list was undoubtedly 1958. It was perhaps ironic that I was by then an Old Boy, although I did return to the school for the Speech Day in question, and received my prizes from the hands of no less a distinguished guest than that Ghost of Christmas Past, Mr C. E. Leese. The three books that I obtained were required texts for my university studies, and went on to become well used, the latter most of all. In handing the books over to me, Mr Leese, himself an amateur geologist, professed profound approval of *The Petrology of the Igneous Rocks*, although his tone was more than a little disparaging when it came to commenting on its sedimentary companion. As to the two volumes at the head of my list, they are sure treasures that remain with me, as unread now as they were then — I hasten to blame myself rather than the quality of the books for that lapse.

The Speech Day ceremonies were held in the same chapel in the heart of Camelford to which we all had traipsed a few scant months previously for the Festival of Nine Lessons and Carols. However, the seating plan for Speech Day was set up to ensure that prize winners could gain immediate access to the podium when they heard their names called, hence they were congregated in appropriate order in the pews at the front. Having them struggle out of pews set further to the rear, where they were certain to be impeded by classmates into whose hands prizes never fell, was thereby avoided.

On the podium at the front of the chapel, from which in normal circumstances local preachers were inclined to give vent to emotionally charged religious invective, a large table groaned under the weight of neatly stacked books arranged in order and ready to be picked up one at a time by a school-appointed minion, opened at the plated dedication page, and handed on to the distinguished guest of the day. The name and nature of the award having been announced, the distinguished guest then shook the prize winner's hand, while proffering the book for acceptance and offering a gratuitous comment or two, depending of course on how the mood of the moment appealed to him or her.

Others among the gathering in the chapel whose seats were strategically allocated but who were not necessarily up for prizes, were those with a role to play in the trappings of the Speech Day ceremony as a whole. They included one or two who were primed to give an inspirational reading to punctuate the action at a set moment; unlucky designates selected to propose votes of thanks to, *inter alia*, the distinguished guest; and then of course various limelight seekers, without whom an event such as Speech Day would always be incomplete.

In one of my Head Boy years I was instructed that the duty of proposing a vote of thanks to the distinguished guest had fallen to me, in which instance it was to be directed at no less a titled personage than Lady St Aubyn, the good wife of Sir John Molesworth St Aubyn, Bart, himself the high-born head of an ancient lineage of landed Cornish gentry, and incidentally the Chairman of the Sir James Smith's Grammar School Board of Governors. Hence, well prior to my proposing that vote of thanks, it was implied to me that nothing less than fawning deference towards Lady St Aubyn's august presence would do.

When I got to my feet to perform my duty, I was rather more terrified than nervous, and since I was nervous to a fault, my fear knew few bounds. All present in the chapel were grateful to Lady St Aubyn, not so much for what she had said in her speech, since it was likely that few had really listened very intently, but more for the relief that she had at last finished saying it.

As I spoke my piece, I felt dissociated from the reality of the moment, but I hoped that I had done the best that I could in terms of the laying-on of slavish admiration. A few days later, however, I was advised by Miss Jones and Miss White that my vote of thanks had lacked a ring of sincerity. Coming from Miss Jones, who was more often than not fair-minded, I could accept the criticism. Perhaps I had spread the obsequiousness so thickly that it contained overtones of my latent lack of admiration for the aristocracy and all its works. On the other hand, Miss White's historically uneven-handed treatment of me made me feel that she would not have recognised sincerity even if it had jumped up and bit her in her holier-than-thou backside.

Each year, the speech given by the distinguished guest of the day followed a template of near-shameless predictability. In its fallow field of patronisation, well-worn cliches were seeded about with an abundance that was both reckless and overbearing. Humility invariably took a back seat.

In his or her speech, the distinguished guest never failed to remind us pupils that he or she had once been young like us (no matter how improbable that seemed). And, oh yes, the Game was there to be played and played up, the straight and narrow way lay ahead of us to be walked; *carpe diem* and so on; the future beckoned us advantageously with many nettles to be grasped by winners and non-winners alike. Evidently there were no losers in a distinguished guest's comfortable experience.

During my time at Sir James Smith's I attended Speech Day ceremonies addressed by distinguished guest luminaries such as Mr J. G. Harries, Secretary of Education for the County of Cornwall; Sir John Molesworth St Aubyn, Bart; his good wife Lady St Aubyn; and the one and only Mr C. E. Leese. Each delivered speech was a virtual copy of its predecessor. Occasionally, the stodgy dough might be leavened with an attempt at a joke that it was mandatory for us to laugh at irrespective of its antiquity, but that didn't happen very often.

Rounding off Speech Day, it was traditional for the assembled school to sing John Bunyan's "To Be a Pilgrim", which contained the opportunely prophetic lines — "Whoso beset him round with dismal stories do but themselves confound — his strength the more is".

With a hey and a ho, and a hey nonny no.

Sports Day

Sports Day, which always lived up to its name, came along towards the end of the summer term, when the grass was green, the sky was blue, birdsong was all around, and the sawing of grasshoppers harmonised with the drone of bees throughout the livelong day.

At least, that is how the recollection of the Sports Day feeling hung in my memory, and in truth, the weather for Sports Days must always have been reasonably fair, as none of them, year after year, was ever called off on grounds of climatic inclemency. Which went on to mean that no one ever got out of having to be there on the day by virtue of an Act of God.

The athletic celebration that was Sports Day took place in the same field across the lane from Mr Sprayson's residence on which those of us with an aversion to football shivered our way through the sodden autumn and winter seasons and went on to lose ourselves in the cricket outfield in the spring and early summer.

The arrangements for the Sports Day competitions were a masterpiece of planning and co-ordination. The event as a whole may not have flowed smoothly, but it always flowed. The Sports Day motto might have been appropriately borrowed from Peter Cheyney's Slim Callaghan Detective Agency — "We get there somehow and who the hell cares how".

The programme of events was focused mainly on running and jumping competitions, yet thankfully enlivened by a range of novelty races involving sacks, eggs, spoons, three legs, wheelbarrows, cricket balls and, last but not least, bicycles.

The objective of the bicycle race was to come in last over a distance of fifty yards or so, or in other words to endeavour to go nowhere while balanced on the bike with your feet on the pedals. Touching the ground with either foot meant instant disqualification. In so many ways the slow bicycle race had much in common with a circus act.

Of course, in order to compete in a slow bicycle race you had to bring along your own bike — wholly owned or borrowed, it made no difference, as few pupils were bike owners and perhaps even fewer bike owners who weren't pupils were prepared to lend their bikes to enhance the slow bicycle entry list on Sports Day. It was therefore predictable who would take part, and even more predictable who would win.

The preparation of the Sports Day field was exemplary, as was the grading of competitors into groups based on age, size and ability to ensure the elimination of unfair advantage. The running tracks were marked out using the mobile whitewash-dispenser that normally realised its purpose in defining the limits of the football pitch and the cricket boundary. Shallow pits were dug and filled with sand to make moderately safe landing zones for jumpers, and a clear area was secured into which the cricket ball could be thrown without threatening the lives or limbs of innocent bystanders.

For very good reasons, javelin throwing was not included on the list of Sports Day events. The availability of a spear-like implement and a cornucopia of targets both animate and inanimate was not a combination devoutly to be wished.

The mile race was for dedicated athletes and was seldom

over-subscribed. Much more interest was applied to running over shorter distances — one hundred, two hundred and twenty, and four hundred and forty yards. These attracted both individuals and relay teams.

Since in principle it was demanded of all pupils that they must enter their names for many events irrespective of ability, multiple heats were staged to winnow out the wheat from the chaff.

I was not a bad sprinter, although my best performances were at the jumping — long jump and hop, step and jump to be specific. The greatest of my flaws in the execution of valid jumps was that I rarely managed to hit the take-off board in the most advantageous way, and concentrating on getting that right was all too often detrimental to my jumping distance. I once did what I held to be such a brilliant hop, step and jump that I seemed to be flying weightlessly. The run up was effortless, and it felt for once that my take-off point was spot on as I soared over the sand and landed a good way further down the sand pit than I had ever gone before. I was really happy, but that was prior to my being disqualified on the grounds that the leading edge of my plimsoll had extended over the front of the take-off board. Miss White wasn't the line judge, but it was a disqualification that might have been quite worthy of her.

In 1956 I managed, probably by the default of others, to accumulate enough Sports Day points to be declared Victor Ludorum. I must have made fewer errors than the others did. That particular lightning never struck in the same place twice, but it did get me a medal presented at the subsequent Speech Day.

The girls' equivalent title of Victrix Ludorum in my year of mild triumph was won by Sally Burnett. She was a much more worthy winner — the girls as a rule were far more athletically inclined and motivated to compete than were the boys. When the girls were good, they were very, very good, and when they were bad, well, they still weren't all that bad.

Sports Day also incorporated a competition for the House Prize, pitting members of the two school Houses, Drake and Wallis, against one another. Drake's colour was green, Wallis' red — together the colours of the school. You naturally scored points for yourself, and then these points were fed into the cumulative pot for the House to which you belonged. It was probably only on Sports Day that the significance of House membership ever came to be invoked as an allegiance for rallying to.

I was assigned to Drake House — gladly of course since the name of Drake had a far stronger ring to it than did Wallis. I knew about Sir Francis Drake, and at one time had seen his statue up on Plymouth Hoe when I went to that city on a Sunday School outing to the annual pantomime. In History class we were told that Drake had been playing a "rubber of bowls" (our imaginations lapped that expression up) when the Great Armada came.

In the recesses of my memory, the House Prize on Sports Day was almost always won by Drake. Wallis may have fared better in the academic sphere, and probably did, although no reckoning was kept of that achievement on which a tale could be hung.

The Hotspur's Red Circle school boasted three principal House subdivisions, namely Home, Conk and Yank, respectively designated for pupils who were nationals of the British Isles; pupils from the colonies, and pupils of transatlantic origin. In addition there was a Senior House for senior pupils, no matter where they came from.

The three principal Red Circle House complements were forever engaged in a tacit contest for supremacy and the then-earned right to refer to themselves as "Cock" House. With Drake and Wallis, we at Sir James Smith's had not quite as much of the competitive drive as did our Red Circle counterparts, albeit that in their case they were all boarders with ample time to plot, whereas we were not.

With three or more Houses, striving for the Cock House accolade seemed most worthwhile, but when there were only two Houses like ours it just felt as if it wasn't worth the effort.

A school united under a single banner felt much more relevant to us. Any residual loyalty that we had to spread around wasn't very substantial in any event once our home villages had soaked away their share, and the little that was left was no more than enough for Sir James Smith's to lay claim to.

The School Photograph

The event that brought the might of the school, pupils and teaching staff alike, together in all its glory, was the formal school photograph, timed to be taken in the late spring or the early summer when reasonable weather conditions had a right to be expected. The school photograph was always done in the main section of the boys' yard using one or other of the inner walls as a backdrop, since the boys' yard offered the only option with sufficient space to rank everyone up in four-tiered fully-uniformed order. It was imperative that the photographic exercise, planned with military precision, should end up a success. Its battle plan, seeking to guarantee that everyone was gathered together in the same place at the same time with no rushing mighty wind or tongues of fire to mar the occasion, all in uncharacteristically neat array and positive of countenance, was not executed with ease.

The front tier of the four tier photographic assembly was occupied by members of the First Form, and, if their physical stature had not yet taken off and flourished, by some Second Formers as well. None of the front-tier boys had yet graduated to the wearing of long trousers. They were all required to squat on the ground and assume a lotus-like position. From the perspective of the camera, boys were all placed to the right, and girls all to the left of an imaginary median line on which the camera stood on its tripod about twenty feet away.

This line, and its *de facto* separation of the boys from the girls, was projected back through all four tiers. In the second tier, seated on hard-backed wooden chairs, were the teaching staff, with Mr Sprayson spot on the line at the core. The shoulder-to-shoulder group of seated teachers was appropriately flanked on either side by the Head Boy, Head Girl, Prefects, and any other members of the Fifth or Sixth Form who had been able to wangle themselves a seat.

In the third tier, in behind the favoured few on seats, Fourth and Fifth Formers stood in close order as if on parade. To their rear, in the fourth and final tier and also standing, although in this case with their feet on a line of benches to allow them to be seen above the heads before them, were Third Formers in the main, plus any overflow from the third tier of matching height.

Once the initial marshalling was done, the assembly was subjected to rather a lot of shuffling, shifting around and evening-up, all the time accompanied by the barking of orders and much pushing, shoving, goading, threatening and cajoling. It was only when a form of four-tiered symmetry capable of satisfying Mr Sprayson's penchant for order was achieved, that he felt justified to take up his seat in between Miss White and Mr Menadue and instruct the photographer to go ahead and do his worst.

The photographer called on us all to hold still, to smile at the camera if we still could, and to avoid any precipitate movement of heads, shoulders or arms while the camera did its work. And by and large that was how it was. Those standing were at virtual attention, and those who sat, whether on the ground or on the chairs, maintained straight backs and folded arms.

The camera was a heavy, box-like device, mounted on a stout

swivel-headed tripod. It was a tracking camera — the lens opened to commence its exposure at the far left-hand side of the assembled school and moved across to the far right in one slow paced and gently sweeping arc. Then the photographer repeated the exercise once or twice more just to be on the safe side.

It was rumoured that if, once the camera lens had tracked past your position, you were to drop out and run around the back, keeping low, so as to reach and stand at the right flank before the camera reached it, you could appear twice in the same photo. I never knew if this was ever done, but it sounded, in Greyfriars terms, to have all the quality of a "great jape".

When the school photo was developed, printed and formalised in conjunction with the school's name, badge image and date, you were able to order and purchase a copy. The photo came to you so tightly rolled up that flattening it out was a monumental task, laden with frustration. It was, when unrolled, about a yard long by nine inches high. You unrolled it, you weighted it down with books to flatten it out, you left it for some time, you removed the books, and the photo instantly sprang back into a roll again.

One copy of the school photo was always formally framed to be hung in the library, there to join a gallery of its fellows spanning quite a number of years, all glorying in the company of the great honours boards.

The School Magazine

The school photo not only recorded all present at the school at a given moment in time, but also symbolised the spirit and character of Sir James Smith's. A sense of community, which few would have readily admitted to feeling, shone from all those familiar faces in every photo, demonstrating clearly that, for all its awkward edges, the school as an entity stood firmly on the rock of greatness.

The school magazine, published at the end of each academic year, was intended to demonstrate and make palatable the strength of that same truth. In this endeavour, the heights that the magazine scaled were creditable, even if sometimes a little less than dazzling.

For what it was, the school magazine was a most worthy publication. It was compiled by an editorial board of selected pupils, and supervised by one or two of the teachers. The role of the supervisors was significant in that it had so much in common with that of the British Board of Film Censors. Their purpose was to prevent any form of editorial content deemed to be inappropriate, or off colour, or inconsistent with school policy (both written and unwritten), slipping through to appear in print. Supervision was, to all intents and purposes, something like "Mr In-Between", accentuating the positive, eliminating the negative, and never to be messed with.

Much to my detriment, I felt the weight of supervisory censorship on an Upper Sixth occasion when I sat in the higher echelons of the editorial board, and by my actions gave Miss White yet another opportunity to play the Gorgon. Those same actions additionally allowed Mr Sprayson to once more shake his head over my conduct, although in fairness to him, I think his head shaking was done more in sorrow than in anger.

The Ship of the Desert was of course the tried and true symbol of the school, and the camel's image was there in all its raised-foot glory on the school badge, a graphic representation of which graced the school magazine's cover. There was a popular observation that the magazine's name, *The Camel*, reflected the fact that its contents gave more than a few of its readers the hump. Some readers were (not entirely unfairly) wont to avow that once *The Camel* publication caravan had moved on, all that was left to provide a reminder of the material stretching far away on the lone and level sands of its pages, was a scattering of shit.

The Camel was not a glossy magazine. No professional typesetter assembled its editorial content for printing, and no jobbing printer ran off a host of pristine copies to satisfy the demands of a great reading public. Colour failed to leap from any of its pages and offer relief to its cover-to-cover black and white. However, bits of good, original writing did manage to worm their way in as if they were making amends for random acts of plagiarism.

Indeed, The Camel was published "in-school" in its entirety, all of it written, censored, edited, approved and typed up on "stencil skins", presumably by Mrs Perry, who was in charge of the school's only typewriter. The skins, once ready, were one after the other tightly draped in place on a manually turned ink-charged Gestetner roller/printer. Printed copies of what was typed on the skins were then cranked for as long as the ink lasted, or until the required print run of two hundred and fifty copies or so (enough to satisfy school and public demand) had been realised.

The ink had an unfortunate habit of oozing through the skins in places where Mrs Perry may have caused the typewriter keys to have been struck with a little too much of her undoubted authority.

It was Mrs Perry who typed up the article that I wrote for The Camel which resonated so badly with the censors. It had originally been rejected by the editorial board supervision on grounds of un-suitability and the likelihood that it would offend readers of all ages. I thought it was quite good, however, and so I was determined to try to get it in. Mrs Perry had not been enlightened with respect to its controversial status, and so I gave it to her and she typed it up on a skin as a matter of routine.

Once again I learned the hard way that what was clear and justified in my mind was not necessarily compatible with such latitude — or private initiatives for the taking of it — as was available at Sir James Smith's. The unapproved stencil was given a page number and inserted in the printing order, only to be discovered, withdrawn by Miss White or someone like-minded, and destroyed before it could take up its rightful place on the Gestetner roller.

In retrospect, this piece for *The Camel* was as well intended as my ill-fated version of "Under Milk Wood", but its chances weren't helped by its coming along reasonably hard on the heels of the unappreciated latter. I was duly, and correctly, taken to task for it.

The offending article was entitled "Slive", in a rather unsubtle reversal of the word "Evils". I intended it to be a humorous and convoluted attempt to describe the art of writing on shithouse walls. Although I had never actually written anything of the sort myself, there had, when I was compelled to spend a penny in a public convenience here and there, been no alternative to reading the works of others inscribed all around me at eye level. I thought that some of those mural witticisms were not unimpressive.

The Camel had a dual function. On the one hand it presented a record of key events marking a school year now almost at an end, and on the other it gave the great opportunity for pieces written by pupils of all ages to be published, such as bits of verse; short (blessedly) stories; descriptions and reviews of specific school functions and field trips; jokes (bland of course); puzzles; non-controversial comment; and miscellaneous articles of general interest.

Notwithstanding the errant "Slive", a few pieces of mine had been accepted for *The Camel* in previous years.

My best published contribution to *The Camel* was written when I was in the Fifth Form, and described a journey to Bristol, including an overnight stay, that I took on my own. Its purpose was for me to attend an interview at which it might be determined whether or not I shaped up as the kind of material worthy of inviting for a second interview and an associated set of physical and aptitude tests that might gain me entry to Dartmouth Royal Naval College.

A tradition of seafaring and Naval service had run through my family for several generations, hence there was always a certain pressure for me to fall in line with the same, aim high, and emulate men like my grandfather and father, both of whom had served at sea with great distinction in peace and in war.

The problem for me was that the sea, ships, and those who went down to the former in the latter, in particular the Officer Class, did not appeal to me in any way. Nor was I suited to maritime affairs, even if I had been more compatible with their commission. Looking back on the Bristol episode, my prospective candidacy for a place at Dartmouth Royal Naval College felt, later on, not only like a joke but like a bad joke into the bargain. However, an attempt to comply with the process was required of me, and I gave it a try, avoiding forethought and holding a blackout-type curtain drawn as tightly closed as possible across my mind to shut out a venture that had "mistake" writ large across it.

My Bristol interview, associated with a few written tests, took place on a small naval vessel moored off a quay somewhere or other. I don't remember the precise location, but suffice it to say that it was as far away from home as I had thus far ever been, and I could not help but feel insecure. Yet, a third-class train travel warrant had been provided to get me there, and accommodation at the Navy's expense was booked for me overnight in a hostel that was so much of a new experience for me that its seediness didn't even register.

Finding the exit at Bristol Temple Meads railway station in order to reach the hostel was my initial challenge — I searched for a footbridge across the tracks in vain, and it was only when a kindly porter directed me to a subway tunnel (the first of such that I had ever seen) that I finally broke free.

Faced at the interview with rather too much gold braid and posh accents, I was intimidated from the start, although I found the written tests, on English usage, basic mathematics and engineering associations, quite easy to get through.

It was not long after the submission of my related article, entitled "Interview", to the then editorial board of *The Camel* that Miss White rushed along to see me. Her first salvo was a barb-laden critique of what I had written. She informed me that I had given an impression of being extremely naive — it was, she said, as if I had never travelled anywhere at all prior to making that trip to Bristol. She had of course hit the nail right on the head, no matter that it had not been her intention to do so. Miss White told me that I should add a final paragraph to the piece to let the reader know that the result of my interview had not been a success. She probably would have preferred me to use the word "failure", I thought.

But then again, it hadn't been a failure — quite the contrary in fact. It was just that I hadn't let anyone know. No one was more surprised than me when a letter came to us at home in Port Isaac to let me know that I had been selected to proceed to the second definitive interview and tests, both written and practical, to take place at Dartmouth Royal Naval College itself over a two-day period. I hadn't expected that to happen, having considered that the Bristol expedition had relieved me of any further obligation to pretend that anything of the Navy coursed in my blood. That the Navy was not yet a closed book made me very anxious over what still lay ahead.

The events of my two days at Dartmouth RN College are best left shrouded in the kinder mists of history. From my very arrival I knew that I had stepped a long, long way out of my league. Every aspect of what subsequently took place seemed designed to get me confronted by people that I not only had nothing in common with but also didn't want to relate to. I was, quite literally, dead in the water, and I knew it. I did my best to do my best, but even that was never going to be enough to suit that strange world. I must have fallen short of satisfying the Dartmouth entry requirements on many counts, and couldn't even feel the comfort of glorious inadequacy.

But then again, it did bring me blessed release. I was disappointed only for my father who, for several days after we received the notice of my inability to gain entry to Dartmouth, angrily declaimed the result in terms of my being turned down because I was the son of a Petty Officer rather than of a Captain. That might naturally have been important had I been officer material, but as I wasn't it was all a bit of a red herring that I had to live with. The brass hats of the Dartmouth interview board would never know how great a favour they had done me.

Yet there was a rose among the thorns of the exercise. On the evening of my arrival in Bristol I went on pure impulse from my hostel to a nearby variety theatre and was taken out of myself by a wonderful programme which featured, among others, a brash young comedian named Norman Vaughan, and that great popular vocalist of the day, Miss Ruby Murray, whose voice with its plaintive catch was so "softly, softly" emotive. The very best of all, however, was the act at the Top of the Bill, a classic routine by the brilliant comedian Mr Jimmy Wheeler.

The enduring memory of Jimmy's bright star thereafter negated any unpleasant "Interview"-related memories, inclusive of Miss White's sniping from the side lines. I didn't see fit to make any of the changes to my article for *The Camel* which she suggested, although regrettably in hindsight I didn't mention Jimmy Wheeler in it. My encounter with his mastery was probably too personal to share, and as Jimmy might have said to Miss White, "Aye, aye! That's your lot!"

There was Bristol and Dartmouth, but then there was Jimmy. And there was no business like show business.

Like no business I know

The marathon of amateur talent in all its shades of grey which characterised Christmas Concerts demonstrated an undoubted truism that, no matter how great the odds were stacked against you, to do your best was a quality at least as important as to succeed. It was to reap the rewards from the more lustrous gems of latent thespianism that every once in a while Sir James Smith's staged a full-scale dramatic production of note, which ran for one (or even two) performances if it didn't fold on opening night, and provided manna for the delectation of a public of a more general nature than that associated directly with the school.

The *dramatis personae* and backstage crew involved in these productions in all their grandness were legion, so much so perhaps that had the general public, in which parents played a significant role, not been admitted to performances, there could well have been a greater number of pupils behind the scenes than there could ever have been in the audience.

It naturally fell to the lot of the members of staff who taught English to direct, produce, cast and co-ordinate the shows, to cajole and threaten the players into doing more or less what the playwright intended, and to organise and oversee the set designers, the lighting experts, the scene shifters, the stage hands and the backdrop painters in order to bring it all together in one glorious whole. Miss White was good at that. There was little doubt that in such situations — when it all eventually came together, that is — the school was seen to be at its best.

Amateur dramatic societies and repertory theatre groups thrived in many of the rural communities of North Cornwall. Their great advantage, also seen by some as a disadvantage, was that they tended to fall under the remit and thumb of BBC-accented "gin and tonic"

295

runners-in. But then again, there was no reason not to accept that any of Shakespeare's Kings, Queens, Nobles or Knaves would ever suffer in interpretation by having their lines declaimed in a local argot.

The most memorable production put on by a school dramatic company during my days at Sir James Smith's was *A Midsummer Night's Dream*, written by the ubiquitous Mr William Shakespeare. The cast, made up of members drawn from all Forms in the school, did an excellent job, and no one could doubt that had Mr Shakespeare been around to see it, the school's version of his comedy would surely have met with his approval.

Dorothy Parker's description of a famous actress running "the whole gamut of emotions from A to B" would have been very wide of the mark if she had dared to try and apply it to the Sir James Smith's production of *A Midsummer Night's Dream*. The emotions on display truly went from A up to Z and then back again. Maurice Brown shone in the part of Theseus; Pat Sleeman as Puck was a revelation; and Jackie Clemmow played Bottom as if the part had been written by Shakespeare with him in mind. The costumes, staging, continuity, scenery and lighting bore a quality that was wholly professional, and there was an undeniable truth that the lilt of Shakespeare's language was given an extra dimension by Cornish tones. It was paramount that Shakespeare's lines sounded right — understanding them was a secondary consideration.

I was not a cast member of the *Midsummer Night's Dream* company, but I did get my chance to tread the boards of legitimate theatre when I was in the Upper Sixth and, under pressure from Mr Williams, was "volunteered" into playing the male lead in a slightly obscure one-act farce written by Mr George Bernard Shaw. Perhaps the great GBS was not having one of his better days when he wrote the piece. It was a farce both literally and figuratively, entitled *Passion, Poison and Petrifaction*.

I was classically miscast as a nobleman, Adolphus by name. Being called Adolphus gave me a moment of unease, but I was grateful for small mercies, and at least it wasn't Adolf. The said Adolphus was induced to swallow building plaster as an antidote to a poison he had previously ingested, only to have the one react chemically with the other and solidify within him. The female lead, Lady Magnesia, was brilliantly taken by Margaret Jasper, also of the Upper Sixth, and it was only my great liking for her and desire to do right by her which pulled me through and served to ease the greater part of any tendency of the audience to shift restlessly in its seats. At the final curtain the audience may have felt more relieved than I did, if the volume of their applause was anything to go on. Aye, aye, that was their lot, but a lot with laughs in rather shorter supply than Jimmy Wheeler might have provided.

Previously, in my Lower Sixth days, I was a participant in another of the school's stage productions for public consumption, this time a "Top of the Form" quiz contest, in a format based faithfully on the BBC radio programme of the same. Under Mr Williams as Question Master, Sir James Smith's version of "Top of the Form" ran for one night only.

"Top of the Form", as it was presented annually on the air, was a knock-out quiz competition involving a select number of what, from a Sir James Smith's perspective, might be regarded as "posh" schools. Each participating school, most of which appeared to take boarders, was represented by a team of four pupils who were, supposedly, selected on grounds of academic capability rather than mere seniority. In principle, "Top of the Form" was an often rigorous test of general knowledge. The quiz proceeded through a number of

elimination rounds to reach the quarter and semi-finals and culmi-
nate eventually in a Grand Final in which the two best (i.e. luckiest
with their questions) teams met to determine which school would
be that year's "Top of the Form" Champion.

Regional accents were not much in evidence on "Top of the
Form". The schools involved broadcast from their own school halls,
opponent linked to opponent by the miracle of wireless technology.
It was well-nigh impossible when listening to a "Top of the Form"
broadcast, to avoid a feeling that for those taking part winning was
everything, and moreover that all taking part could have benefitted
by taking themselves a little less seriously and being much less
obviously po-faced in manner. Humiliation at the hands of their
respective teaching staffs almost certainly awaited losing teams. Any
team member giving an incorrect answer to a question perceived
by the home audience to be too simple to get wrong was courting
disgrace and all that followed in its heels.

A rural grammar school like Sir James Smith's would probably
never have managed to surmount the existing class and social bar-
riers which separated us from "Top of the Form" entrants. With that
said, however, there was an underlying humour in the broadcast
quiz to be savoured, its recipe being so formulaic that regular
listeners always seemed to know what was coming up well before it
actually came.

So it was, on the basis of all these understandings, and with the
golden initiative of Mr Williams to guide us, that Sir James Smith's
set up its own performance of the celebrated "Top of the Form"
elimination quiz, with eight teams in competition. The programme
therefore comprised a first knock-out round of four contests followed by two semi-finals and finally (what else) the grand finale. I
had a place on one of the teams.

I don't remember which of the eight won the final, other than that

298

it wasn't the team I was on as we were eliminated in Round One.

Each contest consisted of three rounds, meaning that each team member was required to answer three questions.

The three that Mr Williams directed at me went something like this:

My First Question : "Who was the author of Paradise Lost?"

I paused for a moment, hoping to give the audience an impression that I was pondering how best to frame an answer which I didn't have. Shakespeare was always a good bet for anything connected with literature, and so I responded with his name, incorrectly as it turned out. The question was then passed to the other team, and of course its arm-waving and gratuitously eager team captain, who was doing A Level English Lit, jumped in at once to declare that it was John Milton who wrote the piece. Mr Williams glossed over my unfortunate answer in his continuity patter by advising the audience that as science was my forte, my getting a first question on literature had perhaps been too exacting. As it turned out, I got no science-related question from him to compensate, although if I had been asked a question in that category, I could just as easily have got it wrong as well.

My Second Question: "What would you expect to find in 'Hansard'?"

I knew the answer to that one all right, thanks to those few tattered and aged copies of that publication of the same name which sat on a shelf in the library. The politicians whose words both relevant and irrelevant were recorded verbatim in the school's collection of "Hansard" were undoubtedly deceased and, sadly perhaps, not even well remembered. "'Hansard'", I said, "gives a verbatim record of goings-on in the Houses of Parliament."

This was not a bad answer, I thought, although Mr Williams and a few members of the audience seemed to find some amusement in my use of the expression "goings-on". Mr Williams repeated it to the audience, and won himself a much bigger laugh. The volume of laughter was such as to suggest that the light relief of my answer had not been unwelcome. With that, my answer record was one won, one lost and one to go.

My Third Question : "What is a censor?"

The key word was spelled out for good measure as if to remove any element of opportunity for it to be misinterpreted. I knew the answer without even having to think, as the word appeared in its grandest association on British Board of Film Censors Certificates, (mostly rated "U", sometimes "A" and once or twice "X") at the commencement of the first reel of every film I had ever seen at the Port Isaac Rivoli Cinema.

However, I wasn't slow to recognise that there was an intended catch in the question, and wondered if, in classic "Top of the Form" style, I should simply step into the trap laid, and define the function of a censer. It felt like the right thing to do, but then again, the making of deliberate mistakes was best left to the discretion of Mr Ronnie Waldman, or better still, to lessons taken under Miss White. Therefore I gave a correct answer, to the effect that "The job of a censor is to cut the ruder bits out of films, broadcasts and published works". This created yet another Mr Williams motivated guffaw from the audience. No matter, the point was won.

In a clarification which to me, and evidently to many others, wasn't clear at all, Mr Williams then said that a censor was "one who examines". It only served to make me think that my answer was better.

After the grand finale of the Sir James Smith's "Top of the Form" contest, when a worthy Champion had been acclaimed, and a large proportion of the audience had set itself to milling around in the vicinity of the tea urn in the hope of claiming a cup of tea before excessive demand accompanied by survival of the fittest techniques denied the refreshment to them, Miss Jones came along to speak me. She was no real stranger to stage presence, as she had mentored extra-curricular drama classes at one time. I attended a few of those classes before coming to realise that there was so much drama packaged up in a standard school day that seeking more of it after hours wasn't what I wanted to do.

Miss Jones told me that a few members of the audience had spoken to her about the laughter at my expense during the quiz. "'Oh, that poor boy,' they said," she observed, "'being laughed at like that! How awful for him.'"

"But," she then went on, "I said to them that he doesn't mind that sort of thing at all — and I was correct to say it, wasn't I?"

As indeed she was. I had made my way up through the school thus far not very brilliantly perhaps, but by and large I had managed to get things right a little more often than I got them wrong, except when it was the other way around. If people could be induced to laugh at or with me when I fell into the shit, then my extrication would never be as problematic as it might otherwise have been.

20

Here Endeth the Lesson

And there it was.

And when the last trump of the organ had been beaten into submission by Mr Turner; when the echo of Miss White's final carp aimed in my direction had faded in the direction of infinity; when Miss Jones' *Pons Asinorum* was burning to the rear of our geometrically advancing column; when the trauma of departed A Levels rested on the charity of examiners whose truth could be rejoiced in; and when Mr Sprayson had, with golden intonation as always, invoked a valedictory address for us, the time had come for me and my Upper Sixth not necessarily happy band of pilgrims to put away childish things and be prepared to view the world through a glass, darkly.

We were reasonably assured that we knew in part, but just what that part was, well, we didn't quite know what it was at all, or for that matter what it might even be about.

In my last autumn term at Sir James Smith's I went away to attend prospective undergraduate interviews at two universities, one being at the faculty of Mining Geology of the Royal School of Mines, Imperial College, University of London, and the other at the faculty of Geology at the University of Birmingham. Both interviews eventuated from orchestration, prodding and prompting by Mr Sprayson.

His *prima facie* rationale, never backwards in coming forwards, was that, come what may, right or wrong, reading Chemistry at Birmingham, his personal *alma mater*, was what going to a university was all about. However, he recognised without rancour that my A Level mix of Chemistry, Maths and Geography might be better placed under the Geological discipline that The Royal School of Mines could provide. Of the many great things that Mr Sprayson did for me, that was the signal one.

The one enduring memory of my trip to the University of Birmingham for interview was of travelling up on an overnight train from Plymouth, and travelling back along the same route in reverse on the following night. Hence the function of a hotel for that journey was provided by the train compartment.

The return journey was preferable to the journey up, as there were only three passengers in the compartment, meaning that there was then room to stretch out without interfering with any other passenger's desire to do a similar thing.

Going up to Birmingham, the compartment was jam-packed with naval ratings from Devonport — those seafaring worthies did not smell fresh, especially when they all proceeded to remove their footwear for the duration of the journey. They also took out all the light bulbs in the compartment and the corridor outside, thereby leaving our sector of the train in darkness. Railway officials tended to frown on such practice, but never chose to act on transgressions when the odds were stacked so convincingly against them.

With the lights out, the host of naval personnel arranged themselves in a close-fitting assembly born of substantial practice, much in the way of a precisely cut jigsaw puzzle. I had feet set in my lap, feet up on my shoulders, and at one moment, feet placed on my head.

The atmosphere became hot, humid and feral. The one blessing was that the compartment was designated non-smoking, not that such a prohibition was ever a setback to the truly determined.

As a result of the two university entrance interviews that I undertook, I was accepted by both the University of Birmingham and the Royal School of Mines. My appreciation of quite what the study of any aspect of Geology implied, whether the scientific direction was to be pure or applied was, shining on it as kindly a light as was feasible, a great and looming unknown. My eventual choice of a place at the Royal School of Mines may well have been influenced by a traumatic train journey in the company of sailors that I would rather not have made.

Naturally enough, taking up the university place that I was offered and had accepted was entirely conditional on my A Level results meeting scholarship requirements, and achievement of a scholarship became my immediate priority.

Leaving Sir James Smith's after seven full years in the company of classmates and teaching staff who had all, for good and less good, become close familiars rose up as a most difficult barrier to cross.

But then, at the end, it was strangely not really hard at all.

Looking back over the seven years of rapidly changing times it was truly remarkable to reckon on how many pupils (and teachers to a lesser extent) came like water and went like wind around the central core of constant classmates who struggled on.

Occasionally a class member might suddenly vanish in mid-term — there on one day and gone forever on the next — but mostly it was the between-term holidays which took them away. We left on holiday, and there they were — we returned for a new term, and there they weren't. A reason for their absence might or might not be forthcoming, but no one bothered about it much, and in a day or so the ranks had all closed up again. It was as if the dear departed had never been there in the first place, a sad reality that would have applied to any of us under appropriate circumstances.

The perspective of the teachers must have taken in a rather broader field than the blinkered outlook of pupils could manage. The teaching staff were faced every year with the twin necessities of saying hello to a new First Form intake, and goodbye to the departing Upper Sixth. Did they think about it, miss individuals and see it as a matter for regret and heartache? Perhaps they did, but it is a cause of much soul-searching for me to have no good answer to put forward.

A reasonable guess would be that some kind of fine balance was drawn, with the sorrow over parting with particular favourites being neutralised by the satisfaction of finally seeing the backs of others of a less favourite stamp. At school we became a family of sorts, and as in all good family traditions, separation came only at a personal cost.

Where departure concerned me, I walked with blunted senses away from Sir James Smith's for the last time as a pupil on break-up day at the end of the summer term of 1957. It was the end of seven years of what until then had seemed to be a regular succession of ups and downs, but which on later reflection felt to be only positive in its balance.

Apart from my return to the school for Speech Day and prize giving in the following year, I never saw any of the teachers again, failed dismally to seek them out, and, to my ultimate detriment, didn't keep up anything much in the way of subsequent contact. It was as if a door had closed behind me and other doors had immediately opened before me. I stepped up to them, and newly minted priorities pulled me through and took my attention away from all that lay behind.

And then again, consider the teachers. They toiled and they span for us who were their pupils, and they lived on in their subtle qualities and their everyday idiosyncrasies that we absorbed from them by unwitting osmosis. Their teachings formed the essence of the mortar binding together the building blocks of our lives.

For all of them — the great, the good, and even the subjectively less good — Solomon in his all his glory would have been hard pressed to be arrayed like one of these.

Not a day goes by but that the advice they passed on, the lessons they taught us, the means of coping with challenge that they inspired and the knowledge that they instilled in us is still being used by so many of us in a meaningful way.

Thanks to them, to every beloved one of them.

Benedictus, benedicat.

And that really is the end of the lesson.

Since Lord, thou dost defend
Us with thy spirit,
We know we at the end
Shall life inherit.
Then fancies, flee away!
He'll care not what men say;
He'll labour, night and day
To be a pilgrim.
John Bunyan (1628 — 1688)

www.ingramcontent.com/pod-product-compliance
Lightning Source LLC
Chambersburg PA
CBHW022102280326
41933CB00007B/222